D0411449

A FINE PLACE TO DAYDREAM

Also by Bill Barich

Crazy for Rivers
Carson Valley: A Novel
Big Dreams: Into the Heart of California
Hard to Be Good: Stories
Traveling Light
Laughing in the Hills

A FINE PLACE
TO DAYDREAM

Bill Barich

CollinsWillow
An Imprint of HarperCollins*Publishers*

For Imelda
bright star

First published in 2005 by
Collins Willow
an imprint of HarperCollins*Publishers*
London

© Bill Barich 2005

1

A CIP catalogue record for this book is
available from the British Library

ISBN 0 00 719180 4

Printed and bound in Great Britain
by Clays Ltd, St Ives plc

The HarperCollins website address is
www.harpercollins.co.uk

Photographic acknowledgements

Colorsport 1b; **Corbis** 4t, 9b; **Cranham Colour Library** 1t, 2tr, 2b,
6b, 7t, 7b, 13b, 16cl; **Getty Images** 16; **Healy Racing Photos** 2tl, 3t,
4bl, 4br, 5t, 5b, 6t, 7c, 9t, 10 (all), 11 (all), 12b, 13tl, 13tr, 13c,
14m, 14b, 15t, 15b, 16t; **Peter Mooney** 3b, 8cl, 14t;
Trevor Jones 8t, 8cr, 8b, 12c, 16cr

'I can also truly say that of all races, that which comes nearest to Paddy's heart is a rattling steeplechase. It is so essentially Irish. There is incomparably more excitement – a chance of a broken limb, therefore more "fun" to be expected. It is regarded with far greater interest than any other diversion . . . The reckless daring of the bold peasantry endears a spectacle which shows so much intrepidity, and there is a sympathy between the rush of the racing hunter and their own impetuous natures.'

'Life and Adventures of Bryan O'Regan',
The Dublin Saturday Magazine, 1865

'The Irish obsession with racing, matched only in fervour of religion and alcoholic refreshment, can with justification be accused of diverting the national intellect from more gainful pursuits.'

FLANN O'BRIEN, *The Hard Life*

'The sport of kings is our passion, the dogs too . . . Nothing human is foreign to us, once we have digested the racing news.'

SAMUEL BECKETT, *Texts for Nothing*

The Crossing

*N*ow *through the night come the horses. They come
from obscure little villages like Lisaleen and
Closutton, Coolagh and Moone, dozing and possibly
dreaming on the long, dark ferry ride from Dún Laoghaire
across the Irish Sea to Wales. They are Ireland's pride, the
finest jumpers in a country obsessed with jumping, with
grand historical leaps over daunting obstacles, so they've
been prepared for the trip with the utmost care. Some have
IV drips to keep their electrolytes balanced, others have
been fed Chinese herbs for an energy boost, and almost all
have had their lungs scoped for infections, their blood
tested, and their weight recorded precisely, down to the
last ounce, to be sure they have reached a peak of fitness
for their annual tilt against the English at the Cheltenham
Festival.*

*They've heard the word 'Cheltenham' countless times,
of course, uttered by their trainers in both delighted antici-
pation and total despair, so it has some resonance. It
might even have some meaning. Horses know more than
they let on, after all, they're in touch with elemental*

1

things. In the old days, farmers in rural Ireland believed their horses could see ghosts. Whenever one stopped dead and refused to budge, they reckoned a shade was nearby. If you looked between the horse's ears, you could catch a glimpse of it, the farmers claimed. To prevent the fairies from stealing a good horse, they tied a red ribbon or a hazel twig to it, or they spat on it. Folklore had it that a wild horse could be tamed by reciting the Creed in its right ear on Friday and its left on Wednesday until it came to hand.

So the legends go. In truth, horses do live by their instincts, and those on the ferry understand that because they're travelling, they'll probably be racing soon. Perhaps they can sense a few ghosts on the horizon, too, since the Cheltenham Festival has been around for almost one hundred years. Originally designed as a showcase for the National Hunt Steeplechase, in 1904, it evolved into a three-day extravaganza of jump racing that features twenty highly competitive races, ten of them Grade One Championships. Now more than fifty thousand fans turn up each day, and they'd raise a mighty roar in 2004 when Best Mate, the current wonder horse, tried for his third straight Gold Cup, hoping to equal a mark that Arkle, the greatest chaser ever, set in 1966.

There was a time when you couldn't walk into an Irish pub without hearing Arkle's name. The horse was an institution, a national treasure. Glasses were raised in his honour, and children around the world sent letters addressed to 'Arkle, Ireland' that were actually delivered by the grace of God. Trained in North County Dublin by Tom Dreaper, a self-styled 'humble farmer', he won twenty-seven of his thirty-five starts, often carrying twice the weight of his rivals. His fans drove past the farm on weekends, eager for a snapshot or just a peek at him. They were loyal and devoted and could describe his favourite meal in detail – mash, dry oats, six raw eggs, and two bottles of Guinness mixed in a bucket. They even forgave his owner Anne, Duchess of Westminster, for being British and royal.

Some experts thought Arkle's feat would never be duplicated, but now Best Mate was on the scene, and every newspaper on the ferry carried a story about his quest. The stories all mentioned his superb physical condition, and told how the bookies favoured him odds-on, and how Henrietta Knight, his sweetly eccentric English trainer, had recently lost two stone on the Atkins Diet and couldn't bear to watch her darling run for fear she'd see him fall. Her husband Terry Biddlecombe, a former jump jockey, also provided excellent copy with his jokes about Viagra and his gruff but emotional manner. He'd wept in public when Matey won the Gold Cup a second time.

A victory in the Gold Cup, with its twenty-one fences over three-and-a-quarter miles, requires speed, stamina, and faultless execution, but those qualities are worthless without some racing luck. Even a wonder horse can make a mistake, hit a fence, and fall. Knight knew this, and so did the Irish trainers dreaming of an upset, including the canny Michael Hourigan from County Limerick, who was sending Beef Or Salmon, his stable star, to the Festival again. A talented but awkward eight-year-old, Beef Or Salmon had run in the 2003 race and had fallen at the third fence, his challenge over before it had begun.

But maybe the horse had improved. The same might be true of Harbour Pilot from Noel Meade's yard in County Meath, who was third to Best Mate in 2003, albeit by a whopping thirteen lengths.

Fortunately, the sea is calm tonight, so the horses can rest easy. In stormy weather, they get spooked at times and need constant attention, but now the grooms and box drivers can take a catnap or stretch their legs on deck, studying the inky water for omens. They talk about the pressure, the stress, and the anxiety of the Festival, all complicated by the hardships of travel and the brain-numbing effect of a three-day booze-up. Cheltenham always produces its fair share of basket chases, but every owner, trainer, and jockey longs to be there in March, if only once in a lifetime. The jumps season lasts virtually year-round now, in both the UK and Ireland, but no other event has the same cachet as the Festival, not even the Grand National. The prize money is excellent, too, at least by the lowly standards of the National Hunt, with the Gold Cup worth £203,000 to the winner, plus the publicity is enormous, affording instant fame to the fortunate few.

For the Irish, though, the Festival has an extra dimension, a metaphorical value. In their familiar role as under-dogs, they accept the disadvantage of shipping their horses to Cheltenham, glad for an opportunity to take on their colonizers on English ground. The contest is friendly, but every patriot in Ireland prays that the Hourigans and Meades will stick it to the Brits. The Irish have an extraordinary way with horses, after all. The earliest invaders from England recognized it, and remarked on how a rider and his mount appeared to be inseparable, a single creature with nothing between them, skin to skin. Often the rider lacked a saddle and used a mere snaffle for control, the lightest of bits. Respect for a horse, empathy with it, those were essential concepts for the Celts, who believed that the Otherworld, a place beyond death, was bright and happy. In their myths, horses transported souls across the divide.

Around dawn, the ferry arrives at the port of Holyhead, north of Caernarvon Bay. The grooms and drivers may be grumpy and a little bedraggled after their hours at sea, but they click into action and make certain each animal is comfortable, quiet, and suffering no ill-effects from the trip. In general, horses manage well on the ferry. They can stand upright and clear their lungs of mucous, something that's more difficult to do on a plane. They don't usually kick up a fuss, either, when the overland part of their journey resumes, with the boxes and vans following a route through Anglesey that crosses the Welsh border into England near Chirk, then cuts through the Severn Vale and skirts Birmingham's suburban sprawl before dropping south toward Cheltenham and the western edge of the Cotswolds.

In time, they reach Cheltenham Racecourse at the foot of Cleeve Hill. The dutiful grooms lead the horses to the Stable Yard, where an official checks their passports to confirm their identity. Next, the grooms give the horses some water (they don't drink much on the ferry) and take them for a walk over the course. Today – a Monday – the weather is overcast, fairly mild and spring-like, and the horses gradually relax and lose any trace of stiffness.

They look contented, returned to a world they know. They're alert and enjoying the fresh air and the feel of the grass, all agreeably familiar sensations, aware that something special is brewing because of the noise, the people, and the frenzied activity everywhere.

With the Festival scheduled to begin on Tuesday, the racecourse is besieged. Lorries come and go, e-mails zip through cyberspace, and callers begging for last-minute tickets jam the phone lines. Letheby & Christopher, caterers to the event since the 1920s, are laying in around eleven thousand pounds of beef, sixteen thousand pounds of potatoes, thirty-nine thousand chocolate bars, and forty-seven thousand sandwiches. The champagne bottles are on ice, and the Guinness kegs are cooling. In the bazaar-like Tented Village, merchants are setting up their stalls. Security guards patrol the entire five-hundred-acre site – no threat, however weird, can be discounted – while the police prepare for the clash of merrymakers and pickpockets.

While the horses walk the course and get their bearings, racegoers all over Ireland are packing their bags and departing for the Cotswolds. The Irish contingent will be large, vocal, informed, and dying for a gamble, their wallets stuffed with notes. Many are repeat visitors, among them diehards who've been staying at the dowager Queens Hotel since Arkle's last run, but there are also plenty of newcomers pouring into Birmingham Airport, barristers and plumbers, publicans and teachers, all mad about horses and often at the mercy of travel agents who broker package tours and must dispatch their clients to lodgings in faraway towns – to Stratford-upon-Avon, say, or Twigworth in the middle-of-nowhere.

There, in a single room at the Twigworth Hotel, you'll find a punter who doesn't quite fit the mould, being an American – a Californian, to be precise – although he lives in Dublin now and is just as obsessed with the jumps as the lads from Kilkenny and Waterford in the rooms around him. He has a bag filled with form books and notebooks, and a corkscrew should he locate a palatable bottle of wine at the hotel – there are no stores nearby and no village, and he doesn't have a car – and he is looking forward to the Festival in a major way since it marks the high point of his own journey, one that began back in October when he joined the Irish caravan of horses, trainers, and jockeys to record its progress on the bumpy road to Cheltenham.

Or you could say that the journey really started when he sold his house near San Francisco and rented a flat in London to freshen himself, fully expecting to go home in a few months and buy a fishing cabin in the Sierra Nevada, where he'd ripen from middle into old age. That was three years ago, but instead he had the good luck to fall in love with an Irish woman and the surprising bravery (given his usual shyness in such matters) to fly to Dublin to pursue her, and now he has a brand new life. The move required a leap of faith, but probably love in any form, at any time or age, demands such a gamble, and at odd moments he feels a sharp kinship with the horses who, when they take flight and leave the earth, hang for a half-second in a cloud of uncertainty before they know what the future will bring.

October: Stirrings

It was early autumn when I settled in Dublin to be with Imelda, my new love. Apartments were scarce in the city, so I took what I could get, a tiny one-bedroom in a fancy complex where the other tenants were all baby stockbrokers and insurance salesmen. The building was a tribute to Ireland's booming economy and dwarfed the Victorian cottages on the Dodder River nearby. Our porter was a fierce-eyed, black-haired rogue, and when he saw me reading the *Racing Post* one afternoon, he offered me a tip on a horse at Punchestown. That caused an odd stirring in me. I felt that I belonged.

The horse lost, of course, but that was all right. I wasn't in it for the money, not yet. In a way, the porter had opened a gate and made me realize how uninformed I was about Irish racing compared to the English scene. In London, I'd fallen into the habit of gambling on the televised races every Saturday, rising early to study the form and poring over it with the rapt attention of a convict searching through law books for a loophole that would set him free. I liked the dense columns of statistics, the oddly poetic jargon, and the underlying assumption that the puzzle could be solved and the brambly nature of existence untangled, if only for an instant.

While the English are fond of their racing, I soon discovered the Irish can't live without it. Their embrace of the sport is passionate, a streak of lightning in the blood. Nothing grips them as powerfully as the sight of horses jumping over hurdles and steeplechase fences, maybe because the National Hunt still carries an echo of the country's rural, agricultural heritage and has the ability to touch people and even move them. Whatever the case, this was new territory for me, and I took to it so readily that the flat races began to bore me. Devoted to speed, they were over in a flash, but a good steeplechase unfolded at a leisurely pace, like a Hardy novel. The jump races were textured affairs, too, rich in subplots and dramatic reversals of fate, plus they had a pastoral aspect that struck me as entirely beautiful.

By the time I moved in with Imelda a year later, into her house in a quiet neighbourhood, I was hooked on the National Hunt and often strolled to our high street to visit the local bookmakers. We had two within easy walking distance, Paddy Power and Boylesports, both Irish-owned chains. The shops were so neat, clean, and wholesome they made gambling appear to be a normal, even welcome part of everyday life. 'Stop in and bring your granny' might have been their motto rather than Boylesports' urgent injunction, 'Bet here!' Indeed, I did see a granny in the shops on occasion, filling out a docket with her poor wrinkled fingers.

Eventually, I became a regular customer and drifted between shops on the tides of fortune, loyalty in gamblers being linked to the flow of good luck. My companions were a diverse crew. The mainstays were retired or on the dole, and they were joined at intervals by punters taking a day off from work or a break from it – a barman, say, or a waiter from our Chinese restaurant – all glued to the action on satellite TV while betting on races in Ireland, England, South Africa and even Dubai, along with computer-generated virtual races and, possibly sinking even lower, the dogs. They were quiet compared to fans in the States, rarely raising their voices to cheer or object (although that isn't so at racecourses), but I did hear a muted cry of 'Go on, my son!' sometimes and also the words 'fookin' and 'feckin' used with extraordinary frequency, often as adjectives applied to certain jockeys.

The more I watched the races, the more I understood how the National Hunt depends on the Irish for its survival. Even in England, the best horses tend to be bred in Ireland, where the best riders also come from – Tony McCoy, Mick Fitzgerald, Ruby Walsh, and Jim Culloty are all stable jockeys for English trainers, while Barry Geraghty often crosses the ocean to ride in big races on a freelance basis. In fact, the British didn't cotton onto the steeplechase when they first encountered it during the colonial period. They dismissed it as a 'bastard amusement', but racing over obstacles has long been a feature of Irish country life, born of the landscape and a profound love of the hunt. To recycle a hoary legend, the first chase supposedly occurred in County Cork in 1752, a race between Edmund Blake and Cornelius O'Callaghan from Buttevant Church to St Mary's Church in Doneraile, its steeple visible about five miles away.

By the nineteenth century, the steeplechase was firmly established as an Irish sport. The courses, noted one observer, 'were laid out over perfectly natural country; not a single sod or stone would be removed nor a fence trimmed, and there was no levelling of places where the going was bad.' A rider picked his own line and jumped whatever he met along the way. The races could be brutal. Every horse fell at least once, and it wasn't unusual for a winner to fall three or even four times. Heroes emerged. There was Black Jack Dennis, for instance, a famous daredevil, who once jumped a five-foot-high fence and the donkey cart right in front. To cash a bet, Dennis rode the intimidating course at Rahasane (ten stone walls, twenty-five fences) without a saddle or bridle, relying on a cabbage stalk for a whip.

I read about those amazing feats at the National Library in Dublin, a grand old building as sleepy and dusty as any scholar could want. On my walk into town, I'd buy a few pencils at our newsagent (ink is banned from the library to prevent some creep from defacing a precious book or manuscript) and head down Leeson Street, then cross over to Baggot Street and pass the birthplace of Francis Bacon, whose father trained racehorses while Bacon had sex with the stable lads. The temptation to stop for a jar of the black stuff at Doheny & Nesbit's was always strong, but I usually resisted and rounded a corner by the Shelbourne Hotel, host in 1842 to William Thackeray, who complained that his room hadn't been 'scoured' for months, though he praised the kind and gentle staff.

Up the library's central staircase I climbed, into the deep silence of the Reading Room with my reader's ticket and its ghoulish passport photo (I'd closed my eyes by accident, so the picture resembled a post-mortem shot) on a chain around my neck. I blended comfortably into the mix of genealogy buffs digging up their ancestors, students doing research, budding writers courting inspiration, and the predictable complement of daydreamers. Quiet, well-mannered clerks disappeared into the tomb-like stacks to unearth the books I'd requested, and I sat and studied and gradually got the lie of the land.

Sometimes when I tired of reading I'd lift my head, stare at the ring of cherubs on the ceiling, and realize, with a profound sense of wonder, that I was actually living in Ireland – in Dublin, a city I had visited only once before as an impressionable young tourist in search of literary landmarks. Out to Howth and Dalkey I rode the train, thinking about Flann O'Brien and his curious archive, and I went to Sandymount Strand, too, where I had an icy stroll by the water and battled a fierce winter wind that removed a layer of skin from my cheeks. Near Mountjoy Square, in an act that now smacks of foreshadowing, I put a small bet on a horse running at Leopardstown, who shocked me by winning and caused a night-long celebration and an awful morning-after.

Now these landmarks were an aspect of home to me. The transition was strange, but also utterly ordinary. Imelda and I often talked about chance – fate, destiny, call it what you will – and how the tiniest missed signal could have kept us apart. We had met by accident at a gallery opening in London, where Dorothy Cross, a friend of Imelda's from Dublin, had a show. As we chatted over glasses of lukewarm white wine, I learned that Imelda was an artist as well, a figurative painter, and that she had two teenage sons and had been separated from her husband for many years. (Divorce in Ireland is still a messy business, legal only since February 1997; I'd been divorced myself for almost a decade.)

The gallery was so crowded and noisy that I asked if Imelda would come to a quieter place where we could talk in peace, but she politely declined. That would be disloyal to Dorothy, she said. She was there to support her friend, so I stalked off in an arrogant huff and wound up nursing a beer in a wretched, noisier, even more crowded pub down the street. What if I hadn't swallowed my pride and returned to the gallery? What if Imelda hadn't called me on her next trip to London? What if I'd complained about the snotty, overpriced restaurant where I took her to dinner instead of keeping my big mouth shut? And so on. Though I have always believed in chance, Imelda frankly surpasses me. She has a mystical side and a deep faith in the power of coincidence, being Irish to the core.

Certainly, I had never lived anywhere on earth where the citizens latch onto 'hot tips' with such enthusiasm, the way a drowning man clings to a piece of flotsam. So-called 'inside information' gets passed along from the most dubious possible sources – from a barber, say, who happened to cut the hair of a man whose son goes to school in Tipperary with a nephew of Edward O'Grady, the trainer. Yet even though I recognized the suspicious provenance of those tips, I wasn't immune to their allure, not at first, so when I was getting my hair cut one day and heard the barber mumbling about Caishill, a 'sure thing'

due to run at Listowel – this was in September 2003 –
I dashed to Boylesports and threw a fiver on the horse.

The race was a chase over two miles and six furlongs.
On the face of it, Caishill was up against it, but he had a
good jockey in Shay Barry and carried at least a stone less
than the other horses. Barry kept him in the middle of the
field and was going reasonably well when Caishill banged
into the ninth fence and fell. Horses hit the ground so
hard, with their delicate legs flailing, I am always surprised at how swiftly most of them recover, upright again
in seconds and often none the worse for wear, except for
the psychological effect. Some jumpers shake off a fall as
Caishill did, winning a chase in November, but others
become scared and inhibited.

In many respects, jump jockeys take a greater risk than
the horses, being more fragile and vulnerable. For
instance, I once read through a list of all the injuries Carl
Llewellyn, an experienced rider in his late thirties, has
suffered in his long career: a broken cheekbone, two
broken collar bones, nine concussions, eight broken
noses, two broken jaws, two broken ribs, a broken wrist,
a broken elbow, and a broken 'pinkie', along with soft
tissue bruising and ligament, tendon, and muscle damage
too extensive to mention. Despite the painful catalogue, I
knew Llewellyn counted himself lucky to be riding at his
age, since most jump jockeys don't last as long.

That same September, we were confronted with some
hard evidence of how abruptly a jockey's life in the saddle
can end when Norman Williamson, a fine rider with over
1,200 wins to his credit, took an awful spill at
Downpatrick, in Northern Ireland. He lay so still on the

ground it scared everyone – he might have been dead. He swore that he felt OK, but he did ask the paramedics to put a brace on his neck for safety's sake, and that meant he would have to undergo an examination before he'd be permitted to ride again. After a subsequent X-ray, he was told that his next fall might lead to paralysis, so Williamson, only thirty-four and in his prime, chose to hang up his boots.

It could have been much worse, really. Only a month earlier, Kieran Kelly, a popular young Irish jockey, who had won the Royal & SunAlliance Novices' Hurdle on Hardy Eustace at the Cheltenham Festival the previous year, fell in a race at Kilbeggan and landed on his head. Though he wore a helmet, he broke his neck and lasted just a week on life-support before he died. Others have survived such horrible accidents and gone on to make a new life, as Shane Broderick did after injuring his spinal cord in a fall at Fairyhouse in 1997. It was as if Broderick had been in a motorcycle crash, tossed over the handlebars and smashed into the pavement head-first, but he fought back and is now training horses despite being a paraplegic confined to a wheelchair.

Jockeys don't dwell on such accidents, of course. They can't afford to, so they stay in perpetual motion, busy all the time. That autumn – the autumn of Best Mate's quest for a third Gold Cup – they were more concerned about the weather and how it was affecting their finances. The month of September was the driest on record in England, and Ireland was almost as dry. Without the soft, safe ground necessary to cushion the jumpers, most horses were behind schedule, not yet wholly fit. Trainers were being careful with their best stock, so the fields in many races were small, sometimes with just three or four entries. Punters sniffed at the short prices on offer and held onto their money, and the bookies were rumoured to be bleeding.

Racing fans are optimists, though, and I had no doubt that the weather would eventually oblige. As a third-year Dubliner, I put the chance of a drought at 10,000-1, based on my experience. In fact, I knew how wet, cold, and sometimes miserable I'd be over the next few months as I indulged my new passion and travelled from race-course to racecourse, trying to learn as much as I could about the Irish and their obsession with horses. I wanted a proper education before I tackled Cheltenham. Walking home from the library one evening in early October, beneath the city's lovely, ever-changing sky, I made a mental note to buy some waterproof shoes and fill my little silver flask, a gift from Imelda, with good Irish whisky.

My journey started the next morning, when I boarded a train for Kilkenny at Heuston Station, off to meet Jessica Harrington, one of Ireland's most successful trainers, at Gowran Park Racecourse. As we travelled southeast through Kildare, Athy, and Carlow, there were more farms with each passing mile, broad fields in the midst of rolling hills. The landscape had an earthy coherence, even a sense of rightness, so that the new cookie-cutter suburbs looked out-of-place – too

American, I thought, wishing I could stop the train and warn the Irish before it was too late.

From Kilkenny with its bright air of prosperity, I took a taxi to the racecourse. We drove through more rich farmland, past woods where the trees were touched with autumn colour. I'd noticed this before in Ireland, a sudden transition from the urban to the rural, as if time itself were switching gears and slowing down to accommodate a country rhythm. Over a distance of eight miles, we'd left behind a bustling city and retreated into a different century. It could have been 1914 at Gowran Park, the year of the track's first meeting. The fans were in no hurry for the action to start. They gathered in little groups, as at a county fair, and talked about local affairs. Elderly men in flat caps were everywhere. I counted twenty-two of them sitting on a long bench outside the Racing Secretary's office.

The atmosphere at Gowran was so intimate and informal I felt as if I were inside rather than outside the races, not a spectator but a participant. At the parade ring before the first race, I could have reached out and touched the circling horses. I could see the pimples on the faces of the youngest jockeys, who were in their teens and still hormonally challenged. When they dismounted after the race, they walked right through the crowd to the weighing room, an unthinkable feat at any American track, where the disgruntled punters, possibly armed, might attack them for their failure. Here they were treated to expressions of sympathy and a bit of soft-core heckling.

'You picked the wrong one again!' someone teased a skinny youth who'd been on a loser.

'But I don't get a choice!' the kid replied. His accent turned the word 'choice' into 'chice'. It sounded chewed upon.

I met Harrington at the weighing room before the second race. Known to everyone as Jessie, she emerged with a purposeful stride and cut a path through the scurrying jockeys. Tall and lean, she has the attractive, outdoors look of someone who has logged countless hours on horseback. She is in her late fifties, with lively blue eyes and blondish hair kept short for a minimum of fuss. I had the impression she resisted fussiness at every turn, unwilling to waste a minute on anything frivolous. In her voice, I heard a hint of Anglo-Irish stiffness, but her manner was cordial and helpful.

Jessie might have inherited her no-nonsense attitude from Brigadier B. J. 'Frizz' Fowler, her father, who moved his family from England, where she was born, to Ireland in 1949, settling a few years later on a farm in Meath he'd inherited from his uncle. The brigadier hunted, played polo, and raced in an occasional point-to-point, so Jessie grew up with horses and farm animals. She can't remember learning how to ride – being on a horse was second nature. She belonged to a pony club and later became one of the country's top eventers, competing in the European Championship when she was just twenty and later travelling to Los Angeles as a member of Ireland's Olympic team in 1984. Her background has given her what military types call 'command presence'. If she had issued an order, I would have followed it without question.

That afternoon, the race card was a mixed bag, with

both jump and flat races as the two seasons briefly dove-tailed. Jessie had a runner, You Need Luck, in the second, and on our trip to the parade ring, she told me she'd become a trainer by chance. She and her husband, Johnny, a retired bloodstock agent, had a few decent home-breds on their farm in County Kildare that they couldn't sell, so she started working with them and did well enough to catch the eye of some owners, who inquired about her services. By 1990 she had a public licence and an excellent reputation. At present, she has about ninety horses on the farm's 115 acres, and she is always among the top Irish trainers in terms of earnings, and the only woman.

In his three outings to date, You Need Luck had produced no wins, nor given any indication he ever would. After Jessie instructed Timmy O'Shea, her jockey, she seemed to forget about me and made a beeline for an open stand with a few rows of concrete steps. The stand was so basic I'd have wagered it had been there since 1914. Since it didn't offer the best vantage point, being several lengths from the finish, I guessed Jessie favoured it as a lucky spot, and she admitted it. As jittery as I am about superstitions, still capable of being undone by the sight of a black cat, I discovered that most trainers are every bit as bad.

The legendary Martin Pipe provides an excellent example. Admired for his intelligence and innovative methods, and interested enough in hard science to enroll in an equine studies course at Worcestershire College of Agriculture to further his understanding of horses, he believes the colour green is so unlucky he once sent an owner home from the races to change her dress. Seeing a chimney sweep on race day is a scary sign for him, too, as is the delivery of a load of straw to his yard. (Henrietta Knight shares that superstition, but a load of hay is OK with her.) He would never wear a red shirt or red socks to the track, or drive over a bridge while a train is beneath it.

Jessie had visited Pipe's yard in Nicholashayne once, and had been impressed with his attention to detail. He even made the wood chips for his gallops. As an outsider, the son of a wealthy bookie rather than a member of the hunt-club set, Pipe had to go it his own way and ultimately rewrote the manual for training jumpers. First and foremost, he relates to horses as if they're human beings, granting them a psychological complexity they're often denied. He is a close observer and listener as well, especially after a horse's workout when he concentrates on its breathing to judge its level of fitness. The faster a horse stops blowing, he says, the closer it is to 'doing the business'.

In his autobiography, *The Champion Trainer's Story*, Pipe revealed some of his secrets. He doesn't let his horses trot at home, because he thinks the gait is unnatural. It puts too much pressure on the joints and can damage the cannon bone. His horses don't come off the bridle on the gallops, but they do sprint over a short distance. Horses who've spent the summer away walk for at least six weeks before they do any serious training, and Pipe monitors their feed carefully, so that they don't overeat and become lethargic. If he can see a horse's last two ribs, the horse is ready to race.

Unfortunately, You Need Luck lived up to his name and dragged in next-to-last. Jessie's mood improved later when Imazulutoo, her best novice hurdler – and maybe the best in Ireland – beat a good field in the Kilford Arms Hurdle for three-year-olds. It was a lovely race to watch over the lush, green, undulating course at Gowran Park. This was racing at its most organic and unforced, without the nuisance of a starting gate or the distraction of a flashing tote board. Again, I had a sense of travelling back in time. The race caller's voice was hushed, as if it would be silly to show any excitement over the sort of contest that had been going on for centuries. He even added a nice writerly touch by saying, 'The jumping of the trailing group leaves something to be desired.'

Under Barry Geraghty, Imazulutoo's performance was sharp enough for Jessie to be considering the Cheltenham Festival for her horse, perhaps as an entry in the Triumph Hurdle. Her tough mare Spirit Leader would probably be going for a second victory in the Champion Hurdle, and she also had other horses in mind, among them Colca Canyon for the Arkle Chase and Pay It Forward for the Stayers' Hurdle. 'All I can do is peddle along and keep dreaming,' she said, knowing how many things could go wrong before next March. Her only certainty was Moscow Flyer, a horse I would develop a strange affection for when I made his acquaintance a few days later.

*　　*　　*

The Harringtons' farm is in Moone, a blip on any map. Tourists do leave the N9 road to explore Moone Abbey with its ruined Franciscan friary and ancient high cross, but not very often. I never saw another soul there while I was wandering around. The friary, like Gowran Park, belongs to another century – the fourteenth. Any horse who happened on the ruins would surely spot a ghost. There were crumbly old gravestones I dared not touch and a vaulted chapel open to the sky. Birds own the friary now – birds and the long grass.

Moone has only a small central market that doubles as a post office. A hardy gent well into his seventh decade was at the front counter, dressed for work in a suit and a tie, an accepted country tradition. He directed me to the farm, saying, 'First one on the right. I mean, on the left. Anyway, you can't miss it.' The farm *was* on the left, with a paved drive that leads to the main house, a sprawling pink place set against a backdrop of the Wicklow Mountains. Mature beeches and lime trees line the drive, their leaves yellow and gold. Cottages are scattered around the property, as are some old stone buildings used as stables.

I found Jessie on horseback, putting her second lot of the morning through their paces. She watched intently as the horses went around a circular four-furlong gallop. Each time they passed, I heard the thump of their hooves and listened to the sound of them breathing, as Martin Pipe might do – an athletic, chest-expanding sound. The air rippled with animal energy.

For the works riders, this was the best part of the day, when they could play at being jockeys. In reality, most were only grooms, a job not everyone would covet. Several came from Eastern Europe, five from Poland alone. They lived like college students in the cottages, and just as messily. Good stable help is difficult to find these days. The Irish lads who were once hungry for a chance to muck out a stall (despite the poor pay and punishing hours) now pursue work in the cities, especially in construction. Jessie's team labours from 8 am to 5 pm, being responsible for five horses apiece, seven days a week. You'd have to be devoted, or captive to jockey fantasies, to accept the terms of employment.

As the horses left the gallop to cool down, Jessie invited me to join her on a tea break. We walked briskly to the house, trailed by a number of dogs. In all my visits, I was never certain how many she has – eight, ten, it could be twelve? – in a variety of breeds. Hers is a peaceable kingdom, where the dogs and horses share equal rights with everybody else. She opened the back door, and we passed through an alcove piled with muddy boots, where silks hung on a rod, ready to be grabbed on the way to the races. The dividing line between work and play doesn't seem to exist for Jessie. Work is life, and she loves it. Driven and ambitious, that's how she comes across.

She doesn't stand on ceremony, either, so Eamonn Leigh was already in the kitchen, boiling the kettle. He's from Dunlavin, a nearby village, and began working for Johnny Harrington about thirty-three years ago, when Johnny ran his bloodstock business full-time. Eamonn is more of an assistant trainer than a groom, someone Jessie looks to for an opinion, and Moscow Flyer is the only horse in his care. He is so close to the Harringtons that he recently built a home for his own family on the property.

At the kitchen table sat Robert Power, a works rider but also a professional jockey with fifteen wins under his belt that season. Only twenty-two, he appeared to have a bright future, but Jessie was always advising him to be careful. If he did manage to reach the top, it would be a long, hard climb. Power has no trouble making the weight now, but that will change with age as his metabolism slows down. Older jockeys don't bounce back as quickly from falls, either, Norman Williamson being a case-in-point, as was Adrian Maguire, just retired at thirty-three with a serious neck injury. Regular riding used to keep jockeys race-fit, but now they need more stamina and must jog, hit the gym, and be even more strict about their diet, though I did see Power nibble at a biscuit.

I looked around the room. On the walls were photos of horses, among them Space Trucker, a home-bred and Harrington's first Festival winner, in the Grand Annual Chase in '99. There were also some framed newspaper clips and photos of Jessie's four children (three daughters and a son), two with her first husband and two with Johnny. They were all grown up, except for Kate, the youngest at fourteen, who is at a Dublin boarding school. One jokey sign stood out. 'Dull Women – Have Immaculate Homes', it read, a sentiment Jessie endorsed. I couldn't imagine her being content with a traditional role, not when the pull of the horses was so strong.

An assistant brought Jessie the mail. 'Junk, most of it,' she said, casting it aside, but one envelope held a cheque from an owner. It costs between 1,200 and 1,400 euros a month to keep a horse in training at Harrington's yard, exclusive of vets' bills, transport, and entry fees. In general, she gets on well with her owners, particularly those who pay on time, but a few drive her nuts. That morning, she'd had a call from a man who asked about his gelding, saying 'How's she doing?', glossing over a distinction Jessie felt he ought to be able to make. The dizziest owners blame her for every failure, and they are all dying to race at Cheltenham and freely offer her plans A, B, and C for accomplishing it, even when their horses are still maidens. 'I wish they'd realize horses aren't machines,' she sighed.

A trainer's headaches are infinite, and we soon witnessed an unexpected one when a Polish groom burst into the kitchen in a foul mood. His English was limited, so he had to rack his brain for the right vulgarities to express his outrage. 'No money!' he shouted. 'No phone! No Katrina money!' It took a while to decipher, but we finally realized that he'd been robbed. In Moone, no less. Someone had broken into his cottage and stolen his stash of 600 euros, his wife's money and both their mobile phones. Jessie asked her assistant to call the guards in Ballintore, a slightly larger village down the road, and report the crime, but that did little to soothe the over-agitated groom, who continued to moan and pace and curse, wondering why he'd ever left Poland in the first place.

After tea, I met Moscow Flyer. He was going to the Curragh for a bit of fine-tuning – a racecourse gallop to keep him from getting bored or lazy. He has his own special paddock as befits a celebrity, probably the best

two-mile chaser anywhere when he concentrates the way
he did when he won the Queen Mother Champion Chase
at the Festival in 2003, a race that's almost as valuable
and prestigious as the Gold Cup. He likes to roll around
the paddock after a gallop, or stand by a fence at a far
corner and look down at the traffic zipping by on the N9.
The flash of distant metal specks fascinates him, and he
won't move for twenty minutes or so when he's really into
it. He could be meditating, lost in his own thoughts. He's
an intelligent horse – maybe too cerebral, because he can
go all dreamy during a race, barely sliding by on the
grease of his talent.

He whinnied when he saw Eamonn, delighted to board
the horse box with three stable mates. I rode with Jessie
in a Mercedes that she drives like a Jeep, speeding around
the yard over bumps and grass and ignoring the rattle of
the undercarriage. She isn't a person who cares much
about possessions, that's for sure. The car reminded me of
an upmarket version of an old junker I used to own,
where all the stuff I never tossed out managed to collect.

On our bracing journey over Kildare's back roads,
often just wide enough for one-and-a-half cars, Jessie
recounted how she'd bought Moscow Flyer as a four-
year-old at a Tattersalls Ireland sale, in June 1998, acting
as an agent for Brian Kearney, whose son, a racing-mad
barrister, had convinced him he'd need a hobby other
than golf when he retired. She had a budget of 20,000
guineas to spend on a chaser, the preference of most
owners. Moscow came up late in the auction, and though
his breeding didn't amount to much unless you went back
three generations – he's by Moscow Society out of

Meelick Lady – she liked the look of him and paid 17,500 guineas, guessing he'd be a nice horse and nothing more.

When we reached the Curragh, I felt I could see for miles. It's among the flattest places in Ireland, a broad limestone plain where the Irish have raced horses for centuries. Bold winds whip across it, and one was blowing that afternoon, lending an arctic chill to an otherwise bright day. Eamonn and the other riders were already there, checking their tack. Moscow's first race, the Fortria Chase at Navan, was still three weeks away, so Jessie urged Eamonn not to push the horse. She was concerned about the ground, still too firm from the lack of rain. 'Look at that,' she said, pointing to some withered clumps of grass. 'That's dry for Ireland.'

While the horses hacked up on their way to the course, Jessie began shivering, so we got back into the Mercedes to escape the bitter wind. 'Training from a car,' she said, amused. 'What a business!' She has such a strong, independent personality I wondered if she'd encountered much resistance when she tried to break into the game. Predictably, the begrudgers were against a woman entering their ranks, she told me, and assumed she couldn't be serious. They took her for a dabbler funded by her husband, who'd pack up and quit in a year or two when the job became too gruelling.

'Nobody said anything directly,' she went on, 'because that isn't the Irish way. I could feel it, though.' She spoke calmly at first, not wanting to complain, but her tone grew more heated, and I could tell my questions had touched a nerve. 'It's still a man's world,' she said. 'We don't have any female stewards. Women are rarely on the boards of racecourses, and all the beat writers for the papers are men.' That chauvinistic attitude wasn't confined to racing, she felt. Instead, it reflected Irish society at large, and she mentioned how she'd once applied for a bank loan for her business, only to be advised to bring Johnny along to sign the papers for her.

She drove closer to the track and picked up her binoculars. Moscow looked so vital, so natural, I could hardly believe he'd been slow to develop, but in his first four races, all bumpers, he'd never finished better than third, and when Jessie tried him over hurdles in a training race at Punchestown in '99, he screwed up completely and dumped Barry Geraghty. 'Moscow ran into a dolled-off hurdle. The horse went left, and Barry went right,' she recalled. 'I was so cross with him!' Since jumping is Moscow's sore point, and since Geraghty has the bumps and bruises to prove it, I once asked him for his thoughts. 'The thing is, Moscow's very brave,' he said. 'He just doesn't worry about it. He's like, "If I get it wrong, fuck it." His style isn't careless – it's carefree.'

After the Punchestown fiasco, Moscow Flyer won a maiden hurdle at last, in October, defeating the highly regarded Young Buck from Noel Meade's yard, so Harrington entered him in a handicap hurdle at Down Royal a week later, where he faced another fancied horse of Meade's. 'I don't know why we're odds on,' Meade confided before the race. 'We're giving you weight, and this horse isn't as good as the last one he beat.' Those were prophetic words – Moscow romped home by fifteen lengths. Later that month, he scored another big win in the Royal Bond Novice Hurdle, a Grade One at

Fairyhouse, and might have gone straight to Cheltenham if he hadn't suffered a hairline fracture of the pelvis.

By the following autumn, Moscow Flyer was a rising star, the young pretender ready to challenge Istabraq, an ageing Irish immortal who had won the last three Champion Hurdles at the Festival. They faced each other in three oddly disappointing races, all at Leopardstown. Moscow won the first in late December, but the result was tainted because Istabraq fell. In January 2001, Istabraq countered with a win, but Moscow was a faller that time. Their rubber match provided no resolution, either, because Istabraq fell again. The races left everyone dissatisfied and unreconciled. They'd been determined by phantom blows.

Istabraq ran just twice more, the last time at the Festival in March 2002, where he was pulled up and later retired. But Moscow kept improving, getting stronger, more battle-hardened and mature, and Jessie allowed him to go chasing, Brian Kearney's wish and her goal from the outset. Again, Moscow was slow to catch on, falling in his first beginners' chase at Fairyhouse, in October 2001, but he won three in a row after that, and then fell at Leopardstown in January, establishing the curious, disturbing pattern that has dogged him throughout his career – a mishap, then three wins and a mishap.

At the Curragh, Moscow Flyer was a vision of power in motion, his head carried low and his neck curled. He was tugging so hard Eamonn had to keep the tightest possible hold. 'He's very well,' Jessie said, pleased with what she saw. 'Eamonn's arms will be six inches longer. The horse has so much ability! He doesn't need to do very much to win a race. He'll look around here, look around there, and he's only in second gear. That's why the Queen Mother Chase suits him. The pace is so fast, and the competition's so intense, he has to pay attention.'

We collected the horses. Moscow was scarcely blowing. Jessie was concerned about his stable mare Start From Scratch, who had a habit of pulling left in his races, as he had done again today. I sensed she was beginning to scrape the bottom of the barrel, unable to solve the problem. She wondered aloud if his teeth were hurting him, and suggested a ring bit and a cross-nose band as remedies for his tendency to hang, but she didn't sound all that positive or confident. She couldn't find the key to him, really. Start From Scratch had a few more runs for Jessie before his owner moved him to another yard, proving the point she'd made earlier. Owners are fickle, and every trainer is subject to their whims.

The weather continued bone-dry. Teasing clouds drifted across Ireland, but they only delivered showers and squalls. Britain fared no better. Late in October, in a 'race' that summed up everyone's discontent, Santenay from Paul Nicholls' yard collected the winner's share of a £5,700 purse for walking over the course at Kempton by himself. Most trainers were still keeping their big horses under wraps and playing it safe. Jessie wouldn't run Moscow Flyer in the Fortria if the going stayed firm, so I was glad to see that Henrietta Knight had entered her old warrior Edredon Bleu, now eleven, in the Desert Orchid Chase at Wincanton.

The Desert Orchid was on a Sunday. After breakfast, I shoved aside the work on my desk to make room for the *Racing Post*. My weekends were a happy shambles ever since I'd accepted the fact I wouldn't get anything of value done until the races were over. Like Moscow Flyer, I needed to concentrate and focus. The process was similar to runic divination, an attempt to break a secret code and reap the reward of untold riches. I began with the form charts and scanned them for recent winners, circling those who'd done it 'impressively' or 'comfortably' – an obvious plus, but one that's easy to miss if you skip the fine print. Next, I turned to the Selection Box and the Naps' Competition to check the experts' opinions, and then read the comments from trainers, an exercise in trying to separate the half-truths from the bare-faced lies.

Around noon, I left for O'Herlihy's, my local pub. Irish pubs can be divided into two categories, the striving-to-be-hip-euro-modern and the insistently traditional, a style that a visiting pal from the States defined as 'still having those little wooden stools'. I was uncomfortable in the euro-modern places, put off by the shrill, unfathomably upbeat pop music and the blinding décor, all mirrors and shiny surfaces repellent to most people of middle-age, so O'Herlihy's, with its little wooden stools, was perfect for me. The light is soft during the day and softer at night, the upholstery is frayed, there are some antique balsa fishing lures in a display case and some framed prints of horses, of course, as well as a pair of bronzed baby shoes behind the bar that a customer forgot once, in the distant past, and never reclaimed. Instead of loud music, we have the gentle murmur of a radio pitched several decibels below the level at which the programme (whatever it is) might be heard.

As usual, my friend T.P. Reilly was already at the pub. Our friendship is an odd one, I suppose, because we never meet except at O'Herlihy's or at a bookies. A semi-retired fellow who only works when he wants, Reilly is large, talkative, and sweet-natured, with a full head of curly grey hair and an expansive belly. He was drawn to me out of curiosity, charmed to see an American studying, and muttering over, the *Post*, and he took it upon himself to contribute to my education, being both a collector of racing memorabilia and an amateur historian. At times, he seems to regard me as his own creation, a punter he has moulded from plain, unpromising clay.

Like so many of the Irish, Reilly fell in love with horses as a child when a farmer-uncle let him ride an old plough mare. He hasn't been in the saddle since, but still believes he is a superior judge of horseflesh and banks on it, in fact, relying on a horse's looks to guide him. As a system, it's probably no worse than any other, and it doesn't cost him any money. He's always good for his round and owns a terraced house nearby, where he lives with two cats and an ageing spaniel called Oliver. He does have one other idiosyncrasy as a gambler, preferring to wager on British races because he believes they're less 'bent'. Despite being immensely proud of his country, he feels the Irish score poor marks for strict obedience to either the rules or the law.

The day of the Desert Orchid Chase, Reilly had finished his deliberations and was busy with a crossword puzzle. I ordered my pint and prepared to be transported.

It's my conceit that only over a beer can I pick the winners of the races on TV. The Guinness lifts me into a state I can only describe as fuzzy clarity, relaxed and yet able to address the *Post* with a more critical eye. Reading the paper again, I saw tiny filaments of meaning my sober, less perceptive self had missed. Horses who'd been attractive at first glance now appeared outclassed or worse, while others I'd glided over gained a new resonance. Thus enlightened, I was certain that Edredon Bleu couldn't lose, even though he carried almost two stone more than the other four entries.

Rare is the pub in Dublin that's more than a block or two from a betting shop, so I was at Boylesports in under three minutes. Besides Wincanton, there were races at Aintree and Towcester, and also some good Irish racing at Galway and Wexford, affording the punters an ample opportunity for confusion. All twenty-seven TV screens in the shop were broadcasting a fluctuating display of odds, live action, and ads coaxing customers to have a flutter, so the clerks were overwhelmed. Edredon Bleu was a heavily-backed favourite at 6-5, but I had learned that you must take a short price on jumpers sometimes and put fifty euros on the nose, elbowing my way through the crowd to do it.

In the old days, the Irish wouldn't be caught dead at a bookie's on the Sabbath, I realized, but the Roman Catholic church isn't the power it once was and even suffers from a shortage of young men willing to be priests. That reminded me of a story about Richard 'Boss' Croker, a Catholic from Cork, who earned a fortune as a corrupt Tammany Hall kingpin in New York, and then set himself up as a trainer in Foxrock, a Dublin suburb. When Croker entered Orby in the Epsom Derby, in 1907, the British hacks wrote off the horse – 'The turf in Ireland has no spring in it, and the climate is too depressing,' they said – but the loyalists at home backed Orby down from 66-1 to 100-9, and lit bonfires around Trinity College after his victory, where an old woman was heard to cry, 'Thank God, we have lived to see an Irish horse win the English Derby!'

That afternoon, Edward O'Grady had a rewarding time at Galway. He saddled Golden Row, who won the Grade 3 Ballybrit Novice Chase, and Windsor Boy, who took a listed handicap hurdle, both with Barry Geraghty riding. Rumour had it that Barry might replace Norman Williamson as O'Grady's stable jockey, a job to be envied. O'Grady is bright and sophisticated, with a dry wit, and he has trained more Cheltenham Festival winners – seventeen – than anyone currently active in Ireland. He also has the dubious distinction of being the only Irish trainer ever to be arrested at Cheltenham, charged with conspiracy to cheat and defraud the British bookmakers.

The scandal centred on a betting coup, later known as 'The Gay Future Affair'. Tony Murphy, a wealthy Cork builder, was its ringleader and borrowed his scam from greyhound racing. It involved a double or treble wager (two or three win bets) that coupled Gay Future with Opera Cloak or Ankerwyke, or both, who would be withdrawn on the day, 24 August 1974, thereby turning the bet into a single on Gay Future, the bookmakers' standard practice. All three horses were supposedly at the yard of Tony Collins in Troon, Scotland, although the 'Gay Future' with Collins was a phoney, a decoy. The real Gay Future was with O'Grady in Tipperary, in serious and secretive training, being honed to a fine edge over hurdles.

Collins declared Gay Future for a novice hurdle at Cartmel, an out-of-the-way track in the Lake District, with the longest run-in in England. The phoney horse departed from Collins' yard in a box, but was switched for O'Grady's horse by a phone box near the racecourse, shades of Clark Kent. Before sending Gay Future into the parade ring, the conspirators further covered their scheming by rubbing the horse with soap suds, so he'd look washed out. They also arranged for Collins' top jockey to be on another horse, Racionzer, and plunged on him at the course. Gay Future, priced at 10-1, soared home by fifteen lengths under Timmy Jones, an Irish rider flown in for the day – a perfect coup, it seemed, except that Collins had messed up.

Instead of sending Opera Cloak and Ankerwyke to their respective engagements at Plumpton and Southwell, and then inventing an excuse for their failure to arrive – a traffic jam, say, or an accident – he just left them at his yard. A reporter who sensed a good story discovered the ruse with a simple phone call, speaking to a stable lass who told him she could see both horses from her window. That alerted the authorities, who launched an investigation, and the police arrested Murphy and O'Grady at Cheltenham the following March, on the Festival's first day, while Collins was detained in Troon. The case dragged on for another year or so, with the accused out on bail. When it came to trial, the prosecutor failed to present any evidence against O'Grady, and he was cleared. The judge, though sympathetic to the others – the fraud was 'very minor' in his opinion – still felt compelled to fine them because a jury had found them guilty.

To the end of his life, Tony Murphy denied that he'd done anything illegal. In essence, there was no fix, he claimed. The right horse had run at the right track, as advertised. But the bookies didn't agree, and only paid out on a fraction of the bets his Cork cronies had spread around London and its environs, investing about thirty thousand pounds as they sped from shop to shop from their base at the Tara Hotel. Besides the notoriety, The Gay Future Affair brought Edward O'Grady an unexpected bonus – a movie deal, with Pierce Brosnan playing him in *Murphy's Stroke*.

Back at O'Herlihy's, we watched the horses milling around before the start of the Desert Orchid Chase. As optimistic as I was, I had a twinge of anxiety since Edredon Bleu is a front-runner, a style of racing I distrust. Often front-runners are like those novelists who publish a brilliant book at twenty-two, then burn out over the long haul and wind up reviewing novels by a new crop of brilliant twenty-two-year-olds. I shouldn't have fretted, though, because Edredon Bleu had class to spare and won by a Gay Futuresque margin of fifteen lengths, setting a track record in the bargain, eleven seconds off the standard time. Henrietta Knight, very gratified, thought she might try the old fellow at a longer distance next time and threatened to write his biography, as she'd done for Best Mate.

A winning bet confirms a man's genius and elevates his spirits. I never told Imelda about my losses, only about my wins, and if I needed another reason to feel affectionate toward her, which I didn't, it would be that she never asks how the gambling is going. Her interest in racing is confined to the glory of the horses and the places where they run, a scene that hasn't changed much since Degas painted it at Longchamp. We talked about such things on an evening walk to town, down Grafton Street through a giddy mass of shoppers to the Liffey. The river, though low and murky, its thrust curtailed by dams, still had a twilight glory, and we followed it to the sea, pleased to be where we were, together.

And how did it happen? I had asked myself that more than once. The initial attraction, the sheer fun of a romance, the falling *into* love, those parts were easy, but there were difficulties, as well. Being older, we were both wary, on guard for each other's fatal flaw, desperate not to repeat our past mistakes, and careful about her children's reaction to the newly minted fact of 'us'. I had friends who thought I was being rash or just plain foolish, while some in Imelda's circle wrung their hands over her choice of a partner, this gent from abroad travelling without portfolio – and a writer to boot. But trust and conviction grow if real love is in the mix, and with them comes the courage to say, I want this to work, an admission that centres you in the midst of swirling waters.

Sunday dinner was a tradition for us now. We splurged on an expensive bottle of Chardonnay, the sort of treat a winner deserves, and a fat chicken to roast, stuffing it with half a lemon and sprigs of rosemary from the garden. There would be roast potatoes, too, at the younger boy's insistence, and a salad with some buttered carrots from the root-crop heaven of Ireland. A new CD to listen to, a coal fire blazing, the *Observer* for the news, and an Irish tabloid for the gossip – how simple life can sometimes be. Amazing grace, indeed.

The rain finally came at the end of the month, a bristly, stinging storm with a harsh taste of winter at its core. It struck while I was on a train to Thurles, a large but plain town in Tipperary, for a Thursday meeting, seated across from a quartet of well-dressed men toting old-fashioned leather satchels. If I hadn't known better, I'd have taken them for OAPs on a holiday trip to Cork, but they were bookies on their way to the racecourse with a rough day ahead, the weather the least of their concerns.

In the pecking order of Irish tracks, Thurles ranks toward the bottom, so the bookies wouldn't see much money that afternoon, but their costs were still fixed, whether the betting ring was full or empty. They pay an annual fee for their pitch at the course, along with a daily fee (five times the price of a ticket) and half of one per cent of their turnover. The internet betting exchanges cut into their profits now, as do the high-street shops where punters can bet on sports other than racing. (Going a step further, Paddy Power offers novelty bets – 10-1 that Bono will become a Buddhist, say.) They also have travel expenses and the cost of hiring a helper to chalk up the wagers. Contrary to the myth of on-course bookies raking in the gold, only about twenty percent of those in Ireland earn a substantial living. In effect, they're an endangered species.

I once visited a retired bookie to learn more about the trade. Kindly and arthritic, in his late eighties, the Old Bookie was a tenth-generation Dubliner. 'Can't you hear it in my accent?' he asked, as he greeted me. He was dressed like a fringe member of the Rat Pack in a powder blue cardigan, neatly pressed beige trousers, matching socks and shiny shoes. He'd made book for about sixty years, following his father's lead. 'I was brainless at the start,' he swore, but he was also adamant that you don't have to be super-intelligent to succeed in his line of work, just reasonably good at maths. 'I knew three fellas who belonged to Mensa, and they were so hooked on theory, they were lousy at their jobs,' he said.

'Is it hard to get a licence?' I asked.

'Nah, the police will licence anybody.' He waved a hand dismissively. 'Unless you have a criminal record or serious enemies.'

'Serious enemies,' I repeated, picturing a row of shallow graves.

He nodded. 'Serious enemies.' At any rate, he'd done all right in the business, flush at times and just scraping by at others. He went broke twice, but he survived. It was fruitless to worry about the flux, he believed. 'I'd put it behind with a stop at the pub, or at the Gresham if I was doing well,' the Old Bookie said, although he admitted that the work was stressful and took its toll on family life. 'The things I did wrong, they haunt me,' he confessed, and his face did look hollow and haunted for a moment. He confirmed what I'd heard before, that most on-course bookies become rich only if they own a betting shop or a share in one, or invest in property instead of pissing away their money on a flashy lifestyle, with too many stops at the Gresham.

The Old Bookie thought he lacked the courage to be what he called a 'superior turf accountant'. 'I didn't have the nerve to ride out a hot streak and take a big gamble when I had the touch,' he told me. 'And if somebody wanted me to take a really big bet, I ran the other way. Care for a drink?' he asked. I watched in awe as he poured me a few fingers of Bushmills whisky from a drinks tray, and when I didn't add any water to the glass, he gave me a look of mock horror. 'Whoa, that'll kill you! Drinking whisky straight!' Then he smiled and hitched up his trousers. 'I'm going to be eighty-nine soon. Think I'll make it?' I had the good grace not to reply, 'What kind of odds are you offering?'

A queue of taxis waited at the train station in Thurles, and the bookies piled into them. The racecourse was a mile or so away, built on some of Ireland's best farmland. Often racing goes ahead at Thurles after a heavy storm, when other tracks are waterlogged. The land is naturally free-draining, and the Molony family, who've owned it for decades, tend it like good farmers, letting it rest during the summer and fertilizing the racing strip with the leavings from a local sugar beet factory.

The rain was coming down hard now, whipped into a fury by a nasty wind. After I entered the course, I searched for a warm corner where I could hide out, a snug little bar or a cosy restaurant, only to discover that they don't exist at Thurles. There are two bars, but they're both under-heated, as is the buffet-style restaurant, where the yellowish fluorescent lighting created a penitential gloom. In a misguided attempt to brighten the room, someone had put wilting carnations on the tables in glasses of water and little cream jugs, a sight so sad it almost brought tears to my eyes. For all their conviviality, gentleness, and politeness, the Irish can sometimes be awfully good at punishing themselves.

I chose the smaller bar as my sanctuary, figuring it would yield more body heat. Thurles draws about two thousand fans on an average Thursday, and I prayed they'd all show up immediately. The race card listed seven races split between the jumps and the flat, but I was distracted by a flickering TV that played an ad for the bookies – all text and no pictures. The jingle went, 'Bet with the Bookies/It's easy/It's value/It's fun!' That would motivate anybody, I thought wryly, as I surveyed the regulars around me, whose ruddy complexions and broken capillaries were the result of braving the elements, or maybe avoiding them in any handy pub. This was desolate territory. I started on the hot whisky myself – Jameson, sugar, hot water, and a lemon slice stuck with cloves.

To be fair, there are trainers who love Thurles. Willie Mullins once told me how much he enjoys the course for the good galloping ground and the knowledgeable spectators. Possibly Jessie Harrington feels the same. She was in high spirits before the first race. 'Don't complain,' she scolded a grumbler in the parade ring. 'It's raining!' The race was for maidens on the flat, and she had two horses in it, but she was up against Shangri La, a classy Sadler's Wells filly from Aidan O'Brien's yard at Ballydoyle, and had no real chance. It's unusual for O'Brien to lose a maiden race in Ireland, so well bred and conditioned are his colts and fillies.

'Things can only digress from here,' said a man at the bar afterwards, tearing up his losing ticket. 'I mean, regress.' Strangely, I understood him. I'd checked the card again and knew what we had in store. Among the entries for the Munster Handicap, for instance, were A. C. Azure (no wins in twenty-seven starts), Callas (none in twenty-five), Camillas Estate (none in thirty-one), and the comparatively gifted Hamlyn (one in thirty-eight). The fifteen horses, a full field, ranged in age from four to ten. They had a combined total of 409 starts in Ireland, and had won just fourteen of them, or 3.4 percent. A few were home-breds trained by farmers, but most belonged to hapless owners who hoped (or used to) that they would amount to something. In every flat race that day, there were fifteen runners plus reserves – the average field in an Irish race is fourteen horses – and that led me to the inescapable conclusion that Ireland produces a lot of racehorses, not all of them good.

Whenever I asked anyone about the boom in racehorses, I was directed to the imposing figure of Charles Haughey, Ireland's former Prime Minister, whose surname in Gaelic (Eachaidhe) means 'horseman'. Like Richard Croker, he was called 'The Boss' while in office, carried himself with the authority of a high chieftain, and shared Croker's ability to reap questionable benefits from his position – a rogue, in other words, despised in some quarters and loved in others. But politics aside, Haughey's affection for horses is genuine. He bought his first for £3,700 in 1962 while serving as Minister of Justice, and gradually built up his stable and sent his mares to a stud farm in County Dublin presided over by Captain Tim Rogers, once an aide to Winston Churchill.

In 1968, Haughey acquired his own stud in Meath, often a perk among the newly affluent Irish and, a year later, as Minister of Finance, he introduced a tax exemption for the breeding industry at an opportune moment, just as similar exemptions were being scrapped in Britain. (In this case, 'tax exemption' meant no taxes whatsoever on a stud farm's profits from breeding.) Haughey's finest hour as an owner came in 1985, when his Flashing Steel won the Irish Grand National under top weight. John Mulhern, his trainer, later married his daughter Eimear, and they run Abbeville and Meadow Court Studs on the Curragh.

Toward the end of his political life, in 1999, 'The Boss' spelled out his views on the breeding industry in a message to *The Irish Thoroughbred*. 'Natural advantages in climate and soil, and favourable taxation treatment, have contributed to our excellent reputation for horse breeding,' he wrote. 'However, it is the skill and innate love of horses in our breeders that have been the decisive factors . . . In more recent times we have seen the development of large specialized stud farms. I consider this a positive development and complementary to the work of the small breeder.'

Though Haughey survived many scandals, his tendency to confuse the national interest with his own caught up with him at last. Dragged before a tribunal, he was accused of accepting lavish gifts from businessmen, and also owed the government millions in back taxes and undeclared income, although this hardly made him a bankrupt – he still owns one of the Blasket Islands off the Kerry coast, for instance. In some respects, his support for big-time breeders smacked of the same cronyism that brought him down. The tax loophole he opened allowed the 'large specialized' stud farms to dominate the market, a hindrance rather than a compliment to the little guys struggling to get by.

The most prominent beneficiary of Haughey's gambit has been the famous Coolmore Stud in Tipperary, a global operation with farms in Australia and Kentucky, too. Coolmore owns many of the world's most desirable stallions, and its racing arm at Ballydoyle provides a showcase for the colts who'll stand at stud some day. The business has been so profitable that John Magnier, its MD, is a tax exile, although he has a home in Ireland and spends as much time there as permissible by law to oversee his concerns. Nobody blames Magnier and his associates for taking such brilliant advantage of the loophole to improve the Irish racehorse, but Coolmore has been criticized for overbooking its stallions. For example, Sadler's Wells may cover up to two hundred mares in a season, doing double duty in Australia and bringing in a reported £40 million annually.

Haughey's legacy, then, is a double-edged sword. If it has allowed operations like Coolmore to raise the quality of Irish runners and hold a pre-eminent position on the international stage, it has also fostered a glut of less talented stock. The number of horses in training continues to rise, up to 5,762 in 2003, as does the number of owners, even though the hobby (that's what it is for most people) isn't cheap. Single owners and partnerships (up to four members) are the main players, but syndicates of six, ten, or even twenty individuals are gaining in popularity. Almost all male chasers and hurdlers are geldings and worthless at stud, while brood mares are only slightly more valuable, so an owner's initial fantasies revolve around the prize money to be won and, more distantly and less reliably, on the glittery pleasure dome of Cheltenham.

That's fair enough, really, when you consider that the average purse in Ireland is the highest in Europe, 22,840 euros compared to 16,389 euros for the UK. Although it's true that almost half the horses in training do win something, that something usually isn't enough to fuel any further fantasies. Many owners become realists as the bills mount up, and they sell or retire their horses, a pet for the kids to ride, or hang onto it for the *craic* if they can afford to, running it for fun at tracks like Thurles. In 2003, the overall attendance at 303 fixtures was up by eight and a half percent, another sign of how much the Irish love racing and are willing to embrace a horse of any kind.

The Irish never let rotten weather stand between them and a good time, either. All afternoon they'd battled the elements, determined to enjoy themselves regardless of the rain, and by the fifth race it appeared that the elements were beginning to surrender. The clouds parted enough for me to see Devil's Bit Mountain, the track's logo, a humped shape on the horizon missing its tip – the bit torn off by the devil in 'a fit of anger' and deposited in nearby Cashel. It was still very cold, but I felt fortified by the hot whiskys, three and counting, and ready for the day's feature, The Irish Stallion Farms European Breeders Fund Steeplechase over two-and-a-quarter miles, worth almost twenty thousand euros.

Again, the firm going in Ireland affected the race. Of the original fourteen entries, only two had stayed in at the declaration stage, so we had a match between Splendour, a winner on good ground at Roscommon earlier in the month, and Risk Accessor, who'd last run (and lost) at Galway in July. Risk Accessor's level of fitness was a question mark, but I couldn't rule him out, not when he belonged to John P. McManus, Ireland's largest owner of jumpers, who has a mythic status among punters. Extraordinarily wealthy and influential, he picked up the nickname 'Sundance Kid' for his raids on the betting ring in his younger days, robbing the bookies repeatedly.

Born in County Limerick, McManus contracted the gambling bug as a child, but he was small for his age and had to rely on adult accomplices to place his bets. When he was nine, he cashed a memorable one on Merryman II in the 1960 Grand National, at odds of 13-2. After leaving school, McManus worked with his father, a dairy farmer who also had a plant hire business, but he quit to be a bookmaker himself at twenty and went broke twice while learning the ropes at point-to-points and greyhound races. The second time, his mother loaned him some money on the sly, promising not to tell her husband, who disapproved of his son's occupation. 'I suppose I had more respect for it than any money I've had before or since,' he told Raymond Smith, a racing journalist, perhaps because the money carried a mother's blessing, no small thing among the Irish.

In fact, McManus was never skint again. Instead, his luck improved dramatically. His agile brain for higher maths and figuring the percentages paid off when he diversified into currency trading later in life. With his profits, he bought prop-erty, leisure assets, and horses, frequently excellent ones. His ambition was (and still is) to win the Gold Cup at Cheltenham. Despite his legiti-mate ventures, he continued to gamble and played high-stakes backgammon for a while, but the bookies bore the brunt of his assaults. In 1982, he was rumoured to have taken them for £250,000 on his horse Mr Donovan, trained by Edward O'Grady, who won the Royal & SunAlliance Hurdle at the Festival.

In those early days, McManus was not yet the con-summate pro. Sometimes he got murdered at the races. Lacking the discipline to quit when his hot hand ran cold, he once wrote to some English bookmaking firms and warned them that if they gave him any more credit, they did so 'at their peril'. Eventually, he gained an icy control, and never chased his losses or tried to get even on the last race. He came to believe that jump racing rep-resents the best value for a punter, because a horse can commit an error or two and still recover, almost impos-sible to do on the flat. For Raymond Smith, he laid out his guiding principles as concisely as any textbook: The going is the most important thing. Set out to make a point or two over the odds, and go in with both fists. And above all, beware of certainties.

When McManus's offshore corporation Cubic Expression sailed into the financial stratosphere, he moved to Switzerland as a tax exile in the 1990s. His office in Geneva reportedly has a fine view of Mont Blanc and a pair of TVs, one tuned to the currency markets and the other to the racing odds. An avid golfer, he sponsors a charity tournament in Limerick every year and has a locker next to Tiger Woods at the exclusive Isleworth Club in Orlando, Florida. With John Magnier, his fellow exile, he is a large shareholder in Manchester United. His string of one hundred-plus jumpers, including such stars as Baracouda and First Gold, is parcelled out among several trainers in Ireland, England, and France.

In the way of folk heroes, McManus often drops out of the sky and lands at a racecourse in his green-and-gold helicopter, the colours of Limerick's South Liberties hurling club. I scanned the heavens for signs of him, but he didn't show up that afternoon. Avoiding Thurles on a stormy day was another tribute to his cleverness, I thought. Still, he missed seeing the match race, a much more interesting contest than I'd anticipated. It began as a tactical stalemate, with neither Conor O'Dwyer on Risk Accessor nor Barry Geraghty on Splendour willing to make the running. After a mile or so, the rain-softened turf worked in Risk Accessor's favour, and when O'Dwyer let him go, the horse never looked back.

*   *   *

Going home on the train, blissfully warm in the sleepy, overheated compartment, I set aside the *Racing Post* for Patrick Kavanagh's *The Green Fool*, an autobiograph-ical account of the poet's formative years in County Monaghan on a farm not unlike those outside my window. I had come across Kavanagh's writing in anthologies when I lived in California, but I didn't know it well and felt I'd made a sensational discovery when I began reading his poems in Ireland, so different in tone and subject matter from those of Yeats, who had laid claim to Irish poetry, at least in the minds of most Americans, as Joyce had done with fiction.

Kavanagh had a farmer's directness, as well as a rough-edged, ribald wit. He loved horses and racing, of course, a logical consequence of growing up where he did, and possibly of being Irish, and he was often seen in Dublin pubs pouring over the newspapers and looking for winners. But as a young man, while practising his craft more-or-less in secret, he was a servant of the land, of his crops and his cattle. He painted a fascinating portrait of his 'clay-heavy mind' bursting into excited flames after reading the Modernists, especially Gertrude Stein. In his poems, he was truthful to his roots, painfully so at times, writing about pinched rural lives and the travail of ageing bachelors, counting himself among them.

Those ties to the land held Kavanagh back when his first book of poems was published in England, but he was ambitious and so hungry for culture that he once walked fifty miles from his village of Iniskeen to Dublin just for a taste of it. Still, he wrestled with his predicament, torn between moving on and staying behind. 'The land is jealous of literature,' he wrote, 'and in its final effort to hold a poet offers him, like a despairing lover, everything, everything.' Yet in the end he broke with the land to pursue his literary future in London, leaving home with £2. 4s. in his pocket.

From Heuston Station, I walked along the Liffey in the early dark and through the city centre, then up Baggot Street until it turned into Pembroke Road, Kavanagh's old haunt, where he rented an apartment for many years. The night air was rain-freshened, and as I followed the Grand Canal toward our neighbourhood, I passed the poet's statue on its bench by the water and sat for a brief while, letting the stillness wash over me. 'Ireland is a fine place to daydream in,' he also wrote, and that's how it seemed to me just then, a realm apart from ordinary cares, where the horses would be running again tomorrow.

November: The Great Unveiling

On the first Saturday of the month, I was at O'Herlihy's again, a pint settling on the bar and the *Post* restored to pride of place. It was the time of year when important National Hunt races start coming in bunches, so Irish trainers would soon have to decide what they were willing to risk, regardless of the going. That blustery afternoon in Thurles, stored forever in my bank of soggy memories, proved to be a cheat. It didn't signal a change in the weather. Instead, the dry days returned, with the English courses being watered almost daily so that they could hold their meetings. There was even talk that the Open Meeting at Cheltenham, the early season's high point, might be in jeopardy.

Moscow Flyer was still penciled in for the Fortria Chase, but I had no idea about the plans for Beef Or Salmon, so I went looking for Michael Hourigan to see what he had in mind. He'd left his yard in Limerick for the Tattersalls November National Hunt Sale, held not far from Fairyhouse Racecourse in County Meath. Hourigan was there to check out and maybe bid on the horses, the unbroken stock and yearlings on offer, more than eight hundred lots. The thick catalogue I picked up at the desk had a painting of a red fox on the front cover, and on the back were photos of Best Mate, Moscow Flyer, and Monty's Pass, the 2003 Grand National winner, all purchased at Tattersalls.

Horses were everywhere around the Tattersalls complex, in all shapes and sizes, constantly on the move. Grooms were combing and buffing them, polishing them up like new cars for their moment in the spotlight. They led the horses from the barns to a holding ring outside the main building, where the buyers gathered to inspect them, and when their number came up, they went through an archway into the sales ring, a little oval surrounded by theatre seats in tiers. An electronic screen dominated the proceedings, flashing the bids in sterling, dollars, and euros. The bidding seldom lasted more than two or three minutes, and the selling price seldom exceeded ten grand. I found it sobering to realize even I could afford an Irish racehorse, so large was the supply.

From an upper tier, I watched the auction. The horses all reacted differently in the sales ring, revealing aspects of their character. Some appeared to be oblivious of the noise, the badgering auctioneer, and the crowd looking down on them, an attitude you could interpret as regal or ignorant – your choice, and buyer beware. Others seemed shocked to be on the market and glared at their grooms in an accusing way, as the very source of their betrayal. Here came a furry little yearling so stunned and needy his entire being shouted, 'I want to go back to the farm!' followed by a gangly, head-bobbing gelding who so resembled a cartoon animal I half-expected him to open his mouth and cough up a one-liner. The comedian was returned to his breeder unsold.

I bumped into Hourigan later by the holding ring. A short, sturdy, ruddy-faced man, he looked the trainer's part in a tweed flat cap, a shirt and sweater with corduroy trousers. His nose is flattened, as if he'd taken a punch, and his small, bright eyes don't miss a trick. *The Irish Field* once said that he 'provides a great deal of entertainment to those who listen to him', and I would agree, with a caveat. Hourigan's joking, often directed at himself and occasionally clownish, masks a keen intelligence, and he uses the mask to his advantage against any fool who underestimates him. He has risen from nothing, liberated from the poverty of old Limerick, to build a yard that wins more prize money every year than almost any other in Ireland.

Hourigan had a foot up on a fence, chatting with his cronies, apparently relaxed. At the same time, he was assessing the horses minutely with those small, bright eyes. I thought he could do it all day long and never be bored. His son Paul was with him, a jump jockey as Michael had been, who'd won about two hundred races and yet would soon be too tall and heavy to ride anymore. Paul was recovering from a cracked shoulder blade, taking the injury and his impending retirement hard. 'The love for it doesn't go,' Michael said quietly when Paul was out of earshot, but it was a relief to him in a way. That morning, Sean Cleary, a flat jockey, was being laid to rest in Athlone, having died in a freak fall at Galway, the second Irish rider to be killed in the past three months. Hourigan shook his head. 'Two dead. You wouldn't believe it.'

The horses kept emerging from the barns in a ceaseless stream. Lot 287 was a chestnut filly by Good Thyne (USA) out of Financial Asset (IRE). When I went back five generations, I found a dam called Sark, who had produced Roll-A-Joint and Sarcastic. The Tattersalls catalogue was quite a document, worthy of structural analysis. As I thumbed through its information-rich pages, I suspected I could get as hooked on bloodlines as I was on baseball statistics as a boy, able to recite Roll-A-Joint's lifetime record (ten wins, nine over fences, including the Scottish National Chase) as readily, say, as Duke Snider's career batting average (.295).

But a pedigree can only tell you so much, particularly about jumpers. It was like searching for poetry in a metrical arrangement of lines rather than out there on the fringes of your psyche where the magic occurs. Whenever I talked to trainers about buying a horse, they used the same phrase over and over again, 'Something about him I liked.' The process sounded weirdly similar to falling in love, involving a glance across the room (or sales ring) and an exchange of meaningful looks that leads to an emotional connection. The horse telegraphs its readiness to surrender, and the attentive trainer feels intuitively that the horse wants to be trained.

The art of judging a horse's potential, of seeing into its heart, is mysterious, and no one in Ireland is better at it, Hourigan told me, than Tom Costello, an old friend. I'd heard the name before, of course. In the pantheon of National Hunt folk heroes, Costello is on a par with

John P. McManus, although he is even more private and secretive. With his five sons, he runs a horse-trading empire in the tiny village of Newmarket-on-Fergus in County Clare, and sells to such top clients as Hourigan and Willie Mullins, as well as to the English, but Costello can be so picky he sometimes rejects any would-be buyers who fall below his unstated yet impeccable standards. I had no doubt he'd be as celebrated some day as James Sullivan, a famous Irish horse whisperer of the early 1800s who – with a single word – taught a horse to lie on its back and remain so still that a glass of beer could be balanced on each hoof.

Costello's exalted status derives from the fact that he has sold six winners of the Cheltenham Gold Cup – Midnight Court, The Thinker, Cool Ground, Cool Dawn, Imperial Call, and Best Mate. There are positives in all their pedigrees, but not enough to justify that level of success. As for Beef Or Salmon, he was another story altogether, with an undistinguished pedigree only his mother could love. Cajetano, his American-bred sire, was such a lacklustre stallion that he was ultimately shipped to the minor leagues in Italy. Beef Or Salmon's original owner acquired him for a mere 5,400 guineas at Tattersalls in 1999 and unloaded him a year later at Goffs, another Irish auction house, where Hourigan snapped him up for 6,500 guineas because he 'liked the look of him'. The horse has repaid his trainer's faith, winning the Irish Hennessy Gold Cup and four other chases in the 2002-03 season, before his unfortunate fall at the Festival.

'I brought four horses to Cheltenham last year, and three of them fell,' Hourigan said wistfully. 'Hi Cloy ran on Wednesday, and he fell. Beef Or Salmon fell on Thursday, and so did Dorans Pride, who died. It's terrible to lose a horse like that. Terrible. But that's how it goes, doesn't it? Can't do feck-all about it.' He hadn't arranged a plan for Beef Or Salmon yet, he conceded, primarily because of the firm ground, but he told me that there was a chance his horse might run in the James Nicholson Wine Merchant Chase at Down Royal in a week or so.

Hourigan stopped talking abruptly, attracted by a yearling on its way to the holding ring. With a sign so subtle I missed it, he conveyed his interest to the groom, who led the yearling up and down a path, like a model on a catwalk. Satisfied with what he saw, Hourigan brushed a hand over the yearling's coat, knelt to feel its legs and then, without a word, dismissed the groom.

'No good? What was wrong?' I asked him. He didn't answer, so I tried another tack. 'Think you'll be buying anything, Michael?'

'I already have,' he said smugly. He'd bought Lot 276 from Carraiganog Stud, a bay gelding by Saddlers' Hall (by Sadler's Wells) out of Lunalae. Farther back, the yearling had some links to Northern Dancer and Bold Lad, and was also related to Beef Or Salmon. Hourigan had paid 72,000 euros cash on behalf of an unnamed client.

That was the highest price of the sale so far, but it was later eclipsed in a bidding war over a Supreme Leader yearling. (Be My Native and Supreme Leader are the top two National Hunt sires, based on the amount of money their offspring have earned.) The yearling, bred at Spratstown Stud in County Clare, was out of a half-sister to two or three Festival winners. Alastair Pim, the flamboyant auctioneer, asked for an opening bid of 100,000 euros. He got just 20,000, but the price escalated rapidly. Only two bidders were still around at 90,000, and only one was left when Pim banged down his hammer at 110,000, a new Irish record for a store yearling. The buyer in absentia was J.P. McManus.

There was still no rain, not in Cheltenham. In nearby Tewkesbury, yes, and in Cirencester, but the race-course continued to parch. I got that information from John Nicholson, the head groundsman, when I called him to check on the fate of the Open Meeting. I hoped to attend the Open as a sort of Festival preview.

Nicholson said he was doing his best to salvage the meeting. He had been watering steadily for about eleven weeks, for ten or twelve hours a day, to ease the going. In a normal year, he went through about seven million gallons of water, drawing on a reservoir that fills from Hyde Brook, a stream flowing through the course, but he'd used most of that already and had to purchase five million extra gallons from the Severn Trent Water Authority. There were fishermen to worry about, too. An anglers' club stocks the reservoir with coarse species such as roach and pike, but if the water level dropped much lower, the fish might perish.

Nicholson's CV is typical of racetrack vagabonds, I learned as we talked. He'd been a rancher in Brazil, a works rider in Australia, and a stud hand at Cheveley Park before becoming head groundsman at Warwick, later moving to Cheltenham where his ties are deep and ancestral. His great-great grandfather was Clerk of the Course in the 1860s, and his father David 'The Duke' Nicholson, a champion trainer with 1,499 wins, 101 of them at Cheltenham, had his yard in Gloucestershire at Jackdaws Castle, now part of the McManus portfolio and home to Jonjo O'Neill and his horses.

Logistics are at the core of Nicholson's work. He has ten staffers to look after the turf, and two of them also care for his twenty-five fences. The fences, made of birch packed into an oak frame, cost about six thousand pounds apiece. They must be rebuilt every couple of years because the birch becomes brittle and rots. (An oak frame can last for about twenty-five years, with only minor repairs.) Nicholson has tried to grow some birch in composted soil but the birch won't take, so he buys it in bundles from commercial foresters. The sixteen sticks in each bundle are graded and trimmed, then packed into the frame, pulled tight with a wire rope for added support, and trimmed again to the proper height – a minimum of four foot six inches – with a hedge cutter. Hurdles are less expensive at £1,000 each, but they require more attention. Horses bash right through them at times, so they have to be fixed frequently – eight to ten after an average racing day. The course has 150 hurdles in all, so Nicholson's men are kept busy.

At the end of a meeting, he hires a special team to mend the turf. Its members walk the track and replace any divots by treading on them. Though Cheltenham only races sixteen days a year, the course still gets chewed up and needs some major reconstruction when the season's over. It must be harrowed through the late spring and summer, and spiked in early autumn. The grass cover gets ripped out, and the soil is subjected to direct-drill reseeding, a painstaking procedure similar to the one on a good golf course. Co-ordinating the effort can be complicated, but Nicholson is proud of the results and hopes, given his sense of history, that what he and his crew accomplish will still be around in a hundred years.

He must be an optimist, I thought, because he was also hopeful about the Open Meeting. 'We're doing all we can,' he said, and even in faraway Dublin, I could almost hear him knocking wood. 'Now if it would only rain.'

The Northern Ireland Festival of Racing was due to begin at Down Royal. It was a two-day affair on a much smaller scale than Cheltenham, but it would still draw a huge crowd as most Irish festivals do, because people who don't ordinarily attend the races like the raucous party atmosphere. There are fifty-two days of festival racing in Ireland every year, divided between the flat and the National Hunt, and they account for a whopping forty-five percent of the total annual attendance.

I planned to go to Down Royal myself, then double back to see Moscow Flyer run in the Fortria at Navan, but I was disappointed Michael Hourigan had vetoed a trip to the James Nicholson Chase for Beef Or Salmon. The ground was still too firm, he told me, as it was at Leopardstown – 'soft on top but like flint underneath,' he said – so his big horse would also skip the valuable

November Handicap there. The earth, eternally itself, refused to bend to the prayers of mortals, and we would all have to wait patiently for Beef Or Salmon's seasonal debut.

My drive to the north went smoothly. The traffic thinned out past Dublin Airport, with only a few cars travelling on the motorway, and I became aware again of how underpopulated Ireland is, the broad fields and even broader skies a kind of comfort. But my reverie ended in Dundalk when I hit the morning rush hour and got trapped in a landscape of gigantic, menacing, banal chain stores whose presence anywhere signifies 'progress' of a most obtrusive type. After a long, slow crawl through town, I was relieved to be climbing toward Newry and Armagh, noticing the first signs for 'Money Changed' and a zealot's singular billboard with the dire warning, 'The Wages of Sin Is Death'.

Soon I was skirting the edges of the Mourne Mountains, a pretty stretch of country. The mountains would only be foothills in my native California, but they were imposing enough here. Clouds drifted by and disappeared, allowing the sun to break through and highlight the topography, the chasms and declivities. Rivulets tumbled down a cliff face here and there. The mountains looked bright and inviting, ideal for a hike or the picnic Imelda always craves, but then the clouds returned and the entire feel of the Mournes changed in an instant. Now I saw gorse-choked browns and purples, the sort of melancholy scenery that has inspired so many woeful folk songs.

The landscape beyond the Mournes reminded me of England. Technically, I was in the UK, of course, so that must have been part of it, but it had to do with the farms as well, very neat and tidy compared to Ireland, where a wild raggedness often prevails. The Irish seem reluctant to interfere too much with nature, maybe out of a Celtic respect for the gods who preside over it, while the English are quick to provide order where none existed before. As attractive as the farms around Banbridge were, with their hedgerows trimmed and the dry-stone walls in perfect repair, I preferred the less manicured countryside of Ireland, and its mystical sense of bowing to invisible yet potent forces.

Hillsborough, a town close to Down Royal, was my destination. Situated on a strategic spot above the Dublin to Belfast Road, it had grown up around a magnificent artillery fort built in 1650 by Colonel Arthur Hill. The grounds of the fort are a park now, with a lake where anglers were casting flies for brown and rainbow trout. I had a fleeting desire to join them, the exercise being similar to casting about for winners, but I checked into my hotel instead and experienced a taste of the mild paranoia one sometimes encounters in the north. My room, booked as a single, had twin beds, but when I returned from a brief tour of Hillsborough, the pillows were gone from one of them. The bathroom had also been edited. I was limited to one towel, one face cloth and a single bar of soap, apparently to prevent me from smuggling in the extra guest I had concealed in the trunk of my car.

Hoping the bookies wouldn't view me in the same light, as a craven opportunist ready to skim whatever he could from the bounty of Northern Ireland, I made for the racecourse. Founded by Royal Charter in 1685, Down Royal is out in the country as most National Hunt tracks are, although the suburbs are marching toward it. The setting is so rural that a three-foot-deep trench had to be dug, then lined with sharp stones, to keep rabbits from tearing up the turf of the course. From the car park, I walked across the turf to reach the gate, surprised at how scruffy it was, sticking up in rude clumps; it hadn't been cut uniformly. When I tried to dig a boot heel into the ground, it barely gave an inch. Firm going, all right.

The crowd was as large as anticipated that mild and sunny Friday, and in an appropriately festive mood. Having swapped the harried concerns of the business world for the freewheeling universe of luck and fun, office workers were shedding their jackets, ties, and inhibitions, like kids playing truant from school. The barmaids were a picture of racetrack cool, all dolled up and ready to be whisked off to Malaga or Corfu should a big winner give them a wink and a nod.

In the first race, a maiden hurdle for three-year-olds, I discovered an old pal, You Need Luck, who'd had two losing runs since Gowran Park, although the last was a decent third at Galway. He was beautifully turned out and won a 50 euros prize for his groom, but I still couldn't bring myself to bet on him. His head was sagging and his eyes looked sad, as if he were mildly depressed rather than high on sublime thoughts of victory. Young Vintage, a Noel Meade filly, was far more appealing as she pranced around the parade ring, a brilliant babe strutting her stuff, but the glow around her was evident to everybody. At odds of 6-4, I had to pass on her and switched to Willie Mullins' Raikkonen at the last minute, though not with much conviction.

I stood by the rail to watch the action and saw why John Nicholson had to repair his hurdles so often. Some horses ran right through them, with only the merest nod toward a jump. The hurdles wobbled and snapped back into place. To my surprise, You Need Luck ran well and took the lead about seven furlongs out. He had the race in his pocket as he cruised toward the second-last, but he jumped so far to the left that Barry Geraghty appeared to be in shock. It was as if the horse had suddenly remembered an appointment in Hillsborough and wanted to get there as fast as possible. Geraghty produced his whip, dealt out some severe correction, and sent his horse on a crashing sprint through the field, all too late. Drift Away, a long shot, slipped ahead to win, with Raikkonen finishing third. For his noble effort, Geraghty received as his reward a one-day suspension for careless riding.

Sentiment betrayed me in the third race. There, in the glorious sunshine, was young Andrew Leigh, Eamonn's teenage son, on Jessie Harrington's Slaney Fox, being led around the parade ring by his beaming father. They talked and joked as they must have done when Eamonn first put the lad on a horse, unconsciously sealing a pact. Yet Eamonn had told me once that he worried about Andrew, who'd recently completed secondary school and had obtained a jockey's licence as a seven-pound claimer, his allowance for being an apprentice. 'Last job I'd want for him,' he said, knowing the dangers involved, but such nagging issues had been shuffled aside, and all I could read on Eamonn's face at present was a parent's glowing pride.

How could I not back the horse? If there was any justice in this life, the father-and-son team would prevail, so I put twenty pounds to win on Slaney Fox. Andrew was a talented kid, after all, and had just won a 50,000 euros handicap at Listowel in September, which was good for his confidence but not so good for Eamonn, who believed Andrew might be getting cocky. 'Already imagines he's a pro,' he'd griped to me. When Andrew moved early on Slaney Fox and sped to the front, I assumed he'd made an apprentice's mistake by asking the mare for too much too soon, but she seemed to have plenty in reserve as she headed for home. A misstep broke her rhythm, though, and she bungled a hurdle and down went Andrew in a heap, his share of the purse vanishing in a second. Somewhere Eamonn must be shaking his head, I thought, and wishing his son had taken up a safe and useful trade, like carpentry or plumbing.

On my return to the hotel, I was delighted to find my towel hadn't been confiscated, and after a pleasant dinner in town, I slept for a dreamless eight hours and woke refreshed and besotted with the familiar punter's notion that today would be the day, all dismal memories of my losing bets having fled. The morning sky was as black as tar, though, a lid clamped on any possible expression of joy, and soon the rain was spitting down while the Union Jacks flying in Colcavey by the track rippled in the wind. The crowd was different today, too. There were still some people taking a break from business, but they'd been infiltrated by a hard-drinking gang of tough guys with copious tattoos and earrings, their hair reduced to nubbins or shaved off entirely to reveal skulls of fearsome dimensions. Their girlfriends looked just as tough.

The wind began to howl more fiercely. I saw a row of marquees near the rail billowing like the sails of a ship on a gusty sea. They were packed with guzzlers and already a little sloppy underfoot from the rain and spilt beer. I could feel the punch-ups brewing. It seemed unfair that the Nicholson Chase, the first major event on Ireland's National Hunt calendar, should be contested on such a foul, mean-spirited afternoon, but the race was devalued in advance, really, having attracted only four runners despite a generous prize of 91,000 euros. No English trainer had bothered to send a horse, and that was curious given the size of the purse, but it reflected a strange pattern of avoidance I witnessed throughout the season.

I skipped the first two races and bet on Edward O'Grady's Windsor Boy in the third, again ridden by the omnipresent B. J. Geraghty, as he had been at Galway, but Vandas Choice, shipped over from Scotland, stole the race at 7-1. The horse's very presence at Down Royal should have sounded an alarm, considering the absence of other entries from the UK. The Nicholson, run over three miles, lacked any drama because of the reduced size of the field, except perhaps for Arthur Moore, the trainer, whose Glenelly Gale battered Barrow Drive, the 11-10 favourite, into submission. 'Pure poetry,' Moore remarked, but he was nearly the only person around in high spirits.

Meanwhile, the afternoon grew starker, more bleak. I heard a drunk badgering jockey Paul Carberry, 'Hey, Paul! Got any tips?' as if Carberry didn't have enough to do trying to ward off hypothermia. The poor jockeys, covered in mud, resembled bog people. I could have wrung a pint of water from my own socks, so when Jessie Harrington scratched Intelligent from the Killultagh Chase, leaving just three horses, I called it quits.

Across from Down Royal is a golf course with a club-house, where you can rent a cheap, tiny room ideal for a single-minded golf nut or racing fan. Simply for the opportunity to change my soaked clothes, I rented one, and when I was inside, nobody else could get in, but at least it was dry and functional. I had a bed the size of a cot, a writing desk for working on the Great American Novel, an ancient TV, and a window with a nice view of some dish towels on a clothes line. A man (although not a fat man) could live here quite happily (albeit sexlessly and alone), I felt, but I was probably a little delirious. My initial satisfaction faded fast, and I was so bored by the early evening that I was looking forward with relish to *The Day of the Evil Gun* on BBC2, featuring Arthur Kennedy as a maniac killer.

Sunday morning broke bright and clear, a promise of better things to come. I was on the road very early, right after breakfast, and when I arrived at Navan well before noon, I learned that the rain hadn't fallen as heavily there. The going was still rated as Good-to-Firm, and that was unfortunate, meaning the Fortria would be as devalued as the Nicholson. Only four horses were entered, including Glenelly Gale, who'd been driven down from the north just a day after his Down Royal triumph. He couldn't beat Moscow Flyer, but the shrewd Arthur Moore figured he could get a place, which he did, earning another 9,500 euros for the trip.

Well, Moscow here we go, I thought as I stood by the parade ring. He was the first horse into it, doing his star turn and nodding to the crowd. The other horses seemed composed on a different scale, carved out of lesser clay. 'He's good enough if he's lucky enough,' Eamonn said, as he led Moscow around, tossing out an old racing cliché. Moscow was still carrying some extra weight because he'd been on his summer holiday longer than usual, and the grass had been particularly good, but he had cut back on his feed as he always did at the approach of a race, mentally on edge. He deserved to be the 30-100 favourite.

In the Fortria, Barry Geraghty adopted a slight change of tactics. He let Moscow go to the lead, and that seemed to help the horse to settle. 'More relaxed,' the jockey said later. 'Not so jazzed up.' I'd read about Frederico Caprilli, an Italian trainer of jumpers, who urged jockeys to interfere with their mounts as little as possible. 'The rider should be at pains to allow the horse to jump with his natural movements,' Caprilli wrote. In other words, the horse knows best, a principal Geraghty appeared to be applying. Only when Glenelly Gale threw down a weak challenge did he shake up Moscow Flyer, and Moscow responded brilliantly, sprouted wings, and was gone in a flash.

For Jessie Harrington, the Fortria was a relief. 'Now I'll be able to sleep at night,' she said. She hadn't been absolutely sure about her horse after the BMW Chase at Punchestown, in April, his last race. It was his first after winning the Queen Mother Chase, and his fourth after three straight wins, and he had unseated Geraghty yet again – predictably, the superstitious might say. But he couldn't repeat the same pattern again, could he? Harrington must have doubted it, because she announced that Moscow would have two more runs before the Festival. Next would be the Tingle Creek Chase at Sandown, and the Paddy Power Dial-a-Bet Steeplechase at Leopardstown after that. I shuddered to hear her plan. Was Jessie tempting fate? Moscow reminded me of the Brooklyn Dodgers of my youth, who soared to unimaginable heights only to undo their ascent for a reason nobody could fathom.

The Open Meeting would go ahead as scheduled, I learned when I got home. John Nicholson's watering programme had done the job. Only one race had to be cancelled, the Sporting Index Chase, because the cross-country course was still too firm. I had a few days to recuperate before taking off again and frankly needed them. In my dark night of the racing soul, in that tiny room with the Evil Gun mowing 'em down, I had almost lost my faith in the jumps, but the afternoon at Navan had restored it with the awe-inspiring spectacle of Moscow Flyer sailing over fences. It was as if I'd been treated to a Bach sonata after many dreary hours of Salieri and had remembered that music truly does have the power to inspire us. That was the beauty of watching a great horse put on a show.

The Irish would send about twenty horses to the Open, hoping for a share of the generous purse money, and the meeting would be a windfall for the bookies, too, especially Paddy Power, the sponsor of four races, including the Paddy Power Gold Cup Steeplechase. (There are probably more gold cups of one type or another on mantelpieces in England and Ireland than anywhere in the world.) The capital outlay was significant for the company, but so was the publicity value, another wedge in the Power group's attempt to crack the British market, virtually a closed shop for decades. 'Time to throw a cat in among the pigeons,' as Paddy Power liked to put it.

When I first saw a distinctive, green Paddy Power sign in Dublin, I assumed the name was invented, a clever bit of wordplay. That would suit the company's colourful way of operating, always tweaking the Irish public on such touchy subjects as sex and religion. Power had recently raised a furor with a pair of controversial adverts, for example. The first pictured two elderly women about to cross a street and quoted the odds for and against their success, while the second featured a teenage couple on a park bench. Would the boy get his hand under her sweater (2-1), or under her skirt (5-1)? Such exemplary bad taste had the clerics and do-gooders howling.

There is a real Paddy Power, though, the son of a company founder and its communications director, who has the gift of the gab and chatted amiably with me before I left for Cheltenham. Bookies are inclined to be sober folk, at least on the course, but having fun is a key element in the Power agenda, even though they are the first bookmakers ever to be listed on the Dublin Stock Exchange. 'We're into entertainment,' Paddy told me. 'We want to enhance the experience of watching a sporting event,' hence the ultra-clean shops and the state-of-the art TVs. 'Our ads push it to the limit without going over it.'

That was the in-house opinion, anyway, one the offended parties probably didn't share.

In effect, the creation of Paddy Power (the company) represents another act of Irish cunning in the face of an English threat. In the mid-1980s, when the tax on betting in Ireland was cut roughly in half, some big British bookmakers, such as Ladbrokes, Coral, and Mecca, viewed it as an opportunity to move in and expand their market abroad, using so-called 'supershops' as a draw. 'You'd take those places for a kip these days,' Paddy laughed, 'but a lot of Irish bookies were still working out of a front room at home. They wouldn't give you a glass of water for free, much less a cup of tea.' Caught napping, the local bookies fought back, led by David Power, Paddy's father, who worked on-course, and his partners Stewart Kenny and John Corcoran.

All three men owned betting shops and sold off a few for cash to compete against the invaders, although they hung onto their most profitable offices. They incorporated as Paddy Power in 1988, with Kenny, a promotional genius, assigned to run the company. 'Stewart wanted to be Mr Bookmaking,' Paddy said. 'He'd accept a bet on anything.' A bold innovator, Kenny instituted the ploy of special and novelty bets. On a special, say, a punter might get his money back if his horse is second to a winner, while the novelties focus on politics and pop culture. Not long ago, Kenny retired from the company and began studying psychotherapy, his interest in the subtleties of the human mind apparently undiminished.

'The novelties don't generate much income,' Paddy went on, 'but they attract attention. We do still try to be innovative. That's an edge we have over Ladbrokes, the only English competitor left in Ireland. They're too big and unwieldy to make quick adjustments.' As if in testimony, Paddy Power's turnover was up forty-six percent in 2003, with a profit exceeding 20 million euros, despite heavy losses at the Festival (too many favourites won) and on the Grand National when Monty's Pass came in, backed by every patriotic granny and child from Munster to Leinster.

'Will the Open increase your handle?' I asked, though I already knew the answer.

'Anything at Cheltenham is huge for us,' he said. 'The Irish bet with the heart, not the head, and they love to beat the English, so we keep devising new specials and pop them in at the last minute.'

'Do you ever lose on the specials?'

'We've come close. At the Festival in '93, we offered double the odds on any Irish winner on St Patrick's Day, and we were doing fine right up to the Bumper, where Noel Meade's Heist was a heavy favourite at 9-4. Our customers could have him at 9-2 – you should have seen the queues outside our shops! If Heist had won, it would have been an all-time low for us, but he didn't. Rhythm Section, another Irish horse, beat him by half a length and saved us.' Paddy paused for a second, as if to savour his deliverance. 'The odds on Rhythm Section were 16-1.'

My guidebook to England described the Cotswolds as 'preposterously photogenic', an accurate assessment. The area had the same prim neatness I'd noticed in

County Down, although even more refined. On the drive to Cheltenham from Birmingham Airport, I passed apple orchards, dairy farms, some fat Old Spot pigs, and lots of sheep, of course, because the hills were once the hub of the English wool trade. The names of the surrounding towns, picturesque but dowdy, could have been lifted from a Monty Python skit – Stow-on-the-Wold, Moreton in Marsh, and Chipping Norton. There were thatched cottages, Norman churches, and shops selling House of Windsor souvenirs. The Cotswolds are where you send your visiting auntie when you need a break, an arch London friend had explained to me once.

All the hotels in central Cheltenham were booked, as expected. Scouting around for a place to stay, I saw signs nailed to trees and telephone poles, way up high where nobody could tear them down. 'Fifty-nine percent of the Public Say Keep Hunting', the signs read. After an hour or so, I found a room at the Beckford Inn – a real room, too, big enough to accommodate a normal human being. The Inn even had a skittles alley, where Falstaffian hijinks could be enjoyed on a summer evening. The Fenns, late of Birmingham, operated *en famille* and served the *Racing Post* with breakfast.

On Friday, I entered Cheltenham Racecourse for the first time a little before noon and felt a silly sense of achievement, as a small town art lover does on reaching the Louvre at last. My arrival was a confirmation of sorts, I believed, and stamped my credentials as a punter and fan. Not only that, I was stealing a march on the Festival, sniffing around to locate the nooks and crannies where good fortune might reside. The size of the complex was intimidating, though, and came as a surprise. From watching the races on TV, with shots of sheep grazing on the hillsides, I'd formed a bucolic image of the course, but tons of concrete covered the 500 acres and created a structure as urban-looking as Yankee Stadium in New York.

I was early enough to do some exploring. The first thing that struck me was the extraordinary amount of tweed on people's bodies. It was as if those grazing sheep were being sheared on an assembly line somewhere to feed an insatiable desire for the stuff. The second thing was how those same people were dressed almost identically, with a degree of conformity I hadn't seen since the 1950s, when the Man in the Grey Flannel Suit (not tweed) was an emblem for such behaviour. The silver-haired gents and fur-hatted ladies were genteel and sociable, and gave off a distinct scent of Old Money. Exquisite air kisses floated about like butterflies. Only when I learned that it was Countryside Alliance Day at the Open did I understand the reason for all the tweed, for the Barbour and Musto, the Bladen and Magee.

The Alliance had a booth on the grounds, where members distributed literature in support of the hunt and other field sports. As protection against the drizzly cold, I bought a baseball cap blazoned across the crown with the slogan, 'Liberty & Livelihood', a rallying cry any American would take to heart. After trying to be entertained by the Worcestershire Gun Dogs, who put on a demonstration in the parade ring, each dog wearing a bandanna, I ducked into the Arkle Bar to read the *Post*. The bar's centrepiece was a framed page three obituary from the *Daily Mirror* (1 June 1970), bearing the headline 'Farewell Arkle . . . The Most Lovable Champ of All'.

After looking up the statistics for the Open, I decided Tony Martin from Meath was the Irish trainer to keep an eye on. His record at the meeting was superb, even better than Martin Pipe's – and Pipe had twenty-three winners from ninety runners in the past five years, a success rate of twenty-nine percent. For Tony Martin, the tally was six out of thirty over the same period for a thirty percent rate. He didn't do nearly as well in Ireland, but he seemed to know how to produce a big run at Cheltenham on the day. Today, Martin had Royal County Buck in the third race, so I circled the name on my card.

Stepping outside again, I heard distant music filtering up from The Cavern Bar, a dark subterranean space, where a sprightly five-piece combo was coaxing the audience to sing along to 'The Wild Rover'. The Cavern proved to be an unofficial meeting spot for the Irish, but the pilgrims were too busy looking for their friends to join in the chorus. Lads from Mayo and Cavan would descend into the pit, blink their eyes, and light up when they saw the familiar face they were seeking. 'Finally! Finally!' one over-joyed man cried, hugging his pal. For an Irishman in England, there's no more comforting sight than another Irishman, especially one from his home county.

I had no interest in singing along either, so I adjourned to the rail to check the going, designated as Good-to-Firm (good in places), rather deceptive as it happened. The jockeys later reported that the watered ground was slippery, and it got worse when the drizzle turned to rain. The stiff head wind also sapped the horses' energy and nearly blew away my new cap. In fact, I blamed the wind for the poor showing of Dermot Weld's Lowlander, my bet in the second race. Though Lowlander was unbeaten in three starts over hurdles in Ireland, the horse came in next-to-last and cost me twenty pounds. Well, no matter, I thought. The Tony Martin factor was about to kick in.

The third race was a marathon four-mile chase. Royal County Buck had never gone that far, but neither had the other entries, so I put fifty pounds on him at 2-1. When the tape went up, Uncle Mick and Rufius, two lesser lights, sprinted to a twenty-length lead, but four-mile chases do not reward such speediness, and they both ran out of gas. Soon we had a duel between Nicky Henderson's Ceanannas Mor and my Bucko, who smacked a fence two out, after which he couldn't cope. Martin was dismayed and said he wished it had stayed dry because Royal County Buck excelled on fast ground, a point I'd missed while studying the percentages. *The going is the most important thing.* J. P. McManus's words rang in my ears, too late to do any good.

Still, I recouped in the fourth race, a two-mile chase, with Cenkos from Paul Nicholls' stable. Though Cenkos was the top weight, Ruby Walsh timed his ride perfectly to beat the fast-closing Kadarann. Whereareyounow, a novice chaser touted as a Grand National prospect, took the fifth race. The sixth, a handicap hurdle for conditional jockeys, had attracted a large field of twenty-three horses, seven from Ireland, but it was the Francophiles who tasted glory when Icare D'Oudairies won at 33-1. The best the Irish could manage was a third, with Edwinna Finn's Better

Think Again, so they would have to file away their hopes of a lucrative outing for the time being.

Paddy Power was everywhere on Saturday. His corporeal self was up in a sky box with the high rollers, while down below, in the humble territory occupied by the hoi polloi, the company's logo and banners were a splash of Ireland's green impossible to ignore. Inside the race card were some prominent ads for the company that posed the question you were probably about to ask yourself: 'How does Paddy Power keep its customers so happy?' After examining the text, I can paraphrase the answer: Paddy Power takes risks, just as its customers do with every bet; therefore, Paddy Power understands what it's like to be a customer!

Friday's rain had changed the going to Good (Good-to-Firm in places). My ledger showed I was down the miniscule sum of eight pounds, Cenkos having repaired most of the damage I'd done to myself with Royal County Buck, so I thought I had a fair chance to boost myself into the winner's bracket, optimism being a disease easily contracted at a racecourse. But I chose to avoid the first race, a four-horse contest that looked like a rerun of a race we'd seen a week ago at Chepstow – a match race, actually, between Martin Pipe's Puntal and Phillip Hobbs' Brother Joe where the latter had won by about thirty lengths. Since the weights were still level, I couldn't imagine a different outcome.

Brother Joe was at evens. He and Puntal were locked

together from the first few strides, and soon left the other horses far behind. While Puntal was going along nicely, Brother Joe seemed to be labouring to stay close, really straining. It was a painful sight, like watching a man lift heavy bags of cement. Each stride was another bag and extracted a further price. Toward home, Brother Joe lost it completely. He banged into four fences in a row before falling two out, leaving Tony McCoy to coast home on Puntal. Poor Brother Joe had fractured a shoulder, and the attending vet judged the injury to be inoperable. In grave distress, Brother Joe had to be put down.

Whenever a horse dies after a fall, the naysayers can be counted on to criticize the 'brutality' of the jumps. It happened again after Brother Joe's accident, most notably in the *Observer*. 'Hideous cold thud to the heart when yet another beautiful horse crashes to the turf in a heap,' wrote Laura Thompson, 'and the green screens go up to shield us from the sight – but not the fact – of death. That, in essence, is National Hunt racing.' In essence? I found this hard to swallow. Never had I been around people who love their horses so much, or care for them as diligently, as those I met in Ireland, nor had I ever heard a harsh word about trainer Phillip Hobbs, and yet when I looked more closely at Brother Joe's record, I did see some cause for concern.

The horse ran an unlucky thirteen times in 2003, a tremendous number of races for a quality jumper. After finishing eighth behind Baracouda in the Stayers' Hurdle at the Festival, he moved on to fences and won seven of eight novice chases during a steady campaign from May to October. He never had more than a month off, although the year before he'd been allowed a five-month rest between May and November. Unlike most chasers, Brother Joe was at his best when the going was Good-to-Firm, so the dry spell had been a gift to him. He'd been thriving in those conditions, winning in those small fields.

But the fences at Cheltenham are notoriously stiff, and a horse who isn't a handy jumper – Brother Joe was not – is liable to falter. If the horse is also tired, the test becomes even harder, and Brother Joe had every right to be tired. Maybe he was asked to run once too often while the conditions were still in his favour. And why not? He appeared to be healthy and in his prime, yet no other horse at the Open Meeting had run thirteen times in nine months, or anything like it. Go to the well too often, a vet once told me, and you'll get an answer, but even so Brother Joe's sad end didn't seem reason enough to accuse an entire sport of cruelty.

A death at the track takes your breath away and alters your view of the world, but the Irish regained a bit of colour in their cheeks when they had their first winner in the very next race – Al Eile from John Queally's small, ten-box yard in County Waterford, who almost missed his appointment with destiny. The horse was supposed to leave for England on Thursday, but the sea was too rough for a ferry passage, so Al Eile was forced to go back to Coolagh, a round-trip of about two hundred and sixty miles, and then returned to the dock in Dún Laoghaire on Friday, only reaching the track at five in the morning on the day of his run. The win was a feather in Queally's cap, although his horse's cover was blown now, and he was worried Al Eile's owner might sell if a serious buyer appeared.

Still, what a miracle! That an Irish horse should over-come adversity to bag a win against the English! Wasn't it grand? To judge by the celebrating, you'd have assumed that every Irishman at Cheltenham had £1,000 on Al Eile at 8-1, and maybe they did, for all I knew. How else to account for the commotion? They spilled from the grandstand, wrestled free of the betting ring, and even emerged from the dank recesses of the Cavern Bar to cluster around Jim Culloty and pat Al Eile, whooping and thrusting their fists into the air, bursting into bizarre little jigs and booze-fuelled arias, with everyone invested in a wildly overstimulated group mania that might have been frightening if so much happiness weren't at its core.

With Al Eile's victory, the fans had bought back a measure of good cheer, so they were looking forward to the Paddy Power Chase, the main course after a tasty appetizer. I was leaning toward Fondmort, but Risk Accessor, the only Irish-trained horse in the race, was bound to improve after his outing at Thurles – a prep race to sharpen him up, really. Timmy Murphy, the Comeback Kid, was riding him, too. It's a fair bet that Murphy is the only jockey ever to do any time in Wormwood Scrubs, a dump of a London prison. Not long ago, he had succumbed to the pressures of the rider's life, a hectic one that barely allows for half a second of contemplation. If a jockey is in demand, the racing day goes by in a blur, and the evening is merely about getting ready for tomorrow. It's a difficult balancing act for the young.

Like most Irish jockeys, Murphy was virtually born on a horse. His dad was a groom in Kildare, and Timmy started riding at seven or eight. He was an apprentice to Michael Halford first, and next to Michael Hourigan, a tough but fair taskmaster who doesn't tolerate any monkey business.

Being ambitious, Murphy left Hourigan and accepted a job as stable jockey to Kim Bailey in England, but already the stress was affecting him. He was impatient and wanted to ride fifty winners in his first season, so he tended to punish his horses, being heavy on the whip. He asked too much of them and earned a number of suspensions.

By all accounts, Murphy is the politest of men, but also quite shy, and he slipped into the shy person's trap of drinking to help him relax and communicate. After a losing ride on Cenkos in the Nakayama Gold Cup in Japan, in 2002, he began pounding down screwdrivers before his flight and got more drunk on the plane, bothering other passengers and groping a woman flight attendant, all totally out of character. He was arrested at Heathrow and sentenced that July, his six months at Wormwood Scrubs ultimately reduced to three. Not everyone would hire him after his release, but Hourigan gave him a second chance, and Murphy was back on top again, with Beef Or Salmon one of his plum rides.

In the ring, Risk Accessor was available at between 7-1 and 9-1, very tempting odds. I saw that Fondmort, trained by Nicky Henderson, was narrowly favoured over Poliantas (Paul Nicholls) and It Takes Time (Martin Pipe), having done well by the handicapper. He would carry thirteen pounds less than the top weight Cyfor Malta (Pipe again), but on the other hand Poliantas had beaten Fondmort at Cheltenham, in April. Poliantas had a nine pounds advantage then, while today Fondmort was the lighter by one pound. That was more maths than I could handle, so I closed my eyes and bet twenty quid to win on Fondmort.

The race, over two miles and four-and-a-half fur-longs, lived up to its billing. Ei Ei, a relentless front-runner, led the field away from the stands and through the first circuit, jumping neatly, while Cyfor Malta sunk under his weight and relinquished a chance to win the race for a third time. Poliantis breezed past Ei Ei four out, and seemed to be going well under Ruby Walsh. Risk Accessor, initially held up, was now tracking the leaders as he came to the second-last, a tricky fence on a downhill slope. Horses accelerate as they approach it, and often misjudge the jump. Risk Accessor failed to manage it, as did It TakesTime. They jumped the fence in tandem and collided, and down went Murphy and Tony McCoy.

At the same fence, Fondmort made his move. His springy leap shot him ahead of Poliantas, and Mick Fitzgerald had five lengths between him and the other horses at the last fence. The result was never in doubt, but the drama wasn't over. After being pulled up past the finish, Poliantas staggered a little, as if his legs were jelly and couldn't support him. He was wobbly and dizzy-looking. Walsh figured the horse must be feeling the effect of his strenuous effort and dismounted. The vets were called, and while they were administering some oxygen, Poliantas keeled over and collapsed, dead of a heart attack at the age of six. It was another blow for Nicholls, who'd been having a devastating season. 'I didn't think it could get any worse,' he told the press, a gloomy state-ment that said it all.

*　　*　　*

Luck is a free-floating thing, settling randomly and then departing, and Ruby Walsh wasn't having any at the Open. Every jockey understands the syndrome because it reflects the quicksilver nature of the trade. Despite their competitive nature, the Irish riders remain a close-knit fraternity wherever they're based. It isn't uncommon to see Walsh, Geraghty, and Carberry sharing a meal, especially when they're camped at the same hotel for a festival. They may play golf and go on holidays together in the Caribbean. Walsh even bunks at Tony McCoy's house in Oxfordshire, a palatial spread with big TVs in almost every room and a framed flag from the eighteenth hole at St Andrews pinned up over the fireplace. The flag is signed by Tiger Woods, whom McCoy admires for his dedication to excellence.

Ruby is a corruption of Rupert, Walsh's grandfather's name. It suits him, since there is a jewel-like quality to his riding. He has an exquisite sense of pace, knowing exactly how much energy his horse has left at any point. Preferring to take his time and creep through the field, he'll pounce on the leaders over the last few furlongs. His father, Ted, tutored him well, being a fine jockey himself with over five hundred winners as an amateur, four of them at Cheltenham. I once asked Willie Mullins why Ruby stood out, and he replied, 'Good racing brain,' meaning the skill to read a race and predict how it will develop. He also raved about Ruby's physical strength and determination. Add to that a bright smile and a distinctive patch of greying hair, and you had the makings of a star.

On Sunday, it looked as if Walsh would stay unlucky. He lost his first ride on Mr Ed in the paddypower.com

Hurdle, producing the horse too late, a rare mistake. No doubt he kicked himself all the way to the weighing room, but he improved in the Independent Newspaper Novices Chase, where he guided Thisthatandtother to an easy win for Nicholls. But Ruby truly earned his keep in the Greatwood Hurdle on Rigmarole, the top weight at eleven stone two pounds, who had been dismissed in the *Post* with the comment, 'limitations well exposed off this mark'. The experts handed the race to Jonjo O'Neill's Hasty Prince, 11-10 against Rigmarole's 33-1. Once more Walsh held up his horse, only releasing the brake four out and swiftly advancing at a hectic pace. It was too much for Hasty Prince, and Rigmarole fought off Caracciola to win in a driving finish.

Along with meals and holidays, jockeys share information. Ruby Walsh gave Barry Connell a tip that helped Connell ride The Posh Paddy to victory in the Bumper, the Open's last race. Of all the Irish amateurs on earth, Connell is the most unlikely, a hedge fund manager in real life, who has such an awkward riding style that he seems to be standing up in his stirrups, as if to see over the heads in front and plot a course. I doubted that any trainer would have engaged his services voluntarily. The only reason he was on board The Posh Paddy was because he owned the damn horse. Though I only had a modest fiver on him, I was still shouting with the rest of the lads when Connell, tall and gangly in the saddle, held on to snatch the prize and take home the trophy.

It felt sweet to return to Ireland after the clamour and exhilaration of the Open. As much as I had enjoyed the wonderful racing, I missed the intimacy and friendliness of the Irish scene. On the drive home from the airport, I stared out a taxi window at Dublin, so understated and village-like, with scarcely a skyscraper on the horizon, and realized how attached I'd become to certain aspects of Irish life that had first struck me as curious, from the scurrying postmen to the gently indirect pattern of speech ('Could you not? Do you not? Would you not?'), to the Irish School of Motoring with its claim that ninety percent of its clients pass the state exam, a statistic any American firm would bump up to ninety-nine percent, whether or not it was true.

I asked the taxi driver to drop me at the Merrion Hotel, a grand Georgian town house, where I was meeting Imelda for a late drink. This was our favourite place for a break from the family, its public rooms hung with paintings by the Irish masters and peat fires burning at the slightest hint of a chill. With its old-fashioned charm, the hotel allowed us to imagine we were swells stopping for a spot of something before rounding the corner to visit Yeats or George Russell, who both lived on Merrion Square for a time, possibly for a session at the Ouija Board or a discussion of the Celtic Twilight. In other words, it felt good to be back. The horses seemed very far away, but only for a moment.

The Great Unveiling continued. Both Beef Or Salmon and Best Mate were finally coming out from under wraps, the first in the Oil Chase at Clonmel and the second in the Peterborough Chase at Huntingdon. To add some spice to the mix, Henrietta Knight was sending Edredon Bleu to Clonmel, an intriguing gambit since she rarely ran her horses in Ireland. The Oil Chase, at two-and-a-half miles, might prove a trifle short for Beef Or Salmon, although he did win the race in 2002, but the distance was ideal for Edredon Bleu and the pot was a good one, worth 39,000 euros.

So I was on the road again, barely having unpacked my bag. In Clonmel, a pretty town on the River Suir, there was a steady rumble of excitement as if a dynamo had been switched on somewhere. A race meeting energizes an Irish community because it's a special event – a carnival, a fun fair, a break from routine. Everyone was going to the track, except the forlorn school kids in uniform, who loitered about in the street. A record crowd of over five thousand turned up for the big set-to between Hourigan and Knight at Powerstown Park, where admission used to be free until one Villiers Morton Jackson enclosed the track in 1913, built a grandstand, roped off the bookies, hired stewards to foil the pickpockets, and charged 2s to get in.

Despite Edredon Bleu's glorious campaign that autumn, the fans, being mostly Irish, made Beef Or Salmon the 4-5 choice, with Knight's horse second-best at 2-1. The two were in sharp contrast to one another in the parade ring, Beef Or Salmon still gawky and adolescent-looking, laid back and pleasantly distracted by all the attention, while Edredon Bleu had the solid, prosperous, mature aura of a razor-sharp businessman about to close a deal. And what a strange history the old fellow had! Only recently had I discovered that he'd won five times as a four-year-old novice in France, where a butcher was his trainer.

Edredon Bleu was accustomed to the lead, but he didn't get it at Clonmel. Instead, The Premier Cat, a course specialist, stuck his head in front. That frustrated Edredon Bleu, who tugged so hard that Jim Culloty had to rein him in. Beef Or Salmon appeared to be lost in dreams. He sauntered along as though he hadn't a care in the world and jumped indifferently, without any flair. Timmy Murphy didn't fire him up, either. Murphy seemed happy enough to just let his horse idle. The punters around me were groaning as they pictured their money going up in smoke, but Beef Or Salmon fooled us by hitting his stride with three fences left, finding a purchase on the ground. He gained momentum as rapidly as a ball rolling down a steep hill, and might even have headed Edredon Bleu if he hadn't botched the last fence and stumbled on landing, third in the end behind Arctic Copper.

After the race, Michael Hourigan stated that he wasn't unhappy with the performance. Beef Or Salmon's jumping was a bit sticky, he felt, but this was the horse's first run of the year. That shotgun burst of speed down the straight hadn't escaped the bookies' notice, and they lowered Beef Or Salmon's Gold Cup odds from 10-1 to 8-1. For Knight, the journey across the water was sheer bliss, Edredon Bleu being her first-ever winner in Ireland. He would be given a good, long break after his three valiant wins, she said, and would return to action in the spring – a plan she soon altered, much to everyone's surprise.

*　　*　　*

Before the Peterborough at Huntingdon, I read Knight's book *Best Mate: Chasing Gold,* a work that revealed as much about the author as it did about her horse. In some respects, her childhood resembled Jessie Harrington's. Her father was also a military man and finished his career as a major in the Coldstream Guards, after which he turned to farming like Brigadier Fowler and rode in point-to-points, although he was never crazy about horses and discouraged his daughter's obsession with ponies. Henrietta's favourite was a Shetland called Florian, who was 'almost human' and had a bit part in the 1960 British film, *Follow That Horse.* On the other hand, Knight's mother loved animals and even wrote stories about them for children.

As a girl, Henrietta showed an early interest in training. She entered her huge black donkey, Sheba, in the East Hendred Donkey Derby, riding him bareback across the fields in preparation. After passing her 'O' and 'A' levels in 1964, she bought Borderline, her first thoroughbred, for £500, plucking him from the advertising pages of *Horse & Hound.* She became a skilled eventer, but her parents wanted to introduce her to a broader social scene, so she was sent to London to meet eligible young men and entered the debutante world. 'Many of the parties were held in beautiful places,' she wrote, sounding a Jane Austen note, 'and even though I didn't enjoy them all, it was most educational, and I loved the food.' Only years later did she meet her Prince Charming, Terry Biddlecombe.

Subsequently, she enrolled in college to be a teacher of history and biology, and trained in the rowdier districts of Oxford, where her pupils once locked her in a book cupboard for nearly an hour and set booby traps to give her electric shocks. But horses were still her passion, and she opened a livery business in 1974 and progressed from there to training point-to-pointers, taking out a National Hunt licence in 1989. When Best Mate reached her ten years later, she was well established and had made many scouting trips to Ireland to look for racing stock, frequently in Cork.

Yet it was in Kildare that she and Terry first saw Un Desperado, Best Mate's sire, a French-bred standing at Old Meadow Stud. That was in 1997, and they were infatuated with the stallion – big, proud, powerful, with an excellent conformation – and given his good record on the flat, they agreed that they'd love to have a horse by him. Here Tom Costello entered her tale, and my ears perked up. Costello had bought Best Mate as a foal at a Fairyhouse sale in 1995, because he liked Best Mate's breeding – his dam Katday ultimately gave birth to Inexorable, Inca Trail, and Cornish Rebel, three other highly regarded horses – and 'his loose easy walk'. He paid 2,500 guineas after a brief but spirited round of bidding, and turned the foal over to his son Tom Junior to be broken.

Until then, Best Mate's life had been tough. He was little more than a month old when Jacques Van't Hart, the Dutchman who bred him in Meath, dispatched him and Katday for a stay at Old Meadow Stud, while he was in Holland on business. The foal was so skinny and weird-looking, having lost most of its hair from lying on wet ground, the stable lads called him Gonzo. They

The greatest-ever chaser. Arkle's favourite meal was mash, dry oats, six raw eggs, and two bottles of Guinness mixed in a bucket.

Charlie Swan on Istabraq, the legendary Irish hurdler, now retired, having won the Champion Hurdle three times.

ABOVE The canny trainer, Michael Hourigan, from County Limerick.

LEFT Vincent O'Brien (right) with Lester Piggott. O'Brien trained 23 Festival winners in just 10 years.

Henrietta Knight with her darling Best Mate, who was so skinny and strange-looking as a foal that the stable lads called him Gonzo.

The bookies at Naas have been using the same basic gear for centuries. It's designed to be cheap and portable, so they can set up anywhere the horses are running.

The gallops on the Curragh, a great limestone plain in County Kildare, where jumps trainers like to exercise their horses.

Dublin's betting shops are so neat, clean, and wholesome they make gambling appear to be a normal, even welcome part of everyday life.

A fiddler at Punchestown, where the first recorded meeting was held in 1852.

Martin Pipe, the son of a wealthy bookie who became a champion trainer.

The parade ring at Fairyhouse, home of the Irish Grand National. In 1929, Frank Wise, who was missing three fingers and had a wooden leg, won the race on his mare Alike.

Victory for Hedgehunter, in the Thyestes Chase at Gowran Park, was especially sweet because the horse had recently fallen near the finish in the Welsh National.

ABOVE A stone wall on the historic bank course at Punchestown.

LEFT When Willie Mullins saw Florida Pearl as a four-year-old at Tom Costello's yard, it was love at first sight.

TOP Bright and sophisticated, with a dry wit – trainer Edward O'Grady.

ABOVE Amateur rider Barry Connell guided The Posh Paddy, a horse he owns, to a big win at Cheltenham's Open Meeting.

LEFT Ted and Ruby Walsh – Ted was an excellent jockey himself, and Ruby still relies on his father's advice.

LEFT 'I'll stay miserable . . . and I'll also keep winning.' Tony McCoy, the National Hunt's finest rider.

BELOW Rule Supreme takes the Royal & SunAlliance Chase, despite a dodgy round of jumping.

LEFT Brave Inca with Colm Murphy, who learned the ropes under Aidan O'Brien.

ABOVE The first novice winner of the Hennessy at Newbury in its 47-year history was Strong Flow.

wondered if he would live or die, but as they nursed him on buckets of milk, his health improved. He was still undersized when he arrived at Costello's yard, so small and light that most people could lift him up with one arm, but Tom Jr approved of his stride, his sound front legs, and 'the nice head on him'.

He was fit and in good health when the Costellos entered him in a point-to-point at Lismore in Waterford, in February '99. Often they use such races as a showcase for horses they're ready to sell. Best Mate didn't win, but Knight, who was there, thought he jumped well and asked Costello about buying him. Costello refused to discuss it until Best Mate had won a race, which he did next time out, although it was only a two-horse race. In mid-March, Knight and Biddlecombe travelled to Clare to examine Best Mate more closely and, satisfied, suggested to Jim Lewis, an owner of theirs, that he buy him. Lewis conducted the negotiations with Costello, but the price he paid has never been disclosed because Costello, ever secretive, would never disclose it.

I had intended to fly to England for the Peterborough, but my energy gave out at last. That was fortunate, because the heavens opened and much of Ireland was soaked and flooded, as were East Anglia and Huntingdon. The rain came down hard and fast; you could forget about firm ground anywhere. At O'Herlihy's, the customers were clustered around the two gas fires, warming their hands and shouting for hot port and whisky. Some of them had settled in early for the Rugby World Cup final between England and Australia, and though they'd already endured a nail-biting, pint-inducing match, they weren't about to budge until they'd watched Best Mate's first run in 254 days.

Knight had coddled her horse with infinite care and discretion, even dishing out his evening oats herself. After the Gold Cup, she had awarded him an eight-week summer holiday and, by August, he had resumed the long, steady canters that build up the muscles necessary for galloping and jumping. Best Mate also received a regular tutorial in dressage for the sake of variety. A week before the Peterborough, he had worked a mile or so up a hill at Mick Channon's grass gallop nearby, and later had a practice session over fences with Jim Culloty schooling him. In between, he and his bosom pal Edredon Bleu grazed together in a field, wearing their outdoor rugs like 'two Little Red Riding Hoods', according to Ms Knight, who must have inherited her talent as a fabulist from her mother.

Television can be a deceptive medium, of course, but I thought Best Mate looked unsurpassed, even bigger and more muscular than Moscow Flyer, with an air of utter authority. He met the criteria Irish folklore once held to be essential in a prize horse – three traits of a bull (a bold walk, strong neck, and hard forehead), three of a hare (a bright eye, lively ear, and swift run), and three of a woman (a broad breast, slender waist, and short back). Of his five opponents, only two seemed genuine, Valley Henry and Jair du Cochet from France. I'd lost money on Valley Henry before, though, and considered him untrustworthy.

Jair du Cochet was more appealing. He might be the Big Bad Wolf to Best Mate's Little Red Riding Hood, I believed. Guillame Macaire, his trainer, swore that his horse had no chance in the Gold Cup – not at Cheltenham, a course Best Mate owned – but at Huntingdon in the mud anything was possible. In an act of Gallic loyalty, Macaire chose to retain Jacques Ricou as his jockey, even though Ricou was criticized and mocked in the English press last spring, when he appeared to move too slowly on Jair du Cochet in the Royal & SunAlliance Chase, which probably cost him the race.

The start of the Peterborough was very curious. As the tapes went up, the horses dawdled, as if they were stuck in a bog. When they did take off, they resembled infantry soldiers slogging through a forced march. The pace was extraordinarily slow, but Ricou kept Jair du Cochet close to it rather than letting his horse lag behind, as he'd done at the Festival. Best Mate simply didn't respond. True, the ground wasn't to his liking, but his jumping, always precise, was very rusty. He even made a mistake four out and never got on terms with Jair du Cochet. I got the feeling he was being deliberately cantankerous, unwilling to rise above the difficult circumstances. The thought occurred to me that he'd been babied too much.

As usual, Henrietta Knight hid her eyes during the race, but her husband described it to her as 'messy', a vast understatement. Being a good sport, she didn't bother with excuses for Best Mate, although she could have. The ground was a horror, the distance of two-and-a-half miles was short of the horse's ideal trip, and the pace was ridiculous, a full seventeen seconds slower than last year. Instead, Knight congratulated Macaire and confessed she had put seventy pounds to win on Jair du Cochet. She likes to back the horses who might beat Best Mate, as if to put a hex on them, but the trick failed this time. As for the emotional Ricou, he shed a few tears of joy, his dignity restored before the English.

Another horse joined the Gold Cup picture that Saturday – Kingscliff, who'd won the 2003 Christie's Foxhunter Chase at the Festival. He ran stunningly in a handicap chase at Ascot, even though his left rein broke when he jumped the third fence. He crashed into the inside rail, but Andrew Thornton held on, rode him cowboy-style for the rest of the race, and still brought the horse in miles ahead. Kingscliff was rated at 140, some twenty pounds below Gold Cup form, but the bookies still dropped his odds to 14-1.

What did the future hold for Best Mate? The customers at my pub were of two minds. It would be foolish to judge a great horse by a single dull run, Reilly felt. He cited some past champions who'd been lacklustre and had recovered, but it was also a fact that Best Mate had always won the first time out before. Moreover, he'd been a winner on soft ground – not as mucky as Huntingdon, perhaps, but still soft. What worried me most was his jumping, not nearly as fluid as usual. I also wondered about his attitude. Was Best Mate overly pampered, spoiled in the way of a handsome, self-centred movie star? When I remembered Beef Or Salmon's burst of speed at Clonmel, I believed it might still be possible for Hourigan and the Irish to win the Gold Cup.

*　　*　　*

Rain, glorious rain. As the bad weather continued, the word 'drought' vanished from the Irish vocabulary, never having belonged there in the first place. If I was disenchanted by the prospect of a normal Dublin winter and another test of my thin California blood, I couldn't argue with the positive effect on the racing. Soggy ground meant larger fields, larger fields meant bigger crowds, and bigger crowds meant increased profits for the bookies. All the trainers I knew were dancing around like Gene Kelly in the rain, delirious with relief and able to implement their plans without further delay.

That November concluded with a bang, when the Irish sent six horses to the Hennessy Gold Cup at Newbury, where all eyes were fixed on Strong Flow, Paul Nicholls' six-year-old novice chaser, who was on a mark of 140, the same as Kingscliff. 'One of the best I've ever trained,' Nicholls had said, although Strong Flow, being a youngster, was prone to mistakes. He was a faller in his first race of the season at Aintree, but he mopped up in a Grade D chase at Newton Abbot after that. I watched the race at Boylesports and marvelled at his jumps. His entire being went into them, every muscle and fibre of his body stretched to its elastic limit, at least when he got it right.

He didn't get it right at Newbury, not immediately. He ran in mid-division and belted the ninth fence so hard that his tail nearly sailed over his head. The fearless Ruby Walsh held on for dear life, and later said the blunder was actually a help. It calmed down Strong Flow and forced him to focus. From then on the horse was in command and became the first novice to win the Hennessy in its forty-seven year history, raising the question of whether

Nicholls should risk him in the King George VI at Kempton or even the Gold Cup rather than waiting for Strong Flow to mature. Fulke Walwyn had won the Gold Cup in 1963 with Mill House, a similarly gifted six-year-old. Trying to repeat the win in 1964, Mill House hit an obstacle called Arkle – a bit of history to provide Nicholls with some food for thought.

On Sunday I went to Fairyhouse, where Solerina was everyone's fancy in the Hatton's Grace Hurdle. Even I had developed a crush on the game little mare. She was a fluke, a case of lightning striking twice for the Bowes of Tipperary. They really were humble farmers who bred their own horses, often from cheap stock, and raced them under a permit held by James Bowe, the family patriarch. He was primarily responsible for Limestone Lad, a heroic stayer, who had won thirty-five of his seventy-one races, including the Hatton's Grace three times, and could lay claim to beating Istabraq fair and square.

Solerina had a storybook background. Michael Bowe bought Deep Peace, her dam, for just £400, but he had high hopes for the future because Deep Peace was from a bloodline he had admired since he was a boy. Solerina was her second foal, a runty thing and a terrible disappointment. 'I don't know what she is, but she's not a racehorse,' Michael complained to his brother, John. Counting on the fact that her sire Toulon was a St Leger winner, he tried to sell her by placing an ad in *The Irish Field*. There were no takers until John, who liked Toulon, made an offer after his mother encouraged him to bid, yet another example of the intricacy of family life out in the Irish countryside.

Even if Solerina never won a race, John believed, she'd still be a decent brood mare. At home, she gave no sign that she could run. She was bored and showed nothing, not a stitch of speed, but when Michael Bowe, now her trainer and not her owner, brought her to the racecourse, she came alive and climbed quickly up the ladder from bumpers to Grade Ones. She lived in a stall next to Limestone Lad, who was laid up with a tendon injury, and John told the *Field* that the elder statesman must be coaching the little mare along, a trope that would warm Henrietta Knight's heart. At Fairyhouse, Solerina took the Hatton's Grace with her usual panache, bowling along in front and moving a step closer to the Stayers' Hurdle at the Festival, although the Bowes weren't certain she could handle either the three-mile trip or Baracouda, the current champ.

The temptation to place an ante-post bet on the Gold Cup was growing in me. Often at night, in the drifty minutes before sleep, I would go over the key races I'd seen and pick holes in all the contenders. I agreed with Reilly that you couldn't write off Best Mate on the basis of one poor run, yet his jumping still bothered me, as did his light schedule. Strong Flow could be scarily-good at times, but also scarily-bad. As for Kingscliff, I needed to know more about him before I could commit, but Beef Or Salmon continued to entice me. He had some Festival experience and was a year older now, and he had looked like the winged god Mercury at Clonmel, so I decided to visit Michael Hourigan in Limerick and see if I could pry any useful information out of him, never once giving a thought to Harbour Pilot, the darkest of dark horses.

December: Glory Days

The perfection of a late-autumn morning at Lisaleen Stables, in Patrickswell, County Limerick: the trees blown free of their leaves except for a last few clinging to the branches, the golds gone to umber, a light frost on the grass, magpies squawking and sparrows singing, and the clip-clop of horses returning to the barns after a gallop. I took a bracing belt of fresh air and felt the dullness in my brain begin to lift. Creeping along a lane came Michael Hourigan in his 4x4, fresh from a trip around his yard, a window open despite the cold, and his eyes less bright and engaged than usual. He jumped down from the driver's seat in his wellies.

'What time did you get home, Michael?' I asked him.

A dour look. 'A quarter-past,' he said.

'Past what?'

'I don't know.'

Hourigan and I had attended a public forum at the Dunraven Arms Hotel in nearby Adare the night before. I went out of curiosity, while Michael was on duty. The event, sponsored by Horse Racing Ireland, the government body that funds and administers the sport, was an attempt to get some feedback about the state of racing, and it drew a large, vocal, opinionated group. To orchestrate their comments, HRI had enlisted Brian Gleeson, a racing presenter on Irish TV, who has the earnest, pink-cheeked face of a choirboy. He performed the job with an Oprah-like aplomb, passing a cordless mike to an OAP who fired the opening salvo and griped about having to pay eight euros to go to the races at Listowel. 'And I'm Listowel born and bred!' he said bitterly, yearning for a discount that would never come his way, not in a million years.

His contribution set the tone. Tickets prices were too high, the food and drink cost too much, and the amenities were few. 'There isn't even a seat to sit on if you bring a lady or a girlfriend,' one man said, as if a girlfriend couldn't, or shouldn't, be a lady. All this amounted to pie-in-the-skyism, I thought, since it was an unwritten law of the universe that every racetrack, like every airport and ballpark, always screws the punter. You might as well complain about having a nose, but other comments were more constructive. How about a covered path to the betting ring? Or hiring local caterers instead of big franchises? Shouldn't an owner get more than two free tickets if he shells out 1,200 euros for an entry fee? And so on.

Toward the end of the evening, Gleeson nailed Hourigan, who was trying to sneak out a little early.

'Don't you go anywhere, Michael Hourigan!' he cried. 'Not until I ask you about Beef Or Salmon.'

'The horse is grand,' Hourigan said, as noncommittal as ever.

'Were you satisfied with his run at Clonmel?'

Hourigan confessed some unease. 'I kept wondering, "Who's asleep? Timmy or the horse,"' he said. But he assured Gleeson that Beef Or Salmon was fit and healthy, although he agreed his horse would have to jump quicker in the John Durkan Chase at Punchestown, his next big race.

After Gleeson's closing remarks, we joined a mad stampede for the bar. Such formal proceedings seem to foster a terrible thirst, and everyone was delighted to ditch the constructive criticism and talk about racing and gambling. There is probably nothing the Irish hate more than saying 'Good night', and when I heard the first few bars of off-key singing, a sign that the session was picking up steam, I retired to my room. It was about one o'clock by then, but Michael was still going strong and had kept at it until the last revellers had straggled out just before dawn. Now his nose was snuffly, and his stomach upset. 'I'm still fairly full of drink,' he muttered, leading me into his kitchen, so we could warm ourselves and chat by the Aga.

Hourigan has the self-made man's outsize and justifiable pride. His yard, just shy of 100 acres, was raw land with only a rundown cottage on it when he bought it in 1985. 'Nobody had lived in that cottage for fourteen years. Two rooms up and two rooms down, go bump your head! Anything you see here, we've done,' he said of his spacious, commodious home. 'The price was 110,000 punts. I had the 10,000 for a down payment, but no idea where the rest would come from. For a time, I thought about backing out of the deal. I was like the fella about to be married and getting cold feet. Jaysus, where am I going to find a hundred grand? That's what I kept asking myself. I hadn't a clue!

'You know who saved me? Jerry O'Connell!' He slapped the kitchen table for emphasis. 'He's a bank manager and my best friend. He saw to the loan, all right. He gave me a chance and authorized my overdrafts. Let me tell you something, I'm a big spender! If I make five thousand selling a horse, I'll spend twenty. If you come to me to buy a horse and decide against it, I'll spend your money anyway!' His eyes were bright and merry again, the previous night's pints burning off like fog. 'My overdraft never drops below fifty grand. I was laid up in bed one time with a bad back, and Jerry called to ask after me and said to my wife, "Nothing wrong with his hand, is there, Anne? He's still writing those feckin' checks!"'

Soon to be fifty-six, Hourigan was on a roll and began reflecting on his past. He is the last of four children, though two others had died at birth. He rued the loss of his father, a cattle dealer and notorious carouser, who dropped dead suddenly at sixty-seven. 'It was like the end of the world,' he said sadly. 'So unexpected! He never saw me train a winner. I still regret it. When I was fifteen, sixteen, I was a thick fucker and thought my father was stupid. But he wasn't. Ah, well, every kid thinks his father's stupid at that age.' He cut thick slices of brown bread, slathered them with butter and strawberry jam, and ate hungrily, the crumbs cascading down his chin. 'I was small as a child and a young man,' he said, meaning 'slight', 'and I was not very good at school. Would you believe I couldn't read or write when I was thirteen?'

'Amazing,' I said. I was on the edge of my seat, in the grip of his tale.

'My parents sent me to Rockwell College, to the holy fathers, and when I completed my schooling on 17 June 1962, I joined Charlie Weld as a stable lad on the Curragh on 17 August. I was fourteen years and eight months old, and the ideal size for a jockey,' he continued. 'I could do six stone seven pounds easily, but I was just terrible. Terrible! Why? Because I was a big coward. In all my time as a jockey, I rode just nine winners on the flat and four over the jumps. The last was Ballybar at Cork in a novice chase, and the crowd cheered for me. They must have been surprised!' He buttered another slice of bread, his fourth, and sent more crumbs flying. I was getting a kick out of Hourigan, who was funny and self-deprecating and gobbled up life in appreciative bites.

'My family owned a grocery store and bar,' he went on, 'and when I took it over, I changed the name from Hourigan's to The Horse and Jockey Pub. That's when I started training, but I didn't have a winner for six years. Six years! And when I did win, wouldn't you know it was on St Patrick's Day? That was in 1979. The problem was, I was always selling off my horses. I used to pray I'd have a five-year-old someday, because the three-year-olds were gone before they were four. I had to make ends meet, you see.' The bar catered to travellers, who were good customers, although loud and boisterous. They always had some cash in their pockets, and sucked Michael into poker games and betting on horses and dogs. 'Gambling!' he shouted, as if I'd stuck his hand in a flame. 'I tried it, all right, but I was a bad man for it.

103

Put your money where your mouth is, and you'll lose your money.'

Over time, Hourigan began to have some winners, but his fortunes really improved when he bought Dorans Pride, known as Padjo around the stable, and sold the horse to Tom Doran. Dorans Pride would win twenty-six of his sixty-one races, among them the Hatton's Grace, the Irish Hennessy, and the Stayers' Hurdle at Cheltenham, and was also twice placed in the Gold Cup, but his life ended in tragedy when Hourigan brought him out of retirement at the age of fourteen, well into his fifties on the human scale of ageing. In the Christies' Foxhunter Chase in 2003, he fell at the second fence, broke a leg and had to be destroyed. This was still a sore point for Michael, who was accused of neglect and worse in some quarters.

'Nobody knew Dorans Pride better than I did,' he said, in his own defence. 'He was restless at pasture and deserved one more chance. He wasn't happy doing nothing, that's for certain. Well, I've been lucky, haven't I? Better trainers than me never had a horse like Dorans Pride.'

All the while we talked, I kept trying to steer Hourigan toward Beef Or Salmon, foolishly seeking the sort of inside information I derided others for believing in, but when he wasn't regaling me with stories, he was fielding a non-stop series of calls on his mobile. 'No, no, I got knocked off my pedestal,' he corrected one caller. 'Noel Meade's in front now.' He was referring to the fact that Meade had just overtaken him and was ranked first among Irish trainers in terms of prize money. Actually, I was mystified that Michael did so well, since his strike rate hovers around ten percent and dips even lower at large tracks. At Punchestown, for instance, he'd had three winners in 116 runs since 1999, hardly a statistic to inspire the fans to contact their bookie.

The reason for such discouraging figures, I learned, is that Hourigan uses races as a training tool. He knows a good horse from Day One, he said, but with most others it's a matter of finding the right level, something he can only do by trial and error. That's part of it, at least. The other part is that he still trains some inferior horses, a job that requires tact. 'You can't say to the owner "Your horse is no good" because he won't believe it,' Michael explained. 'You can say "Your wife is cheating on you" and he'll believe that, but he won't believe the horse is no good.' Hourigan enjoys winning with a cheap horse, but the ultimate thrill for him is to steal a big race on the flat. 'I did it once with Discerning Air at the Curragh – a fifty grand handicap!' he bragged. 'A National Hunt trainer kicking them in their own backyard! I well and truly celebrated that day!'

Remembering our chat at Tattersalls, and how he had rejected that yearling after a cursory inspection, I asked him how he goes about shopping for horses at a sale. He just flips through the catalogue, he said, and might turn down a page if he sees a horse who is related to a good one in his yard, but he'd never buy the horse without inspecting it thoroughly. He watches for the magic, for a glimpse of possibility, even a 'come hither' look. As I guessed he might, he compared it to falling in love and recounted how he fell for his wife Anne the first time he saw her, when she was playing tennis in a short skirt on a summer's night. She was just fifteen, and though he was a little older he pursued her, and they've been married now for thirty-two years and have five children.

'Boy, girl, boy, girl, boy,' Hourigan recited, pleased with the symmetry. 'Mark, the youngest, is ten and riding ponies now. I could be his grandfather! My friends all call Anne "the Queen". When we go for drinks at the Woodlands House Hotel, they ask, "Will the Queen be along?" We do everything together.'

'With Beef Or Salmon, what attracted you?' I asked. 'It couldn't have been his pedigree.'

'Pedigree isn't everything,' Hourigan replied. 'Buying a horse isn't like buying a car. If you want a Ferrari, you can open the bonnet and look at the engine. You can take it apart and check it all over, and you'll know it well and truly is a Ferrari and capable of doing what a Ferrari does. But a horse? You can't take a horse apart. Sometimes a horse with a wonderful pedigree turns out to be a duck. Can't even get out of its own way! But if they're well-bred and trained properly, their pedigree comes out at some point.'

'And if they're not well-bred?'

Hourigan laughed. 'My friend Mick Easterby says, "I'll gallop some pedigree into the fucker!"'

The break from work and the bread and jam had given Michael an energy boost, and now he was firing on all cylinders again. 'Five o'clock I must have got in,' he sighed, amused by his own antics. Ordinarily, he's out in the yard by six-thirty or seven, but he'd stayed in bed that morning to nurse his head. 'The stable lads notice those things. They'll be gossiping about me, saying I was out on the town, same as I did when Charlie Weld was late. You have to show your face at the regular hour,' he confided, 'and then you can go back to bed. Only if you do, you must keep the bedroom curtains open. Very important! That stops the lads from yappin'.'

Around noon, some tourists from Canada arrived. They were visiting Irish yards, doing some hunting, and at least thinking about buying a horse or two, and that was enough for Hourigan to start pitching his wares, but the bloodstock agent in the party had also been at the bar until the wee hours and looked so green around the gills he probably couldn't have ordered lunch, let alone negotiated for a newspaper. When Michael saw the writing on the wall, he showed them around his yard instead, while I tagged along. The first stop was his gallops, three of them – a four-to-five furlong, wood chip gallop, a three-furlong circular gallop, and a new, all-weather gallop of sand.

'I can do anything with it,' he said, snatching up a handful and sifting it between his fingers. 'I can make it fast or soft, and the only tending it needs is some harrowing.'

Next, he moved us along to a ramshackle, two-story building. 'There's my hotel,' he said cheerfully, ignoring its decrepit condition. 'Some good jockeys have come out of there – Timmy Murphy, Adrian Maguire, Shane Broderick, Willie Supple. 'Course, it wasn't such a nice place in the old days. The rain would come down the walls at night, and the lads would wake up and shove their beds away from the wet. It's dry now, though, and even has central heating. Well, I did all right by them, anyway. When I see potential, I encourage it. What a good jockey needs is an old head on a young body.'

Soon we were in the middle of the yard, in the barn area, and horses were all around us, starting for the gallops or just returning from them. Grooms were bathing those who'd finished their exercise, so the crisp autumn air was pungent with the smell of soap, lather and manure, each sharply defined. We were in a vibrant, tactile, physical world constructed out of hard daily labour. Its constants were fixed; there was no confusion. Everyone knew exactly what was required. Certainly, Hourigan was a model of clarity in his role as our tour guide, walking us to a little stream overhung with sheltering trees.

'This is the greatest thing I've ever done, without a doubt!' he crowed. He'd poured some concrete to form a dam and create a deep pool, where up to six horses at a time can have a soak. The gently flowing water cools their hot legs and shins, and they can have a drink at their leisure. 'Sometimes I leave them in overnight and collect them in the morning.'

The last item on the tour was an indoor swimming pool, composed of two concrete rectangles, one inside the other. A horse was in for a swim, doing laps and breathing hard. He had two longish leads attached to his bridle, one for each of the grooms who tugged him along, treading on the concrete. 'Go, boy!' they called to the struggling horse. The swim was equal to a good gallop, especially helpful for horses who have sore legs.

'I used to be the only private trainer in Ireland to have a pool,' Hourigan said. 'I spent fifty-odd grand on it, when I should have spent the money on building a new house, but my wife never complained. Isn't that something? I wonder if I'd do it again?' He tapped my elbow and whispered an aside. 'When you're young and ambitious, you do some stupid things. But they can work out, can't they?'

The following Saturday, I bellied up to the bar at O'Herlihy's to watch Moscow Flyer in the Tingle Creek Chase at Sandown Park. Tingle Creek – the horse, that is – was an extraordinary jumper and had never fallen in any race. He won the chase named in his honour twice and broke the track record on each occasion. My pal Reilly supplied this information, never the least bit shy about showing off. He scoured Dublin's street markets and used bookstores for his racing collectibles, and when I told him I was going to Punchestown for the John Durkan Chase on Sunday, he astonished me by quoting four lines of an old poem from memory. 'A loud hurrah for Ireland, boys/And louder for Kildare/And loudest of all for Punchestown/For I know you all are there.'

'Very impressive, T.P. And will you not join me there tomorrow?' I asked, in my newly adopted indirect style.

But Reilly had no interest in coming along. Punchestown is too roomy for him. It makes him feel as if he's stranded, a stranger in a little country town. 'You go out there,' he protested, 'and your cousin will be there, and the two of you will never meet without the help of a map.' He prefers the more urban confines of Leopardstown where no ancestral link goes unforged.

'So what did your man Hourigan reveal?' he asked me.

'Beef Or Salmon's in the Durkan for sure,' I said.

'That's it?'

'He has to jump quicker if he's going to win.'

'Long trip, small rewards.'

I shrugged it off. 'When you're old and ambitious,' I countered, 'you do some stupid things.'

He turned up the volume on the TV, so that we could hear Jessie being interviewed and congratulated for sending Moscow to England to run against Paul Nicholls' Azertyuiop, his chief rival in the Queen Mother Chase, rather than taking an easier road at home. In Ireland the money was just as good, if not better, but the competition was not as intense, so Jessie had gained some respect for her risk. 'Horses are there to be raced and for the public to see,' she said diplomatically, earning an A-plus in media relations.

By coincidence, Henrietta Knight had just earned a D-minus, having let it drop that she might ship Best Mate to Leopardstown – in Ireland! – for the Ericsson Chase over the Christmas holidays, and pass up the King George IV at Kempton. Was she taking an easier road? I thought so, ever more suspicious about Matey, but Reilly believed she was being smart. 'Best Mate never liked the going at Kempton,' he said. In any event, the mere mention of the potential trip – a desertion, an outrage, even a betrayal of Knight's English roots – already had angry Brits writing tightly reasoned (though mildly threatening) letters to the *Post* that read like legal briefs.

At Sandown, Moscow Flyer went off at 6-4, but I'd backed him earlier at 13-8 and counted it as money in the bank despite Azertyuiop's presence, and it was, although the pace was too slow to bring out Moscow's best. He took the lead at the Railway Fences and had the others beaten at the Pond Fence, where he got a little lazy and needed a couple of cracks from Geraghty. But the Tingle Creek was a true Grade One, with every top two-mile chaser in the mix, so the handicappers raised Moscow's mark to 174, the highest for a two-miler in the past decade. The horse would run next at Leopardstown, then rest for Cheltenham, Jessie said, and I actually rose up on my stool and shouted, 'No, Jessie, don't do it!' since that would definitely make the Queen Mother Moscow's dreaded fourth race.

On Sunday I did go to Punchestown for the Durkan Chase. Originally developed by the Kildare Hunt Club, the racecourse held its first recorded meeting in 1824. Punchestown is as roomy as Reilly had described it, but the gracious country atmosphere appealed to me, perhaps because I had no cousins to find. As at Cheltenham, sheep were roaming the outlying hills. I'd once seen an engraving etched in 1892 that showed several tiny figures clad in black perched on such a hill. They were priests sneaking a glance at the races. A Dublin Diocesan Statute forbade them from attending, and it wasn't rescinded until the 1970s. The only other notable thing I knew about the course was that Harry Beasley, a famous jockey, rode a winner there at the age of seventy-two.

Vowing to concentrate and not bet on Beef Or Salmon just because I had enjoyed Hourigan's company, I borrowed a page from Reilly and studied the six horses in the parade ring closely, judging them by their looks. Only three 'spoke' to me. Knife's Edge was nicely turned out, but I suspected he was outclassed. Tiutchev, the only English horse, deserved respect because Martin Pipe had sent him over, which Pipe didn't do that often. An old-timer of ten, Tiutchev was as buffed up as a bodybuilder with perfect pecs and abs, but Beef Or Salmon was still circling in his goofy fashion, playing to the spectators. 'Hey, Beef, baby!' I wanted to yell. 'Wake up, will you?' His speed alone wouldn't be enough to win a Gold Cup. He had to learn to be more attentive. He had to jump and run.

Still, the spectators at Punchestown were backing him heavily from evens to 4-5, and their support proved correct, largely because of Michael Hourigan's advance preparation. With Timmy Murphy, he'd walked the course before the race and found it so chopped up on the inside that he opted to keep his horse off the rail. From three out, the Durkan was between Tiutchev and Beef Or Salmon, who once again required a smack at the second-last to stimulate his interest. Tiutchev made a hash of the final fence, so Beef Or Salmon's triumph wasn't clear cut, but Hourigan didn't object, not even to the guy in a Santa Claus costume who hugged him in the unsaddling enclosure a good three weeks before the gesture would have been appropriate.

A Christmas tree was blinking brightly at Barry Connell's grand house in Carrickmines, hard by Boss Croker's old gallops in Foxrock. In the foyer, I noticed an oil painting called Thursdays at Thurles, a homage to the track. On a table beneath it, in pride of place, was the trophy Connell had won at Cheltenham on The Posh Paddy. Trim and neatly groomed, he had a formal manner, and his house was so orderly I could see why the ragged edges of racetrack life might make his blood beat faster. 'It's a disease,' he said, in his sober, low-key way, although not one he hoped to be cured of any time soon.

Connell invited me to sit on a couch by the tree and brought out some mince pies from the kitchen. He seemed glad to find them there. If he has a domestic touch, it wasn't in evidence. I had a sense that he was leading a double life, divided between the track and his business concerns, and that his reserve was an attempt, not always successful, to keep the two sides of his nature – the restless and the conservative – in balance. Almost alone among the Irish I'd met, he had taken to horses late in life, although he was a long-time fan of racing, having gone to the tracks around Dublin, to Ballydoyle and Phoenix Park, with his father when he was a boy.

He bought his first horse around 1988 and could not have predicted how profoundly it would affect him. He became so attached to horses and riding that he left the corporate world to start his own business as a hedge fund manager, giving him more free time. At present, he owns The Posh Paddy, who is with Tony Mullins in Kilkenny, and a few other horses at Ted Walsh's yard in Kill, not far from the Curragh, where he rides out two, three, or even four mornings a week, keeping fit at a gym in-between. 'I get withdrawal symptoms if I don't do it,' he told me, and I believed him.

Connell isn't a natural rider, because he didn't start as a child, full of trust and resilience. Instead, he did it the hard way as an adult, enrolling in a riding school, but he was such an avid student and so loved being in the saddle that he was soon skilled enough to ride a winner on the flat at Fairyhouse in a one-off charity race. The race was conducted under Rules, with the jockeys wearing silks, and Barry got a tremendous adrenaline high. Ted Walsh, suitably impressed, urged him to apply for an amateur's licence. 'It wasn't too onerous,' he said. 'I just took a one-day course at the Apprentice Centre on the Curragh and passed a physical exam.' Not long after, Connell guided his horse Ballytobin to victory in a Limerick bumper in July 2003, the day after his forty-fourth birthday. Again he got that adrenaline rush, as addictive as a drug.

His next win came on The Posh Paddy in a Roscommon bumper, and it was accompanied by the first glimmering suspicion that the horse might be special enough for a trip to the Cotswolds. 'He has a lovely, relaxed style,' Connell said, but Tony Mullins was more doubtful. The Posh Paddy is by Be My Native, whose offspring Mullins calls 'hill detectors' because they struggle when they meet rising ground, as they must at Cheltenham.

Connell still liked his horse's chances, but they almost didn't make it to the Open Meeting, their best intentions aside. Two weeks before, Barry took a fall at Mullins' yard. It happened in an instant – no stumble, no warning. All of a sudden, he was soaring through the air and landed on his head, with The Posh Paddy rocketing over him. He was so stiff and bruised afterwards that he couldn't ride for days and needed some physiotherapy to finally set him right, but he was ready for action again on the Sunday of the betfair.com Open Bumper.

He hired a plane, flew to Gloucestershire with eight friends, and walked the Old Course that morning. 'I couldn't believe how tight it is,' he told me. 'It's easy to get lost, to go the wrong way.' The walk was useful, as was the tip from Ruby Walsh. Watering or no watering, the ground was poached inside, Ruby informed him, and he suggested that Barry keep wide for the better going down the back of the course, then swing over to the stand rail when he turned into the straight. Connell did exactly that and forced Richard Johnson to the outside on Alpine Fox, a tactic that made all the difference and probably won him the race.

Beating an old pro to the punch at Cheltenham! Talk about adrenaline highs, this was a hedge fund manager in his mid-forties, who'd just fulfilled every amateur's fantasy. For the first time in our conversation, Barry became animated and relived his moment of glory. 'I was just delighted,' he said, full of enthusiasm, 'and I kept thinking, "What a bloody good horse!" And the cheering along the rail, the way they applauded me. You'd think they'd all backed him!'

'Did you have a flutter?'

'No, but my friends did. Let me show you something.' He left the couch to retrieve a packet of photos from a drawer. After the win, he and his group were having a celebratory drink before dinner at a pub near the Queens Hotel, and when someone at another table lifted a glass and roared, 'Here's to The Posh Paddy!' one of Barry's pals said 'And here he is.' 'Look what happened next,' Barry said, smiling at the memory. He passed me a photo with him astride the shoulders of a big, raw-faced, beaming brute, who was playing the horse to Connell's jockey on a lap around the pub.

The Gold Cup, all but ceded to Best Mate in October, seemed to be up for grabs by mid-December. Exaggerated reports in the papers spoke of the champ's 'slipping crown', an insult that Henrietta Knight did not take lightly. Young Kingscliff, only six and growing by leaps-and-bounds in the minds of punters hungry for a challenger, was the new celebrity. Kingscliff had handled Wincanton's stiff fences easily, a winner by seventeen lengths, and had silenced any pessimists by scoring in the Tripleprint Handicap Chase at Cheltenham. 'I didn't know how good he was before today, but today I got the answer,' said Robert Alner, whose garbled syntax betrayed his excitement. Alner had won the Gold Cup before, after all, with Cool Dawn in 1998.

Cheltenham, Cheltenham. The word appeared twenty-six times in the first ten pages of a recent edition of the *Post*, causing one reader to file a letter of protest. A few diehard English correspondents were still ranting about Knight's possible avoidance of the King George, too, while Knight, unaccustomed to such criticism, had started making belated excuses about the Peterborough, harping on about the 'bottomless' ground, as deep as an excavated pit by now, and its disastrous effect on her horse.

Matey had recovered from his trauma and was quite well again, thank you, although very busy shooting a TV documentary with Jim Culloty in a supporting role. 'Best Mate has an audience most days,' Henrietta said, sounding sniffy. 'He loves being a star.'

Across the ocean, Guillame Macaire, who'd been named the National Hunt's champion trainer in France for the 2002-03 season, was biding his time. Scarcely the sort of person to compare his horses to fairytale characters, he worked them hard and steadily instead of pampering them. Macaire was as tough talking as Jean Gabin in an old gangster movie; none of that three-races-a-year nonsense for him. He could be cutting and disdainful, even of *his* stable star. 'Jair du Cochet is the most stupid horse in the world,' he told a British tabloid. 'The slightest change in his programme and he flips! He has done some very silly things, and I am on a knife-edge worrying about him. And Best Mate scares me in the paddock. He walks around with the command of a lion. He is not an ordinary horse.'

Was this an honest assessment, or merely subterfuge? Macaire kept them guessing about his Gold Cup intentions. And where did that leave Beef Or Salmon? A week after the Durkan, Hourigan ran him in the Hilly Way Chase at Cork, a two-mile tune-up for the Ericsson, and his horse fiddled a win despite more sloppy jumping. The hopes I'd once entertained for Beef Or Salmon were fading fast. That same weekend, pretty Solerina added to her string of pearls with the Tara Hurdle at Navan, while at Fairyhouse Barry Connell chose to let a professional jockey ride The Posh Paddy in a maiden hurdle, his horse's first race over jumps, but Paddy must have missed his master because he finished a well-beaten fifth.

Yet for all the good Irish racing, Cheltenham snatched the headlines again with its Tripleprint Meeting. Kingscliff was the lead story, of course, but Rooster Booster's shocking failure in the Tote Bula Hurdle also made headlines. The race, conducted at a crawl, went to Rigmarole at 25-1, another bonus for Ruby Walsh. Jessie Harrington's Spirit Leader did nothing in the Bula and still hadn't hit her stride, while Nicky Henderson's little Iris Royal, not quite sixteen hands high, hung on to defeat the ill-fated Risk Accessor in the Tripleprint Gold Cup Chase. 'An absolute legend of a horse,' exclaimed Mick Fitzgerald after the ride, but you had to be careful with Mick. He has a history of hyperbole. After winning the Grand National, he once said, 'Sex will be an anticlimax after this.'

The Irish are fond of launches, so whenever a new play, art exhibition, restaurant, hair salon, car exhaust centre or whatever is about to open, you can count on a cheerful party with a dignitary present to extol its virtues and wish it Godspeed. When I heard that Paul Carberry and Barry Geraghty were going to launch a refurbished Bambury Bookmakers shop in Ashbourne, in Meath, I couldn't resist attending the ceremony. Though Geraghty currently had the hot hand, Carberry has a reputation as the best natural horseman in Ireland, bar none, so I thought this might be a good time to meet him and have a talk.

Ashbourne is a country town about to tip over into suburbia. Everywhere I looked, I saw blocks of housing going up on what had once been farmland, with traffic strangling the main road. Just past a sign that certified Ashbourne as Host City to Bangladesh, I noticed a Bambury shop and parked the car. The shop had a piece of cardboard in the front window, half-collapsed and folded in on itself, to advertise the launch. That made me pause, but the shop looked jaunty inside, with new TVs and carpeting, and a new wooden floor gleaming with fresh possibilities. About twenty gents, most of them getting on in age, were waiting for the launch to begin, but I had an inkling that they would have been there anyway, like potted plants, even without the promise of famous jockeys.

Carberry was the first to arrive, his right thumb in a bulky cast. He'd fractured it in a recent fall at Fairyhouse when his whip banged into it, a freak injury. He hated to lose any rides, but it was enough of a nuisance to keep him on the sidelines for a couple of weeks. Soon to turn thirty, he was about to enter the danger zone for jump jockeys, where each new blow would take an increasing toll. His weight wasn't a problem yet – he could make nine stone ten pounds without any serious dieting – and his job as a stable jock for Noel Meade was secure, so he had no reason to worry. In fact, he looked as relaxed as a student in jeans and sweater, while Geraghty was dressed almost the same, right down to the shiny black shoes with silver buckles.

Seeing them up close, I realized how tall for a jockey Geraghty is at five foot nine inches, and how strong in the upper body. He rides at ten stone eleven pounds, and can starve and sweat down to ten stone four pounds, but his normal weight is around eleven stone. While Carberry seemed at ease and agreed to have a drink after the launch, Barry was anxious to hop on a plane to England. He was even toting a set of silks on a hanger. Fame had Geraghty in its grip, but he deserved the recognition. The Irish had six winners at the Festival last year, and he'd ridden five of them.

Jimmy Findlay, the shop's owner, had married into the Bambury family. He was bustling about and urging his clients to hit the buffet. 'Come on, lads, don't be shy, help yourselves, I'm not going to bring it round to you,' he scolded, but they held back, possibly suspecting a catch, some previously unknown bookies' trap that would cost them money. The launch itself was short and sweet. A 'personality' I didn't recognize contributed some patter, and the jockeys answered a few questions but revealed nothing of value to a punter. Geraghty was awarded 200 euros for a charity bet and selected Keen Leader in the Ericsson, a horse of Jonjo O'Neill's he'd just won on at Haydock, in the Tommy Whittle Chase.

And that was about it, except for the obligatory photo op and Findlay's introduction of a regular named Frank ('I inherited him when we bought the shop in 1990'), who was the oldest codger in the room by a decade, no mean feat. Frank stepped right into the picture, as if he were the jockeys' patron saint. While Carberry schmoozed with the crowd, Jimmy led me over to another old guy and said, 'Any idea who this is? Arkle's groom! Isn't that right, Joe?' But it wasn't right. 'I was never Arkle's groom,' Joe sputtered, 'but I worked for the Dreapers for fifty-two years.' He was upset that Arkle got all the glory and started listing some other good horses from the yard, but the din in the shop drowned him out.

Carberry and I left for the Ashbourne Hotel next-door. The quiet bar features portraits of horses etched in glass – Prince Regent, Mill House, and yes, Arkle, no doubt to poor Joe's dismay. I felt a little relieved to be gone from the launch, and I suspect Paul did, too. He can act the part at such events, but it doesn't come easily or naturally. There's something of the loner about him. He ordered a Bulmers cider and tapped out a cigarette with his bandaged hand. His thumb was healing fine, he told me, and he would be ready in time for the big Leopardstown meeting at Christmas.

'I can still hunt, anyway,' he said, with a grin. He loves hunting more than anything, even more than riding a race. He keeps eight hunters at home and rides out with the Ward Union Hunt Club, established in 1854, twice a week. Between sixty and eighty of the club's one hundred or so members follow the hounds across the rolling countryside of Meath, tracking a stag that's been given a twelve-minute head-start. The stag is never killed. Instead, it's returned to the club's park and becomes part of Ward Union's breeding programme. 'I like the speed of the hunt, its unpredictability,' Paul said, plus there are so many different obstacles to be jumped, hedges and wide ditches, and so many decisions to be made in an instant. 'You never know where you'll wind up,' he added. He was about to become the club's honorary whip, as puffed up about that as any of his big-race wins.

Glancing at his thumb, I asked him about his injuries. I was becoming a collector of griefs, fascinated by the battering a jump jockey has to endure. 'Do you have all day?' he replied coyly. He'd broken a leg three times, his ribs, and both wrists. When a horse kicked him in the back, the doctors removed his spleen, but those were just the most severe damages in an inventory he could, but wouldn't, elaborate on. He felt it was dishonourable to carry on about that aspect of a jockey's life, I think. Honour is a concept you could truly apply to Carberry. He reminded me of a shy, laconic sheriff in an old western, the man of principle folks depend on to run the bad guys out of town.

Like most riders, Carberry started early, still in his teens. His father Tommy, a great jockey who later became a trainer, won the Cheltenham Gold Cup three times and lost a fourth through a disqualification, and also won a Grand National. (Paul would win his own Grand National in '99 on BobbyJo, trained by his dad.) Tommy arranged for his son to be apprenticed to Jim Bolger, a flat trainer known for being a hard taskmaster. Bolger's lads aren't allowed to drink or smoke, and they go to church on Sunday or else. 'Your daddy definitely doesn't like you,' Bolger warned his new arrival, but Carberry survived and even managed to sneak in a cider or two.

Though Paul was light enough for the flat, he found the races too boring and always preferred the jumps. At the age of twenty, he tried riding for Sir Robert Ogden in England for a while, but that didn't suit him, either, not with all the commuting around the country and racing almost every day. 'I missed my hunting,' he said, implying that he missed Ireland as well, so when Noel Meade asked him to come home, he settled for a lower profile and a slower pace of life.

The move didn't hurt him financially. Both he and Geraghty were about to pass the million-euro mark in prize money. In Ireland, a jockey earns 130 euros per ride, plus eight percent of the purse should he win or place. His agent carves off ten percent of his earnings, and he must also pay a valet to care for his silks and tack. It's a little difficult to climb onto a horse who's a poor jumper, Paul said, and it can be tough to ride in a maiden race or a race with a large field, but he tended to be most concerned about dodgy jockeys. 'Plenty of those around.'

'Any jockeys you admire?'

'A few.'

'Want to name them?'

Reluctantly, as if the subject were as undignified as his list of injuries, he mentioned Ruby Walsh. 'Ruby knows where to be in a race, the best possible position, and how to save ground. And how to keep out of trouble.' Trouble can lead to a fall.

'Can you tell when a fall is coming?' I asked, remembering Barry Connell's tumble off The Posh Paddy. 'Any signal from the horse?'

'It's always unexpected,' he said. 'There's never any time to think. All you can do is cover up and protect yourself.'

Carberry only travels to England for the big races these days, so his work schedule is fairly routine. He does a bit of schooling for his boss, rides out some mornings, and usually goes racing on Thursdays, Saturdays, and Sundays. 'That leaves you a lot of free time.'

'Not enough.'

'What's the downside of the job?' I watched him take a slow sip of his cider, still close-mouthed as the seconds ticked by. 'So I guess that's the answer,' I said, and he nodded. We finished our drinks and walked out into a mild, sunny afternoon, so pleasant that Paul thought he'd go for a ride on one of his hunters. I wondered why he was so fond of them, what made them so special, and he considered for a moment before replying, 'Guts. They're bold and fearless,' the very qualities that separate a jump jockey such as Carberry from the rest of the pack.

The Christmas Meeting at Leopardstown was fast approaching, and to prepare myself I set up a visit with Ted Walsh, Ruby's dad, who is RTE's racing analyst in addition to being a trainer. I'd learned a little about the sport and the Irish so far, but Walsh is a real insider, and I hoped he could contribute to my education. I was supposed to meet him at his house in Kill at noon, but his wife Helen told me was running late, still on the Curragh with some horses. 'I don't know why racing people make appointments,' she said. 'It never works out.' She offered to let me wait, but rather than sit like a lump on the couch I went to town, bought a *Post*, and had lunch at the Dew Drop Inn, a cosy spot with a good fire, where Shane McGowan was singing 'Fairytale of New York' on the radio.

I returned to the Walsh's house an hour later, but Ted still wasn't back, so I became the lump I had tried to avoid becoming, seated before a TV tuned to the races at Folkestone, where Ruby had three rides for Paul Nicholls that afternoon. He'd won the first race on Lord Lington, and as he was at the post on Harapour in the second, Ted showed up. Compact and energetic, he's outgoing and outspoken, but he didn't waste any time on introductions, flopping into an armchair and asking to see my paper.

'What number is he on?'

'Three,' I told him. 'Harapour.'

He ran a finger down the card and isolated his son's colours. 'Black-and-white,' he said, leaning forward, his eyes glued to the tube. Helen came in from the kitchen to watch the race, as did Jennifer, Ruby's sister, who acts as his agent. Sometimes the Walshs dash down to the only bookie in Kill – in a house next to a beauty parlour – when they can't get a race on their own satellite service, and the local punters read that as a signal and plunge heavily on Ruby's mount. Today, though, it was clear that Ruby wouldn't win the Mr Michael & Miss Kelly Regan Birthday Novices' Hurdle (Grade E), so Ted threw a leg over an arm of his chair and hit the mute button. 'Fire away,' he said, the consummate media veteran.

Walsh was born in Fermoy in County Cork, fertile ground for racing men, as he noted; the great Vincent O'Brien is from Churchtown, for instance. His father owned a pub and did some farming, dealt in horses, and raced them in point-to-points, and Ted worked with him and took over the present yard when his dad died in 1990. He doesn't view training as a precious art on a par with alchemy, just a job like any other. 'If you get a decent horse, the trick is not to mess it up,' he said. 'About ninety percent of our trainers are on a level. Only ten percent are lacking. But this life isn't easy. Don't do it if you don't like it. If an owner wants to go to Thurles and watch his horse finish feckin' ninth, you've got no choice but to go.'

The phone rang. It was Ruby calling from Folkestone. He still relies on his father for criticism and advice. Ted apologized for missing the first race. 'I didn't see it, but you won. Good man, good man!' After hanging up, he said, 'Ruby's at the top of the game and he enjoys the buzz, but it's risky at the top. Some jockeys stay in the comfort zone, and they can last for years at the second or third level. It's safer. But if a top jockey slips, he falls all the way to the floor, and he won't get up again. It's a tough business. So many heartbreaks, so many hopes are dashed.'

In fact, Walsh believes the National Hunt in Ireland is in a precarious position, too dependent on government investment for its survival. Charlie McCreevy, the current Finance Minister, has a soft spot for racing, but what would happen when he was gone? The policies of any government are always ripe for change. 'We're on slippery ground,' Ted said. To build an audience, attract a younger crowd, and ensure the sport's future, the racecourses ought to improve their facilities and provide the sort of amenities an increasingly sophisticated Irish public has come to expect.

'Nobody wants to stand around eating bad food and drinking overpriced drinks when their feet are all wet,' he explained, an argument I could support from personal experience. 'Not long ago in Ireland, when you checked into a hotel, you asked if the bathroom was on the landing, so that you wouldn't have to deal with the stairs. Now you wouldn't stay in a room that isn't en suite. What the National Hunt needs is a Paschal Taggart, someone with a business head and the common touch. He's the most innovative, down-to-earth entrepreneur I know.'

Taggart is Ireland's greyhound chief, responsible for transforming a mug's game into a going concern by upgrading the facilities at dog tracks. Ever searching for louche entertainment, I once tried to reserve a table in the restaurant at Shelbourne Park, Dublin's premiere dog stadium, and wound up on a three-month-long waiting list. So popular is Taggart that when he quit as chairman after a dispute with some members of the Irish Greyhound Board, more than one hundred and sixty industry figures, from Derry to Kerry, convened in Portlaoise to insist he be reinstated, and the offending board members be sacked.

Tossing out Taggart as a model is the kind of loaded remark that sometimes gets Walsh in hot water on TV. He started as a presenter about thirty years ago, while he was still riding as an amateur, and beat half-a-dozen other candidates after a series of auditions. He thinks his honesty helped, as did his knowledge of the sport. 'Before it was just like the news,' he said. 'Actors read the script, but they didn't know fuck-all about racing and couldn't answer a simple question.' His transition from the saddle to a spot in front of the camera didn't go smoothly at first, though. He was a little too honest and had to acquire a knack for diplomacy. He gave me an example. 'When a jockey screws up, you don't say, "What an awful ride!" You say, "I believe he's had better days."'

Walsh received further coaching from Tim O'Connor, a former boss at RTE, who taught him a few more broadcasting tricks. 'Four trainers are in the parade ring before a race, OK?', he asked, sounding like a coach himself. 'It does no good to say, "And there's Paddy Mullins." You have to say, "And there's Paddy Mullins in a trilby!"' O'Connor also taught him to tailor his remarks to the image on-screen. 'Say there's a picture of a Mercedes on the TV, and the camera shifts to a red school bus. O'Connor told me, "That's when you stop talking about the Mercedes." I didn't get it right away, I said, "But I didn't finish with the Mercedes, Tim." He said, "I don't care, Ted." And a producer added, "Just talk about the feckin' schoolbus."'

'So you enjoy it now?'

'Ah, yeah, I enjoy it. Racing's been good to me, and I wouldn't knock it, but I don't give a shite for the establishment. I'm a friend of the real National Hunt enthusiasts,' he continued, loosening up. 'I don't have much interest in the gambling side. Even when I rode, it was never about the money. I was as thrilled to win a little maiden race as a big handicap, bar Cheltenham, of course. That's the be-all and end-all of the jumps. The winner's enclosure is like an amphitheatre, and you don't have hundreds of spectators, you have thousands, and they're the most appreciative on earth, that mixture of the Irish and English. When you head for the enclosure, the crowd parts like the Red Sea. Isn't that the one Moses parted?'

'It is.'

He could barely contain his exuberance now, and reached for another comparison. 'It's like walking into this huge cauldron of cheering people! There's no greater atmosphere anywhere. Nothing in the world compares to it!'

This was hyperbole on the Mick Fitzgerald scale. With the mention of Cheltenham, I took the opportunity to tap into Ted's expertise. 'Who'll win the Gold Cup this year?'

'Best Mate,' he replied emphatically, with no hesitation. 'He has all the attributes. He jumps, stays, and has a turn-of-foot. And he loves Cheltenham.'

'Any idea what Jim Lewis paid for him?'

'Around a hundred grand, I'd guess, but it's only a guess. Tom Costello doesn't boast about those things. Costello is the king of dealers. He's produced more top-class horses than anyone else in Ireland. Did you know Kingscliff and Strong Flow both came out of Costello's nursery? Two more Gold Cup winners, maybe. Tom's a lovely fellow, but he's not in good health at the moment.'

Kingscliff and Strong Flow. Every horse this mysterious man laid a finger on was a potential champion, it seemed. Walsh has been a friend of Costello's for ages, and he described to me how Costello operates. 'There are breeders, you see – small farmers – who don't go to the sales because they hate all the claptrap,' he said, 'and Tom knows them all, and he knows from the stallion masters in the area the pedigrees of all their foals. Take Un Desperado, for example. Tom will know Un Desperado has covered a mare over at Mike Smith's farm, so he'll arrange a meeting. And maybe Smith will have some other nice foals, as well, a Be My Native, a Supreme Leader, and so on.

'Smith will have a price in mind, maybe 38,000 euros for the lot. Tom will dwell on that for a minute and write a cheque for 25,000. Probably Mike won't accept, so they'll have a pot of tea, and Tom will write a cheque for 28,000. Sooner or later, he'll close the deal at a price he likes.

'In the old days, Tom paid cash to the farmers who didn't trust banks. He'd have a wad of bills in a satchel. And he's a master of psychology, too. If a buyer suspects he has a special horse, Tom might say, "I do, but I don't want to sell it", and that drives up the price. Or he'll play off one of his sons. "Tom Junior believes that horse jumps like Best Mate," he'll say, "but I don't think so." His horses are always beautiful jumpers. When the Costellos put a horse through its paces, it takes the sight right out of your eyes.'

I wanted to know even more about Costello, but it was almost three o'clock, and Ted still hadn't eaten lunch, so he invited me to join his family in the dining room. I reckoned I'd never lived in such an hospitable country as Ireland. On a wall, I saw a framed photo of Ruby on Papillon, Walsh's Grand National winner in 2000, but that was about the only racing-related material around. Some trainers are workaholics, Ted said, and don't have a life beyond the horses, while others develop outside interests, as he has done with travel.

'I love America!' he bellowed, when I told him where I was from. He spent two years there in the mid-1950s, when the family emigrated to the States so that his father could try working with Mickey Walsh, his brother, who trained jumpers. The Walshs spent their summers in Queens Village in New York, then moved to Southern Pines in North Carolina during the winter, a peripatetic existence that didn't suit them.

As I was shovelling in some homemade apple crumble and ice-cream, I realized we hadn't got round to Leopardstown at all, but Ted assured me that I didn't need any special advice. 'You'll have a grand time. They take a horse to heart there,' he said, clearly a high accolade 'They clap to the horse. The horse is the hero.'

'And the horse knows it?'

'And the horse knows it,' Walsh said, with a laugh.

The sky over Dublin Bay was a flinty grey on the afternoon I visited Leopardstown, a week before Christmas. The temperature was in the low thirties, and the Dublin Mountains, looming up behind the grandstand, were almost black in the stormy light – brooding, foreboding, the stuff of bad romantic poetry. Tom Burke, the track's Racing Manager, was in his office, a cubbyhole piled so high with cardboard boxes I had to sidle this way and that to get to his desk. The desk too was buried under papers, so that the overall effect was of a place under siege, although Burke had the calm look of a seasoned veteran used to surviving in the trenches.

'Feels like snow,' I said, shivering as I unbuttoned my overcoat.

Burke looked horrified. 'Don't say snow.'

The fickle Irish weather was his enemy these days, the source of his worst nightmares. The Christmas Meeting begins on Boxing Day and is the track's biggest earner, but Burke needs the heavens to co-operate if he's to bring it off, and the heavens don't always oblige. In 1995, he lost all but one of the meeting's four days because the ground froze solid, and that could happen again. Anything could happen, really, so Burke's sleep could be restless. Whenever he felt on top of the situation, all systems go, Mother Nature knocked him off-balance with some torrential rain, say, or a pounding of hailstones the size of golf balls. If frogs dropped from the clouds some day, Burke probably wouldn't bat an eye.

'No matter what you've experienced in the past, there's always a new trauma waiting,' he said, a truth he has learned to respect after some sixteen years in the job. Though Leopardstown carries insurance to cover any weather-related losses, it's expensive, and a cancelled meeting is costly in terms of goodwill. Irrational punters blame the track for depriving them of their holiday fun, and forcing them to stay at home with the relatives and eat yesterday's plum pudding.

Burke had a call to make. To keep me occupied, he handed over a brief history of the racecourse, prepared for its centenary in 1988. The 200-acre site, chosen for its scenic qualities and its access to a railway line, once housed a leper colony, hence the somewhat devious permutation 'Leopardstown'. In the 1860s, an order of English Benedictine monks bought the land for a charitable model farm to introduce the latest agricultural technology to impoverished Irish farmers, but it went belly-up when the Father Superior spent too much money on machinery.

The land then fell into the hands of some Dublin businessmen, who wanted to build a track that would be a rough replica of Sandown Park. They opened in August 1888, on a date that coincided with the Dublin Horse Show, an important event on the social calendar, to a crowd estimated at fifty thousand. People poured into Foxrock Station by train on the old Harcourt Line, but the bridge to the course was only three feet wide and almost collapsed under the crush. The roads weren't much better, becoming so jammed that some of the crowd never even reached Leopardstown. The turnstiles couldn't cope with the pressure, either, and malfunctioned. The main gate was too small to admit horse-drawn carriages, while Mr Street, the caterer, was singled out for abuse in the newspapers and trashed for supplying such 'execrable food'.

His phone call finished, Burke flipped to a favourite page. 'Disgraceful bungling,' he read aloud, with a fair degree of drama. 'That a number of lives were not lost must be ascribed to a miracle rather than to any precautions on the part of the management.'

'The press was tougher in those days,' I said.

'Obviously.' Burke, it seems, has a dry sense of humour, but I could see how he might lose it in the run-up to Christmas, while he was putting in sixteen hours a day. His duties are manifold. He is responsible not only for the state of the ground, but also for printing the race cards and posting the sponsors' signs. He has to liaise with the police over traffic control, still a problem, and massage the egos of the corporate bosses with private boxes. All the fences and hurdles have to be checked and repaired if necessary. The course has very good drainage, so the principle threat to racing is a severe frost, as in '95.

It could have been the paragraph I read about the Benedictines, but I thought Burke had a monkish aspect as he bent to his work. His office is cell-like, and no doubt he entertained a prayerful attitude toward the weather. The stress is most intense on Christmas Day, he told me. One of his younger children (he has eleven, ranging in age from four to twenty-five) ordinarily wakes him early, just after dawn, and if Willie Gibbons, his course foreman, reports the tiniest hint of trouble, he hurries over for an inspection. But if the day is benign, he attends Mass with his family, enjoys his Christmas dinner, and retires around ten o'clock, surely counting his blessings.

Two days before Christmas, Henrietta Knight dropped a lump of coal in British stockings and added to Tom Burke's stress by confirming that Best Mate would run in the Ericsson at Leopardstown and not the King George VI in England. All she would say for the record was that the Irish ground was easier and safer, and that Best Mate had never been fond of Kempton because it was too quick for him and had once given him sore shins and shoulders. On hearing the news, Michael Hourigan welcomed the challenge against Beef Or Salmon, while the wily Guillame Macaire, whose Jair du Cochet was in the King

George, remarked, 'Well, it isn't bad news, is it?' although Macaire was in for a shock.

I was on my way to O'Herlihy's when the story broke. The pub was in a fine holiday mood. A diligent staffer had found some old decorations in an attic corner and put them up, and they matched the tenor of the place – there were a few plastic wise men and some cardboard angels with missing wings, and a strand of glittery letters wishing everyone a Happy Christmas. In honour of the season, the regulars were defying their usually inflexible routines, popping in at odd hours and even standing or sitting in spots other than their normal ones, and that resulted in a topsy-turvy effect, forcing them to talk to people they'd been avoiding all year and reminding them of the reasons why.

Reilly sat at a table with his dog Oliver dozing at his feet. He was excited about Best Mate coming to Leopardstown, yet suspicious about Knight's motives, more so than in the past, and was beginning to share my doubts, though from a different perspective. 'The harse is not right,' Reilly said darkly. 'Your woman lives in mortal fear of Jair du Cochet. She couldn't stand another beating.'

'Maybe she's ducking Strong Flow,' I said. Paul Nicholls was still torn between the big race and the less competitive Feltham Novices' Chase.

'Now there's a proper harse,' Reilly raved. 'Jumps like a bloody stag.'

'Except when a fence gets in the way.'

'Ah, you Americans are so critical! The harse is green, he's still learning. Strong Flow has Gold Cup written all over him, next year if not this one. Have another, will you?'

It didn't require a great deal of arm-twisting to convince me to break my own inflexible rule and have a second pint in mid-afternoon, indulging in a guilty pleasure and basking in the atmosphere of bonhomie. Peace on earth, good will to men, that sort of thing. The faces along the bar had a burnished glow, teased out by the beer and the whisky, and as I sipped my Guinness I thought dreamily about my travels and all the people I'd met, struck again by the relative purity of the National Hunt – purity always being relative – and how the love of the game coloured and enriched the lives of those who cared for the horses, a simple but powerful equation.

Dubliners do Christmas with a vengeance. The next morning, I joined the throngs of last-minute shoppers on Grafton Street, each on a special mission, searching for the right digital camera or pair of woolly red socks for Uncle Fergal in Ballymurphy. Ornaments, tinsel, they danced on the breeze. The air was crisp, the sky sparkly. A little boy was belting out carols, and coins clattered into the bucket at his feet. From Brown Thomas wafted the scent of a thousand perfumes, the aroma of a harem. Gypsy women, sad-eyed but gaily dressed, begged for money, a palm outstretched as they clasped their infants to their breasts. Somewhere, in one pub or another, I knew Shane McGowan could be heard singing, 'Got on a lucky one, came in at eighteen to one. . .'

At Sawers on Chatham Street, I bought a side of wild smoked salmon and a dozen Dublin Bay prawns to be pan-fried in butter with garlic and shallots, then served with crusty bread to mop up the sauce. It was Sheridans for cheese, Gubeen and Durus from Ireland, plus a wedge of Gorgonzola and a tub of bocconcini in olive oil spiced with flecks of red pepper, maybe the work of an Italian artisan in Tuscany – underpaid, undervalued, his horse a loser at Grosseto – trembling in his icy studio when the village beauty knocks on his door with a bottle of grappa under her arm and says in a husky whisper, 'Buon natale, caro.'

Our Christmas tree came from the Wicklow Mountains, freshly cut and still smelling of the pine forest. A neighbour's son delivered it. Matt is ambitious, a real go-getter, and his tree business would earn him enough for a trip to New York over the summer – to the Hamptons, no less, where he'd seek his fortune on the golf courses. He'd done his research and knew what a caddy could make at the better private clubs (if the tips were as advertised), and though he wound up stuck in a ratty trailer in Montauk swabbing out boats for a crazy old sailor, he would be the first to tell you what a grand time he'd had on his American adventure.

The ham and the turkey were ordered from our butcher. That was another Irish tradition, Imelda had explained to me during our first Christmas together. Why both? I couldn't understand and thought she must be joking until we made the rounds of parties, where hunks of pig and bird were heaped on platters, as inseparable as, well, ham and eggs. Salt beef was another new one on me, a pricey seasonal delicacy as tough as shoe leather, but our guests ate it without objection and even murmured a few polite compliments, just as I'd done as a kid when my mother served us the stinky lutefish she'd bought by mail order from Minnesota, a tribute to her Norwegian ancestry.

With the tree up, the lights out, and dinner in the oven, Imelda and I walked to town for a drink at the Shelbourne on Christmas Eve. Always at the hotel she met someone she knew, often a friend she hadn't seen since her school or university days, Dublin being small and the lives of its residents intricately linked, with no secret ever truly secret. And so it was that night, with a round of merry introductions, and when we left after two drinks instead of one, the streets were alive with couples and families on their way home with the last presents wrapped up and under their arms. Horse cabs trotted along the fringes of Stephen's Green, and we heard laughter ringing out like bells from the bundled-up passengers, a complement to our own jolly mood.

Christmas morning broke mild and breezy, with a spattering of rain. I remembered Tom Burke and wondered which of his eleven children had roused him from bed, and if the absence of frost would grant him an untroubled day. I hoped so. Lying in bed with Imelda beside me, I was filled with good wishes for all mankind, as silly and trite as that may sound, thinking that we all deserve big plates of turkey and ham at a table surrounded by those we love at least one day a year. I'd been around long enough by now, and had certainly seen enough, to cherish such rare, full-hearted moments and accept them for what they are, a gift.

On Boxing Day, the ground came up soft but testing at Leopardstown. I couldn't rouse myself from a chair by the fire and stayed home to watch the King

George VI on TV, suffering from a familiar post-Christmas sensation of being overstuffed and never in need of any food again. Two words, Edredon Bleu, rattled around in my brain – blue eiderdown in translation, a comforting image on a cold winter day, probably even to Guillame Macaire, the French tough guy, who looked to have the big race sewn up with Jair du Cochet and might have viewed Henrietta Knight's gesture of sending her second-best horse to Kempton as a sop to her outraged fans, as many did.

For me, the matter was not so clear. I was aware that Edredon Bleu had tried the race once before and failed to last the three miles, but this season he had been so spectacular, with each win an admirable endorsement of his ability to surpass himself, that it seemed possible he could do it again. Then, too, Knight was so finicky about her horses I didn't think she'd risk one of her finest just to placate the vocal minority. With that in mind, I made my way to Boylesports, where Edredon Bleu was on offer at 25-1, and promptly bet on Fondmort because I'd won some money on him at the Open, as if that had any bearing. I can only blame the ham and the turkey.

Best Mate's desertion was a hot topic, of course, and Tony McCoy took a pot-shot at Knight after riding a winner for Martin Pipe in the first race. 'I don't want to start a controversy,' McCoy said, being disingenuous, 'but it's beautiful ground. I'd like to ride Best Mate over it.' This was payback time. Actually, McCoy had ridden Best Mate twice in the King George as a replacement for Jim Culloty, who was out once with an injury and next with a suspension, and he'd even won it for Henrietta in

2002. But Knight was still critical of McCoy in her book, suggesting that his aggressive style didn't suit her sensitive horse. Best Mate is so intelligent and capable, she implied, that all any jockey has to do is sit on him, a notion that McCoy, who isn't known for his lack of an ego, must have found galling.

The King George might have been more competitive if Paul Nicholls had thrown Strong Flow in at the deep end, but he chose the Feltham instead, a conservative play. The horse was a cut above his rivals, backed down to 4-11. Again Strong Flow demonstrated his potential when he jumped well, giving each fence plenty of air, but he also jumped horribly at times, taking off far too soon. He smacked two fences almost square, stuck out a single leg on landing, and remained upright long enough for Ruby Walsh to gain control and pursue Ballycassidy, who had jumping problems, as well, veering to the left. Strong Flow had to put in a good jump at the last to win, and he did it. The look on Ruby's face, seen in close-up, combined relief and disbelief, the standard emotions of a survivor.

Willie Mullins had run Rule Supreme, one of his better horses (although not much of a jumper) in the race, and had even booked McCoy for the ride, but Rule Supreme let him down, or rather, the going did. 'I sent a horse to Kempton, and he came back with sore shins,' Mullins complained, contradicting his jockey's opinion of the ground, thereby siding with Knight's assessment. I had a feeling Willie wouldn't mind seeing the present year end, and a new one begin. Like Edward O'Grady, he could use a change of luck. Davenport Milenium hadn't scoped clean and would miss the big holiday meetings, plus Mullins couldn't quite find the right spot for Hedgehunter, who fell in the Welsh National that same weekend over a distance just a little too long for him.

Jair du Cochet was installed as the 2-1 favourite for the King George, with some money for First Gold and Swansea Bay, much improved this season after two wind operations to improve his breathing. In an act of charitable self-sacrifice, his trainer Peter Bowen had driven him from Pembrokeshire to Kempton on Christmas Day, a trip of some two hundred and forty miles. As expected, Edredon Bleu grabbed the lead when the tape went up. Though only a week shy of his twelfth birthday, he was as frisky as a colt. Going along with him was First Gold, who'd won the race in 2000. Jair du Cochet looked as stupid as his trainer had once described him. He showed every possible sign of disinterest, lagging behind the field and clipping the fourth fence, a ditch. It wasn't a bad mistake, but Jacques Ricou almost left the saddle and never recovered. Jair du Cochet was soon pulled up, and Ricou was treated to another helping of scorn.

The never-to-be-trusted Valley Henry, sold to big spender Graham Wylie and transferred from Nicholls to J. Howard Johnson, was a faller, and so too was Le Roi Miguel. The suspect stayers began to unravel at the fourth-last, Fondmort among them, and First Gold became one-paced, allowing Edredon Bleu to forge ahead again. The old warrior was still full of running, but I feared the worst when Pipe's Tiutchev, the near-master of Beef Or Salmon at Punchestown, challenged him. Nobody coaxes the last shreds of energy from a horse better than

Tony McCoy, but his efforts on Tiutchev were to no avail. Edredon Bleu rallied for a crowd-pleasing win, every bit as brave as his trainer, who had the courage to abandon her habit of shielding her eyes. 'Hiding in the bushes has not brought me much luck lately,' Knight said, 'so I stood by the railings and watched it.'

On Saturday, it was Paddy Power Day at Leopardstown, with the bookmaker sponsoring all the races on the card, including the big one, the Paddy Power Steeplechase, worth a total of 170,000 euros. It looked to be a thriller with twenty-seven horses entered, among them World Wide Web from the O'Neill and McManus team, but I could only focus on the Paddy Power Dial-A-Bet Steeplechase, where Moscow Flyer would go up against a soft field of five other horses. For once, I might be rooting against him.

More than most courses on the Irish circuit, Leopardstown reminds me of an American track. The scenery might be rural with mountain views and a glimpse of Dublin Bay, but the atmosphere is urban and lively, and that attracted some slick young people from the city centre. The older generation still outnumbered them, flat-capped or trilby-topped, often travelling in from country towns by coach. Among the crowd, too, were some lads from the north, from Belfast and Derry, who appeared to be surviving on lager, Bulmers and crisps. If they had a woman with them, she was dressed to the nines. Ireland was the centre of the jump-racing universe for now, having stolen England's fire, and the buzz had everyone on edge.

I could feel the buzz as I went through the gate, past a cash machine where a long queue had already formed. This was puzzling. Had they all forgotten to bring any money? Or had they already lost their stake in a secret craps game under the stands? Many were the mysteries, all right, and just ahead was another, the Leopardstown crèche, a dreary-looking mobile home where a child could be deposited, although a forcefully worded sign urged parents to 'Collect immediately after the last race.' Had tapped-out mums and dads left behind kids in the past, and how were they disposed of? One had to wonder.

I ducked into Jodami's Bar for a beer, where some students pressed into part-time service were doing the pouring, acting cool and storing up incidents of adult misbehaviour to retail later to their pals. The meet-and-greet dance was in full swing, with cousin Jimmy shaking hands with uncle Tommy, while aunt Maeve was searching for her niece Fiona, who had hooked up with her old piano teacher, and so on. All this was carried out in a merry way alien to most racing venues, where the gambling aspect traditionally takes precedence over any human values.

I was too anxious to appreciate the early races, a pair of hurdles, but I did pay attention to the Future Champions Novice Hurdle, where Mariah Rollins deprived Newmill of another victory. Then Moscow Flyer's hour came, and though he destroyed the weak field as I expected, taking the lead six out and hanging on well when Native Scout challenged him, the race was still very tense for me because I almost hoped he'd finish second. Instead, he scored his third straight win and laid the foundation for disaster at Cheltenham if you believe in such things, as I was tempted to do at the moment.

Redemption was the theme for the Ericsson Chase, held appropriately on Sunday. Even though I arrived at the track before noon, the car park was jammed, with Best Mate throwing off so much star power that more than nineteen thousand people bought tickets to see him. Not that he was the only attraction – Pizarro and Sacundai from Edward O'Grady's yard were also out to polish their tarnished reputations. The weather couldn't have been better, cold and clear, with the last traces of frost melting under the winter sun. The drying ground wasn't so testing any more, providing ideal going for Best Mate and the eight other horses in the race.

The spectators were stacked up twenty-deep around the parade ring when Best Mate made his entrance. If there was anything wrong with Henrietta's horse, I couldn't see a single sign of it. Best Mate is an elegant specimen. He seemed to like being alone and on parade, used to being loved at home and adored in public. He was clearly fond of Jackie Jenner, his groom, who also cares for Edredon Bleu, and nuzzled her once or twice as they circled. She understands all his quirks – he only likes his tail and mane being groomed, for instance – and often rides him out. She was on him the day he had an accident that might have ended his career, in fact, when he stepped on a rusty nail on a bridle path. It missed penetrating the navicular bursa bone by a fraction of a centimetre. Matey, the vets said, had been lucky.

Henrietta Knight soon joined her horse in the ring, as did Terry Biddlecombe and Jim Lewis's gang. They had a studied nonchalance, that McManus-like talent for concealing their emotions. Biddlecombe may have a heart of gold, but he looked a rough customer, I thought, the sort of man who once had a temper but had learned to control it. In contrast, Knight projected an aura of innocence and sweetness. I felt I could trust her with my life, with my darkest and most damaging secrets, and that any hideous thing I confessed to her wouldn't shatter her composure or alter her positive outlook. You wanted Hen to like you, to approve of you and tell you that you were a decent fellow, so I could understand why those rowdy pupils in Oxford had locked her in a cupboard and given her electric shocks.

The ever-increasing Irish part of me hoped that Beef Or Salmon wouldn't let us down. The bookies gave him a fair chance at 2-1, while Best Mate, available at even money early in the day, closed at 8-11. (The bookies raked in about nine hundred and fifty thousand euros on the Ericsson, most of it on Best Mate.) Jonjo O'Neill had left Keen Leader at home in England, so Barry Geraghty switched to ride Le Coudray. In spite of the odds, I couldn't bring myself to back Beef Or Salmon. He still had that distracted air of youthful inattention, while Best Mate appeared to grasp the exact nature of his mission. When he took to the track, he showed none of the hesitation or slight puzzlement some horses do. Instead, he was off at a gallop, tossing his head about and eager for the flag to be raised.

For Best Mate, the race was a cakewalk. His performance blew to shreds all the paranoid theories about his health. Jim Culloty let him travel along in no hurry – Culloty was unruffled, a picture of calm. There was really no point in chasing Batman Senora, the leader, because this Batman didn't have any supernatural powers and started banging fences immediately, bumping the third and crashing into the fourth, as if he'd been assigned to knock it down. Next, Tony McCoy on Colonel Braxton began forcing the pace, but Culloty still didn't twitch or make a move. As I suspected, Beef Or Salmon wasn't right in himself. Timmy Murphy had to smack him on the shoulder at every fence, but he still jumped without any enthusiasm.

So Colonel Braxton pressed on, with McCoy digging in, but Best Mate had no need to accelerate. He tracked the Colonel from a leisurely second or third and approached each fence as he might a *divertissement,* not an obstacle, flying over it flawlessly, in a rhythm all his own. When Culloty let him go at the second last, he vanished in an instant, as though he'd been waiting for that very moment, as a child waits for Christmas in a state of suspended animation, and now he was released from it and ran free. His official margin of victory over Le Coudray was nine lengths, but it could just as easily have been forty.

'As good a feeling as I've ever had on a racehorse,' Culloty said afterwards. Though Knight was there to unsaddle Best Mate, her courage had deserted her again, and she had listened to the calling of the race in a car park. The applause that greeted Best Mate on his return from the track was extraordinary. 'I've never heard the Irish cheer an English horse like that,' said Willie Mullins, but Best Mate was only technically from England – marooned there, as it were – and had been born and bred on the Auld Sod.

Lost in the uproar were the fine efforts of Pizarro and Sacundai, equally redeemed. In the Grade One Neville & Sons Chase, Pizarro hung on to defeat Knight's Rosslea, a boost for his trainer after the horse was pulled up in the Drinmore, his last race. Under top weight, Sacundai beat a strong field in the Christmas Hurdle and was reinstalled as a Cheltenham worthy. For O'Grady, it was a pensive afternoon. Had Pizarro's jumping errors killed his chances in the Drinmore, or had O'Grady himself done something wrong? 'I honestly don't know,' the trainer said, after thirty-two years on the job. 'I'm a slow learner.'

On Monday I was at Leopardstown again, for the Bewley's Hotels December Festival Hurdle, a Grade One over two miles. An unusually spirited race, it featured such first-rate Irish hurdlers as Back In Front, Solerina, and Hardy Eustace, as well as O'Neill's Rhinestone Cowboy, a favourite for the Smurfit Champion Hurdle at the Festival, but none of them figured at the finish. Instead, the race was between two long shots, Flame Creek (14-1) from Noel Chance's yard in England and Spirit Leader (11-1), until an even longer shot – Golden Cross at 66-1 – zipped past them like a greyhound to capture the prize on his very first run of the year.

Nothing in racing is quite what it seems, of course. The sport deals in illusions and deceptions. In Richard Holmes' book *Sidetracks*, I'd recently come across an account of Theophile Gautier's visit to Royal Ascot in 1842, a high point on one of his periodic trips to London. Gautier was enthralled by what he saw, the 'vegetable velvet' of the lawns and the emerald turf, where the 'cherry-red horses' ran, while the jockeys caps were 'like poppies, cornflowers, and anemones carried away on the wind'. Our Frenchman waxed poetical about the flock of white pigeons released into the sky after each race, too, only to discover later that the birds were hirelings of the bookies, charged with delivering the odds and the results to their employers.

January: Deep Freeze

For Irish trainers, the New Year began with some distressing news. An equine virus was sweeping through their yards. It was a devastating one and sometimes undetectable. Horses scoped clean and then ran badly, as Beef Or Salmon had done in the Ericsson, gurgling because of the mucous in his throat. 'He'll be grand in a few days,' an optimistic Michael Hourigan told me, which was a better report than the beleaguered Paul Nicholls delivered about Strong Flow, who had cracked a knee bone in his near-foreleg in the Feltham. Whether the fracture was due to his sloppy jumping or to another factor remained uncertain, but Strong Flow's season was over, along with any chance he might duplicate Mill House's feat in the Gold Cup.

Noel Meade's yard was the hardest hit. On the Monday before Christmas, he had eight horses with a fever and runny nose, on Tuesday sixteen, and on Wednesday forty-five. Meade went ten straight days without a runner, and that dealt a whopping blow to his operating costs. Jessie Harrington was also affected. The bug had knocked out Imazulutoo, her Triumph Hurdle hope, but she still had Moscow Flyer to cheer her up. Moscow had done all she'd asked of him and more, so she was awarding him a break to conserve his energy for the Queen Mother Chase. There would be no more prep races along the way. The future was carved in stone. Jessie might have her superstitions, but she wasn't afraid of what I now thought of as The Pattern, a malign and possibly alien condition from the genre of science fiction.

In the *Post,* I saw that Andrew Leigh, Eamonn's son, was still pursuing his career as a jockey. He had a decent ride coming up at Thurles, and I was tempted to go, even though it would make me a pervert rather than a philosopher in the eyes of Voltaire, but a horse fancier always has a ready excuse. After the holiday banquet, the National Hunt had turned into a meagre meal in early January, mostly burgers with little prime rib. Trainers knew more about their stock by now and weren't so involved in trial-and-error on the racecourse. They were exercising caution with their big horses as well, saving them for the major races on the weekends, so if you craved some excitement during the week you had to lower your sights. You had to consider Thurles.

Once bitten, twice shy. That was another maxim I recalled on the train ride to Tipperary, looking out at frosty fields, Ireland's deep freeze. The same old bookies sat opposite me, as weather beaten as their satchels. True winter had arrived, with bone-chilling winds, pelting hail, and dustings of snow high up on the hills. All the talk in the papers about a false spring, about wildflowers blooming months in advance and bird migrations affected by global warming, went into the bin. Well, I reassured myself, at least it isn't raining. I'll be cold but not wet. I experienced a twinge of sympathy for the jockeys when I remembered a remark of Paul Carberry's about Thurles. 'No matter how cold it is outside,' he said to me, 'it's colder in the weighing room.'

Thurles on a cold, dry day was pleasant, really. Even pretty, a little. Once more the elderly crowd made me feel youthful, and with a bounce in my step and a hot whisky in my belly, I cashed a couple of bets before Andrew Leigh's race, a three-mile hurdle, rolled around. Leigh was on Sixtino, the people's choice, who had 'won on the ice at St Moritz', according to *Spotlight's* commentary. Had the horse worn skates? Clearly, my knowledge of the jumps was still incomplete. But Sixtino also had two wins in Ireland, not on the ice, so I had to take him into account, given the quality of the opposition.

Sixtino faced a bevy of non-winners. Only the whim of an owner or trainer kept these nags in competition. Like supposedly gifted children who fail every exam, they were being indulged. Furthermore, they were untried at this distance and could not be expected, by any stretch of the imagination, to find their form. Any horse who could stay on his feet and last the three miles had an honest chance, and since Craigmor Hero had performed that marvel, although not much else, I cast my lot with him. The race went exactly as I'd figured. Most horses quit at the two-mile mark, leaving Sixtino and Craigmor Hero to slug it out, and their battle, hardly epic, devolved into a photo finish with Craigmor Hero ahead, a belated Christmas gift I collected at 10-1.

I felt sorry for Andrew, but good about myself. The trip back to the city was sweet. Having neglected to bring along Paddy Kavanagh for company, I picked up the *Post* again, but I'd read all the articles about horse racing and flipped back to the greyhound pages I normally skipped. The classified ads were a wonder. There were Super Pups for sale and, less ambitiously, Quality Pups, and in the bargain basement greyhounds for under £500. I wondered what it would be like to own a bargain dog, and if the fall from grace would be truly spectacular, although I guessed it wouldn't be since Noel Meade, a classy trainer and member of the Dog Gone Syndicate, held an eleventh-share of a hound called Springwell Arctic.

On my walk home from the station, I fell into full alliterative mode and soon was boring Imelda with Triumphant Tales of Thurles. After dinner, I went online to check the current Gold Cup ante-post odds with Paddy Power. Best Mate had hardened to 5-6 after his Leopardstown show, but Beef Or Salmon had slipped to 12-1. Kingscliff was holding steady at 6-1, while Keen Leader, a winner at Haydock on his last outing, was down to 10-1. On the novelty front, Britney Spears and her quickie Vegas marriage were all the rage. What would that crazy girl do next? Enter rehab (3-1), announce she was pregnant (7-1), become a wedding planner (100-1), or run for president (500-1)?

O ver the next week, the virus continued to spread, leading to fears of an epidemic, something Dr Ned Gowing, who owns and operates Anglesey Lodge Equine Hospital on the Curragh, understood well. He was so busy with sick and injured horses I had difficulty arranging a meeting with him, and when I did manage it, I made sure I got to Kildare early and had some tea at the Stand House Hotel, where I found a splendid photo of Arkle (yet again) and Tom Dreaper, who was chomping contentedly on a pipe stem and petting Arkle's forehead. You could see the affection between the two, as if they were sharing a secret.

The lodge, I discovered, is a white, one-storey building opposite the track. It resembles a house rather than a hospital. A horse box was parked by a vacant paddock, and nearby a gloomy man in the soiled clothes of an overburdened groom paced around, on edge about his appointment. My wait for Dr Gowing – or Dr G as one of his staff called him – wasn't long. A big, easy-going, snowy-haired man, he has the sort of gentle, benevolent presence that often earns an endearing nickname from his colleagues. He led me to a spare room and seemed tired at first, as if talking with me didn't rate high on his list of desires, for which I couldn't blame him, but he slowly warmed to the subject of veterinary medicine, his life's work.

Dr Gowing had graduated as a vet in 1965 and later chose to specialize in horses. He was familiar with the virus plaguing the yards. He hadn't heard of anyone identifying it specifically, but he assumed it was a respiratory strain of influenza and quite contagious. The virus could be detected before a race through a simple blood sample seventy-five percent of the time, he advised me, but it stayed hidden in all other cases and only manifested itself during a race when it was triggered by stress and caused a horse to falter, as Beef Or Salmon had done. Worse still, it could take the horse a month to six weeks to recover, depending on the severity of the symptoms – quicker with a mild cough than with a full systemic infection. (Imazulutoo would still be under the weather in March, knocked out of Cheltenham.) Rest and antibiotics were the only cure.

'I shudder to think of the huge economic losses to owners and trainers,' Gowing said. He might have added jockeys and bookies.

Viruses come and go, of course. Ordinarily, Gowing deals with a variety of familiar injuries, the most common for jumpers being a bowed tendon. He believes the length of the races and the pressure that puts on tendons are responsible for the damage. A bleeding nose is the second-most common ailment he treats. But what about the fallers? Didn't he have to repair a panoply of broken bones? Those crashes looked so vicious I imagined he must have a hospital wing filled with horses whose legs were bandaged or in plaster casts, but he doesn't. 'The soft ground protects them,' he said. 'It cushions the fall.'

We talked for a while about how medical technology had altered his practice. In the past, trainers would come to Gowing worried that a horse might have a heart murmur, and he would do an exhaustive exam to see if it were true, while today there are simple diagnostic tools to detect such problems. One of the simplest ways to assess a horse's health is by its weight, he said. A horse can lose up to twenty pounds during a race, but should put it right back through rehydration in three or four days. If the horse doesn't, something is wrong, probably something latent.

'Where's the fun in this for you?' I asked, an angle I'm always exploring, and he blinked as though startled by the question, one he might never have asked himself, and laughed. 'Every day has a little surprise,' he said. 'You're never bored.'

'Not even with horses? You still like them?'

'Why not?' His fondness for horses aside, Ned confessed he'd never been much of a rider himself, although he admired Ireland's great jockeys. I mentioned how Paul Carberry lived for the hunt and painted him a picture of Carberry ripping across the fields of Meath on his hunter, leaping over stone walls and thorny hedges, as wild and wilful as Black Jack Dennis. 'That would be a very dance,' he said appreciatively, at which point he rose to show me around the hospital, moving through it with a big man's shambling gait. Like Michael Hourigan, he'd started from scratch in a cottage that still stood by the road, and he too was proud of his achievements.

Gowing has a pristine room for his lab work now, and two surgeries, one for the messy stuff such as colic and abscesses and the other for orthopaedic jobs. The horses arrive at a receiving barn and are sedated and anaesthetized with gas before being transferred to an operating table. Further on were two isolation boxes for horses with contagious diseases. He has fifteen boxes in all, and the overburdened groom stood by one, waiting for his horse to undergo an X-ray. It was difficult to say who looked more apprehensive, the groom or the horse. In another box, Emma, a young vet, had a gloved hand inserted into the anus of a mare. It must be a bowel complaint, I guessed, but no, she'd suffered a rectal tear when a stallion had mounted her. 'She's in bad shape,' Gowing sighed. 'It happens.'

Our next stop was a room where he keeps his modern equipment – a video endoscope for searching out infections, a machine to administer electrotherapy to knotted muscles, and a digital X-ray that makes it possible to see precisely what's going on inside a horse. He'd just used it on a poor, shivery little creature who stood quietly in a nearby box. From a distance, I thought the animal was a malformed donkey, even a weird half-breed, but it was a thoroughbred foal and gave off such an air of loneliness and misery I felt a tug at my heart. Gowing touched a shaved area on the foal's ribcage, where he'd performed some sector scanning, but the results weren't encouraging.

'He's pretty sick,' the vet said. 'He was sick before he was sold. His owner got a raw deal. We'll try to save him, but it may be too late.'

I rubbed the foal's nose and wished him luck. In the end, a vet's job didn't seem very different from a regular doctor's. At Anglesey Lodge, I sensed the same blend of hope, despair, relief, and even prayer you feel in any hospital. The melancholy groom could be any anxious relative, eager to hear some good news about the patient. That anybody at all cared about the wretched foal was something of a miracle, and his owner must have known it since the foal wasn't going to win any races if he did survive. The caring was a simple act of obligation, another example of the ancient, honourable covenant between horses and those who own and ride them.

*　　*　　*

By the second week in January, we were nearly over-whelmed with important races. On Saturday, there were meetings in England at Ascot, Haydock, and Warwick, so I was camped at O'Herlihy's for the dura-tion. The pub has many virtues, not least its policy of ele-vating racing to a status above all other sports. In some pubs you have to beg the barman to show the jumps if a decent, or even halfway decent, football match is on, but at our local it isn't an issue, mainly because T.P. Reilly is in charge of the remote control and flicks between Channel Four and the BBC with the exquisite timing he has honed to a fine edge on his couch at home.

Reilly takes his position very seriously. When he arrived, he set a batch of papers on the bar and shuffled through them. The most important was a handwritten list of all the televised races. He used it as a memory aid. He also had tip sheets from various tabloids and a stack of betting slips from Boylesports to be filled out after a look at the horses. On his feet were a new pair of sneakers to facilitate his sprint to the shop. He tried to complete the round-trip before the start of a race, and if he failed and got back even a few seconds too late, he groaned and let his docket flutter to the floor. 'Why bother?' he'd ask. 'I can't win now.' Irrational, yes, but he was always right.

That Saturday, we were keen on the Peter Marsh Chase at Haydock, a three-mile race regarded as a superior Gold Cup trial. Four horses had come out of the Peter Marsh to win the Gold Cup in recent years, so the presence of Kingscliff, still very much in the Festival picture, made the event even more auspicious. He was stepping up in class, but the experts predicted he would handle it. Woe betide those who believed them, though, and backed the horse at 4-7, because he didn't run or jump with his normal skill, and Arctic Jack defeated him soundly. The result puzzled Robert Alner, who thought Kingscliff must have a muscle problem.

'They'll never get that harse right in time,' Reilly said in disgust, his ante-post wager on Kingscliff in jeopardy. 'Might as well give Henrietta the trophy now and save us all the bother.'

He switched the TV channel to Ascot, where the featured race was the Victor Chandler Chase, a two-mile prep for the Queen Mother. Donal Hassett's Native Scout, who had run well behind Moscow Flyer at Leopardstown at Christmas, received some enthusiastic support because he was twenty pounds lighter than the top weight, but that was Azertyuiop, Paul Nicholls' pride and joy, who looked intimidating. Unbeaten as a novice chaser, Azertyuoip hadn't yet won a handicap, so Nicholls and Ruby Walsh were hoping for a solid display after their horse's failure in the Tingle Creek.

Native Scout gave a brave effort, staying close until the fast pace found him out, and from then on the race was between Isio from Nicky Henderson's yard and Azertyuoip, whose leap at the second-last put him in front. Yet Isio showed some real tenacity and fortitude, fought back, and held on to beat his rival by a neck. Still, Azertyuiop's performance was exceptional when you considered that Isio had a nineteen-pound advantage. Ruby Walsh had insisted his horse wasn't right at Sandown when losing to Moscow Flyer, and the Victor Chandler seemed to confirm it and created a certain amount of fear and trembling in those of us who were already concerned about Moscow's ability to transcend the evil grip of The Pattern.

'Like Desert Orchid beating Panto Prince,' someone said on the TV, and Reilly nodded, as if they'd been speaking directly to him, and showed off by replying, 'A twenty-pound pull, and Dessie won by a head.'

In the late afternoon, we had the Tote Classic Chase at Warwick, a marathon for stayers at three miles and five furlongs, with twenty-two fences to be jumped. In general, I am more paranoid than Reilly, ever alert to the possibility that things are not what they appear to be, but he surpassed me for once. He swore that the 'villainous' Martin Pipe was about to try something tricky, and after an analysis of Pipe's three entries, he was convinced that Jurancon II, the least fancied of them, was the key to the plot. Tony McCoy, the stable jockey, had decided to ride Akarus, the favourite, but that was part of the cover-up, according to Reilly. Didn't I see that McCoy was in on the scam? Take Control, Pipe's third horse, was mere window dressing and hadn't won a race in ages.

'Twenty each way on Jurancon II at 50-1,' Reilly said confidently, lacing up a sneaker for his sprint. True, he knew his stuff, but I refused to follow him down that particular path and asked him to put a tenner for me on Bindaree, a Grand National winner sure to go the distance. 'You'll be sorry!' he shouted, ducking out the door.

The Tote Classic was an ugly, punishing, even gruesome spectacle. Fallers were everywhere, and some were good horses, too – Gunner Welburn, Carbury Cross, and

Behrajan, for example, who broke his neck two out. Take Control was another victim, falling at the sixth fence and having to be put down. We didn't hear about the deaths until after the race, when they cast a pall over Reilly's dazzling gamble. Though I doubted that Pipe had planned it, Jurancon II was there at the end to battle it out with Southern Star, another prize pupil from Henrietta Knight's academy, who landed the heavier punches and won. Reilly's pay-off for the place was still substantial, but we didn't have it in us to celebrate after seeing so many horses come to grief.

Sunday dawned bright and blue in Dublin, perfect for an outing. Imelda and I planned a drive to the country for the Shillelagh & District Hunt's point-to-point races at Tinahely, a first for both of us. Such races are the cradle of the sport, and many great horses have come out of them. Only last year, former pointers like Florida Pearl (King George VI), Binadaree (Grand National), The Bunny Boiler (Irish National), and Supreme Glory (Welsh National) had won major prizes, so we hoped to see a diamond-in-the-rough that afternoon.

Imelda packed a sketchpad, a camera and her traditional picnic lunch, and we left before noon and took the motorway past Dún Laoghaire and Bray. We were your typical carefree lovers on holiday until we crossed into County Wicklow and encountered a sudden, profound change in Ireland's famously changeable weather, with dark clouds massed on the horizon. An instant later, showery rain drummed against the windshield. 'It'll probably blow over,' I said, more a wish than a belief.

Turning inland, we went through Aughrim, where the River Ow flowed under a bridge. Farms were a constant of the landscape now, set amid familiar rolling hills. Irish Draught horses, strong, short-legged, and lighter than the Draught breeds preferred in other parts of Europe, once pulled the ploughs here. Multi-purpose animals, they were used for hunting as well as farm work and could keep going all day long, jumping any obstacle. When crossed with thoroughbreds, they produced the Irish Sport horse. The cross has been so successful that pure-bred Draught horses are vanishing from Ireland, despite the efforts of the Irish Draught Horse Society.

In the village of Tinahely, there was a sign for the races, but it offered no directions, so we dashed through the downpour to Seavers Bar for help, almost colliding at the front door with a gent in tweed, who had his wife on his arm. I assumed they were a local couple out for a drink after church, before their Sunday lunch, but they were potential racegoers, too, and just as lost as we were. 'You're here for the pint-to-pint races?' asked the barman, as if no other reason could account for strangers being in Seavers. As it happened, we were only a mile or so away from Fairwood, the site of the course, but I still had to fight an impulse to stay warm and dry in the pub and go from one pint to the next, a suggestion the barman, with his rural accent, had planted in my head.

Imelda wouldn't buy into that idea. She intended to see those horses and have that picnic, the weather be damned, so we ran back to the car and drove down a side road until we came to another sign that could have been written in blood. 'Eight euros,' it said in bright red ink, a warning to sundry farm lads with empty pockets that they couldn't sneak in without paying. Two members of the hunt club were selling tickets, and they wore so much waterproof gear they looked ready for a monsoon. Only their faces and hands were visible as they waved us through a gate and into a sodden field, where the wheels of our car sank inches into the slop.

A tiny hole appeared in the sky, revealing a patch of blue. That lifted my spirits. Maybe we'd have our sunny picnic, after all. A good crowd had already assembled despite the rain, mostly in family groups. We bought a race card from a giggling red-haired girl, whose brother was making mud pies at her feet. Inside the card were ads from almost every business nearby, including The Crocodile Lounge and Black Tom's Tavern. We fell into step with the crowd and walked up a muddy path, propelled forward by a wintry wind. Mud was everywhere, really, and our marching anthem became the slurp-slurp sound of boots and shoes being sucked into it. The kids enjoyed it, though, splashing in puddles and stomping through bogs in their wellies.

What a scene at the crest of the hill! The panorama was worthy of Breughel, as busy and animated as one of his canvases. Teenage boys wrestled with each other to impress the teenage girls, young mothers held bottles to the mouths of their babies, well-dressed squires leaned on their walking sticks and filled their pipes with tobacco, and rosy cheeked farmers with bits of straw in their hair discussed the price of crops. Everybody seemed to know everybody else, or almost. A large marquee for drinks was doing a brisk trade, as were a pair of chippers-on-wheels that smelled of greasy cooking oil. The bookies were gathered in their own soggy enclave, and they didn't look happy about it. This was just a notch above a dog track – or maybe not. Bundled in layers of garments, they had to make a book with only an inkling of what a horse might do, based primarily on word-of-mouth.

Around a fenced parade ring, spectators had gathered for the second race, among them a few bloodstock agents and trainers' scouts. Though the fans were ready for the horses, the horses weren't quite ready for the fans. They turned up at the parade ring one-by-one, as if the starting time of the race had yet to be established, led right through the crowd by their grooms and narrowly avoiding infants in strollers and toddlers on the loose. Hunt clubs from around Ireland, from Killinick and Laois, Kilmoganny and Bree, had brought them to Fairwood, and they each had a following of friends and neighbours, who had fed them carrots at home and reached out to touch them tenderly. Some of the horses wore blankets against the cold with handwritten numbers pinned to them, frequently on scraps of paper too tiny to read.

The Shillelagh & District Hunt began preparing for their annual meeting every autumn, Mary Dagg, the Honorary Secretary, had told me when I called in advance to ask about the races. When the leaves start to fall, the club members cut the birch themselves and build the fences at night after work, a labour of love. Most clubs depend on volunteers, Mary said. The point-to-points may hold a significant place in Irish culture, but they struggle to survive because the costs keep escalating. Mary's club pays 7,000 euros a year for the insurance alone, for instance. Fortunately, HRI has pumped in some funds to keep the clubs afloat and provide an opportunity for 'not so good' horses, Ireland's overflow, to compete and maybe win a little money.

Four of the six races today were for maidens. Owners shelled out an entry fee of thirty euros against a winner's purse of 700, escalating to 950 euros for the feature race. Almost all the races were oversubscribed and would have to be run in divisions over a standard distance of about three miles, the minimum in point-to-points. The horses were certified hunters, meaning they'd hunted with a recognized pack of hounds to prove their jumping ability. In the two open events, their average age was twelve, and most had failed at major tracks under rules. The jockeys, all amateurs, held the status of qualified riders. Some aspired to be pros, but most were in it for the *craic*, the women as well as the men.

We watched the horses in the second race, first division, continue to assemble at the parade ring, still arriving one-by-one. They were maiden geldings of five and six, and this would be the first run for many of them. If they had raced before, they'd usually fallen, been pulled up, unseated their rider, or been brought down. Lost In The Snow's record was typical – BFPPU-P. It would take a courageous, or perhaps self-destructive, jockey to risk a ride on Lost In The Snow, but the same could be said for much of the field. The jockeys were already a mess, covered in the same mud that had threatened to swallow us whole. You might expect young riders to find this sort of thing fun, but there were leathery guys in their forties saddling up for another dose of misery.

Fairwood is one of the most testing point-to-point courses around. It has five fences, and the riders follow a hilly route marked in places by hay bales. There isn't a grandstand, so we took up a spot just a few feet from a fence, near enough that we could hear the horses' bellies brush against it when they didn't get high enough. Imelda was captivated by the loud thump of their hooves. It was sublime to be so close to such tremendous energy, she said – energy barely held in check – and she offered a quote from Edmund Burke, who wrote that our astonishment at such moments, coupled with a degree of terror, caused the soul's 'motions' to be suspended, and our hold on such comforting concepts as clarity and order to slip.

The jockeys rounded a turn, bowled downhill and disappeared from sight, then came thundering back toward us. Just three of the ten horses completed the race, and Louisburgh, the winner, who was trained by Ted Walsh, had many lengths in hand – not that you'd know Walsh was involved by reading the race card, since it didn't list the names of trainers or jockeys. The lack of finishers was routine for a point-to-point. In Louisburgh's last race, where he fell, only five of seventeen horses had completed the entire trip.

If the race could not be described as exciting, the loose horses certainly were. Two riderless geldings were on the rampage, galloping hell bent toward the vans selling chips. I saw an old woman practically do a somersault to avoid being trampled. Grooms and jockeys chased the horses, as did some robust spectators, while less courageous types hid behind a tree, as we did. The geldings were corralled after a few minutes, though not before they'd caused some serious chaos that seemed to delight rather than upset the fans. 'There is a sympathy between the rush of the racing hunter and their own impetuous natures,' as it said in *The Dublin Saturday Magazine* long ago.

Everyone regrouped at the parade ring for the race's second division, won by The Royal Dub, a Carberry family production, with Tommy the trainer and Nina, Paul's sister, the jockey. Those facts weren't on the card, either. I gleaned them on the fly, by listening to the gossip. The chief attraction of a point-to-point, I was beginning to understand, was its glorious informality. If the event became too orderly or organized, the sport might lose its grassroots' appeal. The race card was only a document, just a rough guide, and if you relied on it you revealed yourself to be an outsider with no links, say, to farmer Mathews, a dairyman from Carnew, whose speedy mare had a big chance in the fifth race.

Yet long before the fifth race, it began to snow. That might have been acceptable and even romantic, but when the snow turned to sleet driven at us like a scatter of nails by a vindictive wind, we looked for some shelter in the drinks marquee. It was so packed that the smallest, most undernourished jockey on the premises couldn't have squeezed inside. For some reason, this got Imelda thinking about the mass evictions of Irish farmers early in the century, their doors barred or padlocked and the roofs torn off their cottages for good measure, with whole families tossed out into just such a hostile environment, but I wasn't the best audience for her history lesson since I was running for the car, where we cranked up the heater and ate our little picnic, scarcely able to break off hunks of bread for the cheese because our fingers were so icy and numb.

On that same Sunday, while we were at Fairwood, I missed two good races at Leopardstown, the Pierse Hurdle and Pierse Handicap Chase. Charles Byrnes, a trainer from Limerick, scooped up both prizes for a total haul of about one hundred and forty thousand euros. Confidence oozed from Byrnes, who isn't a big name by any means. 'I would have been fierce disappointed if either of them got beat,' he said of Dromlease Express and Cloudy Bays, both headed for Cheltenham now, with Cloudy Bays pointed toward the William Hill Chase and Dromlease Express toward The Coral Cup.

Beef Or Salmon was back in training again and recovered from his virus, although Michael Hourigan, being cagey, couldn't or wouldn't say when or where his horse would run next. In England, an equine physio was treating Kingscliff for muscle problems in his shoulders and withers, but Robert Alner still had the Gold Cup in mind, while in France Guillame Macaire was readying Jair du Cochet for the Pillar Property Chase at Kempton. Asked to account for the horse's abysmal performance in the King George, Jacques Ricou replied, 'I don't understand why, and he isn't able to tell us.'

In other news, the rabbits were wreaking havoc at Down Royal. They'd burrowed under the chase course and made it unsafe for racing. Paddy Power joked that the track should change its name to 'Watership Down Royal'. Elsewhere, the Irish Turf Club had released the results of its random drug-testing programme. The sixty-five samples taken from jockeys had all come back negative, even for alcohol, a balm to punters and bookies alike. Finally, I read a story in the *Post* about Florida Pearl, maybe the most popular chaser in Ireland, whose trainer Willie Mullins had deemed him fit and healthy, ready to resume his illustrious career after a long absence.

If the National Hunt in Ireland has a true dynasty, it would have to be the Mullins' clan, a family even more entrenched than the Carberrys. Paddy Mullins, the revered patriarch, still trains horses at the age of eighty-five ('I'd like to be Paddy Mullins!' Michael Hourigan once exclaimed, envying Paddy's longevity), and his four sons are also in the game, Willie and Tony as trainers, and George running a horse transport business, while also sharing a farm with Willie and selling shredded newspapers for bedding as a sideline. (The paper generates less dust than straw, so it's easier on a horse's breathing.) Tom, the youngest son, helps out his father and will take over his yard when the time comes, all this despite Paddy's claim that he discouraged his boys from following in his footsteps.

'I could not get them to do anything else,' he complained to his biographer. 'I wanted them to try other things because there was not room in it for all of them. When some of the boys were in school at Roscrea, I preached to them every time I got a chance. "Go and do something else." I might as well have been talking to the table.'

As the most established trainer, Willie tends to attract the best stock, Florida Pearl being his treasure. He saw the horse at Tom Costello's yard and bought him as a four-year-old, later selling him to Violet and Archie O'Leary. For Willie, it was love at first sight. 'The size of him, the scope of him, it's tremendous,' he enthused to me. 'He's a beautiful athlete!' The bay gelding, by Florida Sun out of Ice Pearl, was quick to prove his worth, winning both the Champion Bumper and the Royal & SunAlliance Chase at Cheltenham, and the Irish Hennessy three times, with only the Festival's Gold Cup eluding him, although he has been placed in the race.

Yet the current season had been trouble for Florida Pearl so far. Originally slated for the King George, a race he won against Best Mate in 2001, he suffered a sprain and had to be scratched. Nearly twelve, he was slow to recuperate and failed to show his usual spark around the yard – a worry to his trainer, who had more than his share of them, the most serious being a legal battle with the British Jockey Club over Be My Royal, also owned by the O'Learys, who won the English Hennessy in November 2002. The purse had been withheld, though, because Be My Royal (along with several other horses) tested positive for morphine, later traced to a particular batch of feed. Mullins hoped to reverse the decision at an upcoming hearing before the Jockey Club's disciplinary panel.

Frustrated by Florida Pearl's lack of progress, Willie had recently tried a new tack and turned over his injured horse to Grainne Ni Chaba, an animal physiotherapist, who has a practice on the Curragh and has spent much of her life around horses. In her early twenties, she broke yearlings in Florida and held stable jobs with a few American trainers. At home in Ireland, she has run a livery business, ridden as a lady amateur jockey for Dermot Weld ('I didn't win any races') and on her own mares in bumpers, and cared for abused animals for the RSPCA. Currently, she treats horses for a number of clients, among them Lady O'Reilly, whose savage mare Rebelline left an indelible mark on her.

'I still have a scar on my bum,' Grainne told me, when we talked.

'How'd she do that?' I pictured an explosive fall and an extremely hard landing.

'She bit me!'

From the start, Grainne was fond of Florida Pearl. 'He was an ideal patient,' she said. 'He wanted to get better.' As an expert rider, she did lots of slow, steady work with him, both dressage and *caveletti*, or pole work. By being on his back, she could better isolate and understand his problems and then fix them. He had a sore ligament in a near-side knee, for example, and Grainne didn't approve of the way he looked from behind because he wasn't properly balanced. He ran with his neck too high instead of down low, and that created a little hollow in his back and put extra pressure on the muscles. Though Florida Pearl had only fallen once in a race, Grainne believed that fall had thrown him out-of-kilter.

Her job was to 'rewire' the horse completely. 'It was, like, OK Mister, time to sort yourself out,' she said. In essence, she had to teach him how to run correctly again – to let down, relax and regain his confidence. She addressed his imbalance by using balancing reins to strengthen his back and hocks. For his minor pains, she administered electrotherapy. Florida Pearl received some laser treatment on his sore knee and did plenty of stretching, and Grainne put him on Cortaflex to build up his cartilage. Soon he was following a daily routine that included an hour or so of dressage, a forty-minute massage, and thirty minutes of physio.

The routine was a great success. Florida Pearl stayed with Grainne for over two months, and when he returned to Mullins' yard, he was in super shape, transformed into a racehorse again. Grainne confessed that she still missed him a bit. 'He had a stall next to a horse called Chubaka, and they became wonderful pals. Chewie's the kind of horse who makes other horses happy. He's huge, too, at seventeen hands three, even bigger than Florida Pearl. They were mad about each other. They'd jump up and start playing the minute they met,' she said. 'You should have seen Florida Pearl. He had this great big bum on him. I should have taken some before-and-after photos, but I always forget.'

As it happened, I did see the rejuvenated Florida Pearl shortly after our conversation, when Willie Mullins sent him to Fairyhouse for the Normans Grove Chase, a Grade Three over two miles and a furlong. The race was a probe of sorts. If the Pearl did well after his 238-day lay-off, he might be granted a chance at his fourth Irish Hennessy in February. He was the class act in the field, but the punters shied away from him because he'd been

away so long, letting him drift out to 8-1. Richard
Johnson had flown over from England to ride him,
though, and since Johnson rarely competes in Ireland, I
interpreted his presence as a sign that Mullins wasn't
fooling around.

The other horses in the race – Rathgar Beau, Knife
Edge, Rince Ri, Beachcomber Boy, and Arctic Copper –
had been knocking their heads together for months
without any of them winning a race, so it seemed obvious
to me that a fresh, classy horse such as Florida Pearl could
spring a surprise. I felt smug about working this out,
another indication that my education was advancing
nicely, but as I waded into the ring to bet, the earth must
have wobbled because I heard myself yell, 'Twenty to win
on Arctic Copper.' Then I watched glumly from the
grandstand as Florida Pearl took an early lead and won
the prize without extending himself.

Sadly, my confusion followed me from Fairyhouse to
Gowran Park, when I travelled to Kilkenny for the
Thyestes Chase in mid-January. The Thyestes, a prestigious Cheltenham prep race for stayers first run in 1954,
drew a record crowd of almost nine thousand, and the
Irish gift for sociability was at its most expansive. Even I,
the wandering American, met someone I knew, Tamso
Doyle from HRI, and as we took a little pre-race prome-
nade, she introduced me to friends along the way.

The first person we ran into was Mary O'Grady,
Edward's mother. Known affectionately as Grannie

O'Grady, she was bright and chipper and had her fingers crossed for her son's Takagi in the Thyestes. Next we ran into Brian Gleeson, last seen as our moderator at the Dunraven Arms. He leaned toward us in a posture of utmost confidence, as the Irish do when they deliver a tip, and let it drop that Takagi had been used very lightly by his jockey in his last race at Leopardstown to save some zip for Gowran Park. 'The horse was laid out perfectly for the race,' were Gleeson's very words.

He spoke with such authority I began to waver about Rule Supreme, the horse I'd selected on the train, but Phil Rothwell, a young trainer who'd studied under both Jessie Harrington and Aidan O'Brien, put me right again. The son of a dairy farmer, Rothwell has a small yard near Tinahely, and when we met at the parade ring, I asked him whom he liked, and he said, 'Rule Supreme.'

'That was my first choice,' I replied, reeling a bit. 'But everybody's talking about Takagi.'

'Always stick with your first choice,' Rothwell warned me, with an oracular firmness that made me recall Allen Ginsberg's motto regarding writing, creativity, sex and, who knows, maybe even life. 'First thought, best thought,' Ginsberg had said, so I put twenty euros on Rule Supreme with Paddy Sharkey, violating a motto of my own, 'Never bet with a bookie whose name has a negative ring.'

There is always a relief in placing a bet. Like boarding an airplane or going broke, you're delivered into the hands of fate. Freed of my obligation, I walked to the stand Jessie prefers, but I couldn't find her in the swarm of people, so I edged into the first available space and landed by chance next to Edward O'Grady. He was just back from a Caribbean holiday and still bearing the traces of a tan, his healthy glow like a beacon in the midst of his pale-faced, sun-deprived countrymen. This was an unsettling moment for me – Grannie O'Grady, Brian Gleeson, and now the man himself. Could the gods have made it any more clear? Takagi was destined to win.

It was too late for me to make amends, though. I was stuck with Ginsberg and Rule Supreme. With every glance at O'Grady, I sank a little lower because he looked so serene and unflappable, a veteran of the sport with impeccable bloodlines. His father W. T. O'Grady was a champion trainer, and when he died suddenly, Edward, who was twenty-two at the time, gave up his veterinary studies to take over the yard. He had scored many triumphs since then and also weathered many setbacks, none more painful than the loss of Golden Cygnet, the best horse he ever trained, killed in the Scottish Champion Hurdle in 1978. In fact, he had been dealt another bad hand recently when Sacundai, revived at Leopardstown over Christmas, had developed a leg problem that would keep him out of the Festival, reducing O'Grady's Cheltenham probables to just two, Pizarro and Back In Front.

Takagi emerged as the second favourite to Willie Mullins' Hedgehunter, who was giving it another try after his near miss in the Welsh National. O'Grady watched the race through binoculars, and though what he saw must have upset him, he didn't reveal it. He kept his cool, even though Takagi was struggling – no, worse, the horse appeared to be mired in a pot of molasses for all the headway he was making. Barry Geraghty was flat to the boards on him, but it didn't matter. Takagi was in slow-mo. After a mile or so, O'Grady muttered through clenched teeth, 'Not today,' and added seconds later, 'Horse didn't run,' speaking not so much to me as to a spectral presence, his spirit guide. Takagi's lack of pace was apparently a mystery to him, but Rule Supreme was still galloping well, jumping with more abandon than finesse.

One horse who did run was Hedgehunter. Mullins had located the right niche for him at last, but a change of tactics also helped. As a substitute for Ruby Walsh, off toiling in England, David Casey took the ride and let Hedgehunter go to the front rather than hold him up as Ruby did. The horse seemed thrilled to be out there on his own, demonstrated a number of gears, and romped to an eight-length win, while Rule Supreme botched the last two fences and finished third, no thanks to Allen Ginsberg. That confirmed Hedgehunter for a possible run in the Grand National, Mullins said, indicating his horse might go directly to Aintree without another race because Hedgehunter is light-framed and doesn't carry much extra weight.

Gowran Park is the hometown track for the Mullins' family, close to all their yards, so they had a grand time that afternoon. Tony won the first race with Three Mirrors, while Boneyarrow won a novice chase for Willie. Noel Meade also enjoyed the outing, back on his feet again after the virus scare had run its course. Meade's Rosaker boosted his Cheltenham stock in the Galmoy Stayers Hurdle under Paul Carberry, who was nursing a bruised kidney from yet another fall, this one at Fairyhouse. That was the nature of the Festival beast, I could see – Sacundai was out, and Rosaker was in, at least for the moment. Meade seemed pleased, at any rate. 'Happy days are here again,' he said, firing up a victory cigar.

That afternoon at Gowran Park left me in a shaky state. Having committed the gambler's mortal sin of thinking too much, I needed a break and spent the next day strolling around Dublin in a Bloomish mood, turning a cold eye on every betting shop and letting my thoughts range far and wide. After I bought a couple of books at Hodges Figges, I stopped for a noon pint at Davy Byrnes, where poor snuffly Nosey Flynn, a dewdrop trickling from one nostril, tried to pry a tip on the Ascot Gold Cup – due to be run that day, 16 June 1904 – from the proprietor, who refused to co-operate.

'I wouldn't do anything in that line,' Byrnes scolded him, with a hint of disapproval, his pub being a moral one. 'It ruined many a man the same horses.'

A wise gent, you might say, but not a typical Dubliner as Joyce well knew. Nosey's attitude was (and is) more prevalent. 'True for you,' he told Byrnes. 'Unless you're in the know.'

In the know! That was every real Dubliner's dream. Tips were circulating through the city with extraordinary brio as the Festival drew near, and I had been blessed or cursed with one that morning when I stopped for my newspaper, stepping widely around the *Racing Post*. Our newsagent, Brian, is a devoted racing fan, privy to the clouds of opinion his customers trail through the shop from dawn till dusk. With a discerning ear, he tries to separate the conceivably momentous information from the blatantly outrageous fantasies, Hasanpour being an example of the former.

'I only got word of the horse the other day,' he confided, tapping my forearm, a warm, congenial man often seen poring over the *Post* behind the counter.

Twice a winner on the flat in England, Hasanpour was purchased from Sir Michael Stoute's yard by an Irish buyer presumed to be the spendthrift John P. McManus, or so Brian thought at first, although when Hasanpour ran at Cork on the Sunday just past, his owner was listed as a Mrs G. Smith. But Mrs Smith could be related to McManus, couldn't she? Ah, whatever. The thing was, rumour had it that Charlie Swan, the horse's new trainer, called Hasanpour the best horse he'd ever sat on, and Swan had ridden Istabraq! And McManus owned Istabraq! That was all Brian needed to hear. He backed the horse at even money in the Millstreet Hurdle at Cork, and when Hasanpour shot out to a twenty-length lead, he began reciting a familiar punter's prayer, 'Jaysus, please don't fall!' He didn't have to worry, though, because Hasanpour delivered the goods.

Tap, tap. 'The horse was 66-1 ante-post for the Triumph Hurdle,' Brian said, his voice dropping almost an octave. 'You wouldn't get him at that price anymore, but still . . .' So I added Hasanpour to my Cheltenham note-book, while crossing out Nil Desperandum, who had knocked a bit of bone off a front-leg pastern and would miss the Royal & SunAlliance Chase. Hasanpour in, Nil Desperandum out.

And who would be the next Pope? There was an article in the paper addressing that very question. The favourite was Diogini Tettamanzi of Italy at 2-1, according to Paddy Power Bookmakers whose spokesman, the Paddy Power, expressed some wholly contrived shock that anyone in a Catholic country would be offended by a firm accepting bets on religious matters. Yet everyone from ordinary churchgoers to devout followers of Padre Pio *had* taken offence, especially since the current Pope was still 'alive and strong', as the Right Reverend Thomas McMahon noted. In his firm's defence, Paddy replied, 'It is something people talk about in pubs, and because people have opinions, I think it is something we should be betting on.'

Fair play to you, Paddy, I thought, although I'd never been involved in any gossip about the papal succession at O'Herlihy's. How would the man on the next stool react if I asked him if he liked Tettamanzi? I imagined the blank stare I'd receive, accompanied by the unstated assumption that I must be completely bonkers.

As the lunch crowd filtered into Davy Byrnes, I packed up my little library, bought a fancy sandwich at Avoca, and moved on to McDaid's, where they don't serve food and a peaceful midday calm prevails. Down the bar, the ghost of Patrick Kavanagh consulted the racing pages, irritable and hung over until the magical spirits lifted his own. Here, too, Paul Carberry was known to pop in of an evening. 'You've been seen at McDaid's,' I teased him once, and Paul grinned and said, 'I've been seen at a lot of places in Dublin.'

McDaid's is a proper bookish spot, quiet and conducive to study, so I cracked open my new copy of Liam

O'Flaherty's *A Tourist's Guide to Ireland*, published in 1929. Though I wasn't a tourist anymore, I was curious about O'Flaherty's take on tourism in general. He wasn't all that serious about it, as it happened. Instead, he used the premise to launch a witty, satirical attack on the four pillars of Irish society – the parish priest, the politician, the publican, and the peasant, whose influence could be ranked in that order. Maybe it was the business about the Pope, but I turned first to the pages on parish priests, a dodgy bunch of characters in O'Flaherty's eyes, who were always looking for donations. Tourists were advised to give only to a priest who was 'fat and jovial and owns a good horse and wears riding breeches and goes around everywhere with a horsewhip', perhaps because the author was an obsessive punter.

The parish priest is wary of outsiders, O'Flaherty wrote, and inclined to regard Ireland as the only moral country, although his personal view of the Irish is 'a very poor one'. The English were considered immoral, and the French were even worse. Americans were dubious because they allowed divorce. Germany was acceptable on account of Catholic Bavaria, but Russians were 'beyond the pale of civilization', having overthrown the church. The Italians, Spaniards, and Belgians were 'very nearly as pure as the Irish', O'Flaherty said. As for the Chinese, they might still be saved through the efforts of the Irish Mission to China, but the Mexicans were doomed, and it was the duty of every parish priest to lobby Ireland's leaders 'to get the English to get the Americans to make war on Mexico'.

* * *

Shortly after I read O'Flaherty's book, I paid a visit to Father Sean Breen, who is known as the 'Racing Priest' and also, warmly, as The Breener. He takes pride in being the only priest in the world with two racecourses in his parish, Naas and Punchestown. 'Isn't God good?' he likes to say, in praise of his bounty. I'd been wanting to meet Father Breen ever since someone told me he dispenses an occasional tip on the Festival to his congregation.

Though I had been to both Naas and Punchestown, I got lost on my way to his parish, and when I phoned for directions while on the road, he asked, 'So you're a lost soul, are you?' That gave me a moment's pause, but it was only an example of the gentle humour The Breener brings to bear on the complexities of being human. In his seventies, he has a sweet, boyish, untroubled face, and a talent for light banter and offering comfort that ageing can confer. His house was next door to the Church of the Immaculate Conception, at a rural cross-roads in Eadestown.

'You're very welcome,' he greeted me, apologizing for the non-existent mess inside, as courteous older people do. 'Come into my bachelor pad.' He escorted me into his kitchen, describing it as his neatest room, and made a pot of tea.

Originally from Cavan, Father Breen had held his current post for about nine years and served about four hundred families. (He has recently moved to a new post in Ballymore Eustace, also in Kildare.) He grew up in a small town in farming country, but he didn't have any particular feeling for horses as a boy, once falling off a neighbour's pony when he tried to ride it, a deterrent to any further efforts in the saddle. Only later, as a young priest in North County Dublin, did he become entranced with races, largely through his friendships with such people as Jim Dreaper, Tom Dreaper's son, and Joanna Morgan, a trainer. (He owns a piece of two horses stabled at Morgan's yard in Meath.) On his very first trip to Cheltenham, he had the good luck to see Arkle win his first Gold Cup, and he has returned for every Festival since, barring illness.

Horses are integral to Irish culture, Father Breen thinks, and not all that long ago the priest in his parish would have visited his parishioners on horseback.

'Racing is a marvellous social thing in Ireland,' he said, his eyes twinkling. 'So healthy out in the open air! You meet all strands of people, too. It isn't just the upper classes go racing here. Sure, there are those who overdo the drink and the gambling, but life is a temptation, after all. Anyway, I love it. I absolutely love it! It's so relaxing it takes me right out of my head. Nobody knows what goes on in our heads, thank God.' Of all the Irish meetings, his favourite is Galway in July, a seven-day indulgence. 'It's tremendous fun. Everybody's there. Even the politicians have caught on,' he joked. 'Fianna Fáil has a fundraising tent, and you'll see the Taoiseach for sure, he wouldn't dare miss it. The first three men I ran into one summer were the Ministers for Justice, Finance, and Agriculture.'

As for Cheltenham, The Breener was looking forward to his annual trip. He'd travel with his usual group, some friends who'd bonded together over the last twenty years or so, and he would say a Punters' Mass at his hotel on

St Patrick's Day, which always coincides with the Festival. He expected to have a good time, but the journey would also be melancholy.

'A lot of people die, you know,' he said. 'You don't see them there, and you say to yourself, "He isn't at Cheltenham, he must be dead." The Festival's sort of a check on who's still alive.' When I told him I was going for the first time, he assured me I'd be ecstatic about the quality of the races, although he had some reservations about how things have changed and become less intimate since his earliest visits. 'It's got very commercial. The corporate side ruins everything, doesn't it? The Tented Village, all those shops, they're a distraction.' He didn't say this angrily, just in a resigned way, with a priestly tolerance for what others might prefer. 'I'm a purist, I guess. It's the racing that matters to me.'

He poured more tea and passed the soda bread. Tacked to the kitchen door, I noticed a calendar from *The Irish Field*. On the table was a well-thumbed copy of the *Post*. Through a window over the sink, I could see a neatly kept back garden. The house was very still and peaceful, the kind of place where you can hear the tick of a clock and the drip of a tap.

'The Irish used to ask me to bless their horses before a race at Cheltenham,' Father Breen went on, 'but I don't do it anymore. Do you know where the word "blessing" comes from? It means "to speak well of". I'll tell you an old joke, it's been around for ages. Seems this trainer had a horse he wanted blessed, so he got a priest to do it, and the horse won. A COI fella [COI being shorthand for Church of Ireland] witnessed that, and the next time he saw the priest do a blessing, he backed the horse, and the horse won again. That happened three more times, but the fourth time the horse finished last. The COI fella was upset because he'd lost all his money, so he cornered the priest and asked what went wrong. The priest gave him a look and said, "Ah, you Prods don't know the difference between a blessing and the last rites!"'

'Old but good,' I laughed. 'Are you a gambling man, Father? Who are your Festival picks?'

The Breener does enjoy a punt, but he worried about getting carried away in the reckless atmosphere at Cheltenham, so he put his bets down in advance, three each morning with David Power before he could be swayed. He was considering a treble on Moscow Flyer, Best Mate, and Rooster Booster, even though he understood that history and the statistics dictated against all three champs winning.

'Bookies love trebles,' he said merrily. 'Three chances for the punter to lose!' He already had an ante-post wager on Willie Mullins' Sadlers Wings at 8-1 and was pondering a further plunge on Brave Inca, whose trainer Colm Murphy, a protégé of Aidan O'Brien's, was new to the game. 'No young trainer would get his hands on a good horse like that in the past,' he told me. 'The horse would have been sold right out from under him, gone from Ireland.'

Soon Father Breen would become a seven-day wonder, the subject of a media feeding frenzy during the week before the Festival. 'They pick my brain,' he said, joking again. 'If I'm not being presumptuous about having a brain.' He would do telephone interviews with radio chat shows in Ireland and England. His passion for the races was particularly intriguing to the English, so much so that an interviewer on the BBC once pressed him to account for it. 'What does your vicar do for entertainment?' Breen replied. Alert to being manipulated, he refuses to play along with those who sniff around for tales of drink and debauchery. He savours his brief burst of celebrity, but he could relinquish his grip on it without the slightest care.

As a good Christian, The Breener tired of talking about himself after a while and asked me some questions, what type of books I'd written and why I was in Ireland. 'I met an Irish woman in London,' I began. . .

'End of story!' he cried, interrupting me. 'Best women in the world! And they're great mothers. They have to be.' He halted for a second. 'Why is that, I wonder?'

Father Breen didn't fit O'Flaherty's satirical definition of the parish priest, I thought, being too good-humoured and self-aware. It was a bad time for priests in Ireland and elsewhere, of course, and yet through the ages there had been many decent, committed men like The Breener who have accepted the foibles of their congregation and done what they could to meliorate them. His was a life lived in service, rich in the rewards of community. As I was leaving, I asked if I'd meet him at the track any time soon. 'Oh, yes,' he said ardently. 'If I didn't see a horse for a week, I'd be unwell.'

The next trainer to swallow a dose of castor oil was Jessie Harrington, who brought Spirit Leader to Leopardstown for the AIG Europe Champion Hurdle toward the end of the month. After Spirit Leader's second-place finish in the Bewley's, the form students were supporting her in the other Champion Hurdle, the one at the Festival. Her ante-post odds had fallen to 14-1. Gutsy and genuine, the mare thrives on a fast-paced fight, so Cheltenham's hilly racecourse would be another bonus. If she ran well in the AIG, the theory went, she might peak in the early spring, a trick Jessie had pulled off a time or two in the past with other horses.

But Spirit Leader was hardly a banker at Leopardstown. In the AIG, a Grade One worth about ninety two thousand euros to the winner, she faced a strong contingent of opponents. Golden Cross, the Bewley's winner, was entered, as was Noel Chance's Flame Creek, who was third in that same race. Wille Mullins had the troubled Davenport Milenium ready to go. His horse had come up against Spirit Leader once before, finishing second to her sixth in the Tote Bula Hurdle at Cheltenham, in December, while carrying one pound more. Today Spirit Leader had a five pound advantage, as she did over two horses from the J. P. McManus stable, Fota Island and Foreman, the latter perhaps the more feared of the pair. German-bred, Foreman had done well as a hurdler in France and was a decent fourth in last year's Royal & SunAlliance, prompting McManus to buy him for a princely sum.

The AIG was an odd contest, with an upside-down result. Fota Island made much of the running and wound up third, while Georges Girl, who'd only won a single handicap hurdle in her life, was a surprise second. Under a confident ride from Thierry Doumen, Foreman picked up at the last and soon had the measure of the others, a dramatic spectacle to watch on the big screen because Doumen's face was smeared with blood from a nosebleed he couldn't staunch while riding. He was overjoyed to win, doubly so because Foreman belonged to a string of horses he trained in Chantilly. All the favoured horses failed to place, including Spirit Leader, whose name now had a big question mark next to it in my Cheltenham notebook.

After the AIG, Willie Mullins travelled to London where, on 29 January at Portman Square, the Jockey Club's disciplinary panel began its inquiry into Be My Royal's tarnished win in the Hennessy Gold Cup at Newbury. A total of thirty-seven horses had tested positive for traces of morphine in Britain during the period under scrutiny, sixteen of them winners, and the source in each case was the same – Connolly's Red Mills 14 Per Cent Racehorse Cubes – so the outcome of the hearing would have a ripple effect on the other cases.

Morphine occurs naturally in feed, usually in trace amounts. All the parties agreed on that. At issue was the question of a threshold level, or how much morphine it takes to affect a horse's performance. Experts had submitted scientific papers that proved trace amounts of the substance can have no effect either way, and yet the Jockey Club insisted on a 'zero-tolerance' policy. A horse is subject to disqualification if any morphine at all turns up in a urine sample – a rule Mullins and the O'Learys objected to as antiquated, given the sort of precise analysis that can be achieved with twenty-first-century technology.

To get some background information, I spoke with Noel Brennan of Connolly's Red Mills, whose head-quarters are in Goresbridge, Kilkenny. The company is family owned, with no outside shareholders, and has been around since 1908, initially selling seed and later diversifying into horse feed in 1963. 'With this morphine business, some of us feel like we've been here since 1908,' Brennan kidded, having a laugh at his own expense. The case sounded bad to the uninformed public, he agreed, a black mark on Connolly's proud history because morphine carries a connotation of race-fixing and doped horses.

'Red Mills fed fifty-six percent of the winners in Ireland last year,' Brennan said, doing some understandable image-polishing. 'In 2002, we fed thirty-three percent of winners at the Cheltenham Festival.' In truth, that's a noteworthy accomplishment since Red Mills has ten or fifteen competitors. The morphine incident was predictable, Brennan felt, a bomb just waiting to explode. Everyone knew about the potential for feed to be contaminated, but no one was willing to do much about it. 'The science is there, but the Irish Turf Club and the Jockey Club won't spend the money,' he objected. 'They say it doesn't happen often enough for them to bother.'

As well as being a publicity nightmare for Red Mills, the disciplinary panel hearing was expensive. Not wanting to lose a big customer like Mullins, the company had agreed to foot all the legal bills, but that would raise the cost of their insurance premiums – a waste, in Brennan's opinion. Red Mills would much rather have tossed the money into a kitty to fund the scientific studies needed to rewrite the rulebook. He believed the Turf and Jockey Clubs were blinded by tradition, age-old bodies resistant to change.

The two-day inquiry did not go well for Mullins and Red Mills after their fourteen-month wait, despite the evidence compiled on their behalf. The Jockey Club stuck to its guns, upheld the disqualification, and ordered Mullins to reimburse the Club for its legal fees of about five thousand pounds. Mullins was aggrieved, as he should have been, since during the hearing Dr Peter Webbon, the Jockey Club's chief veterinary officer, stated that any concentration of morphine up to fifty nanograms per millilitre couldn't possibly affect a horse's performance, and Be My Royal's level was far below the benchmark.

In light of that, Mullins suggested the samples be tested again to demonstrate the point. His suggestion was rejected, but there was still a bright spot for him. The disciplinary panel also heard that the Jockey Club had instructed the Horseracing Forensic Laboratory, in March 2003, to apply the fifty nanograms per millilitre threshold level to all samples tested in the future. Mullins' solicitors grabbed at that as a hook on which to hang an appeal, but Willie was still bitterly disappointed, as upset as a child scolded unfairly by a doddery old teacher out of touch with the times.

Another Saturday in Dublin with a coal fire burning and a wet, inhospitable evening outside. On the roof a steady drip of rain, in the oven a leg of lamb, on the couch Imelda reading *The Irish Times*, and in their rooms the boys doing whatever it was they did in their private realms, the older writing in his journal, maybe, while the younger careered through the streets of Vice City playing 'Grand Theft Auto'. The heart of winter, the day's racing at Fairyhouse over and the races at Punchestown just ahead, on the first Sunday in February.

I was back from O'Herlihy's after a pint with Reilly and sat at the table now with my notebooks and old copies of the *Post*, charting the course of the season so far, a record of the usual ups-and-downs, of the mighty ascending and then brought crashing back to earth. What had I learned in the past four months? Chiefly, how difficult it was for any trainer to keep a good horse healthy when faced with a vast array of perils, with viruses and injuries and a random dagger of misfortune that could strike anywhere, at any time, all in the hope that the horse would be fit and ready to shine, however briefly, at the Cheltenham Festival.

Best Mate and Moscow Flyer were resting now and wouldn't be seen in public for another six weeks. After Jair du Cochet's return to form in the Pillar Property Chase, Guillame Macaire had decided to try for the Gold Cup, after all. Michael Hourigan remained tight-lipped about whether Beef Or Salmon would run in the Irish Hennessy next Sunday, or be shelved until mid-March. The ante-post odds for the top horses, though they varied from bookie to bookie, stood roughly at Best Mate 4-7, Jair du Cochet 6-1, Keen Leader 8-1, The Real Bandit 12-1, and Beef Or Salmon and Kingscliff 14-1.

As I carved the rosemary-scented lamb, my thoughts

drifted to Tom Costello and his sons in their enigmatic kingdom in Newmarket-on-Fergus. No doubt they felt an emotional attachment to Best Mate – Tom Junior had broken the horse and must still feel close to him – and would eagerly follow his Gold Cup bid, but I was curious as to whether the Costellos were already focusing their energies on a future champion, the stuff of tomorrow's dreams, a few steps ahead of ordinary mortals again. Their horse trading had acquired such an air of mystery I couldn't possibly consider my education complete without a visit, although how much of their programme they'd divulge to an outsider was an open question.

February: The Waiting Game

Along the River Barrow in Leighlinbridge, County Carlow, magpies were flitting about over a field, their flashing colours distinct against a drizzly sky. It was the sort of morning that makes you want to stay in bed with your book or your lover, or both, but I had an appointment with Willie Mullins to talk about Florida Pearl and the Jockey Club's ruling. After breakfast at The Lord Bagenal Inn, I drove down an overgrown lane to Mullins' farm, a 100-acre property where he lives with his wife Jackie and their kids in a lovely stone barn refurbished shortly after their marriage. On the front lawn, a sculpture of a horse and jockey fashioned from wire and hammered metal was caught in the act of scaling a hedge, with some Christmas lights still threaded through the mesh.

I found Willie up at his gallops. He has a pair of them, a newer one of about a mile and an older one of two-and-a-half furlongs. He keeps about a hundred horses at the yard now, and he was standing by a sand ring and studying a dozen of them as they circled. He offered me a formal handshake, more reserved than the other trainers I'd met, concentrating intently on the movement of his stock and not inclined to chitchat. Whereas Hourigan comes at the job with a boisterous sense of fun, and Harrington with an equestrian's ardour, Mullins is conservative and business-like, meticulous by nature.

When the horses had finished exercising and were cooling down, we headed for his office in a converted outbuilding to escape the rain.

'Been here long?' I asked, making polite conversation.

'Not long. About eighteen years.'

'Did you grow up around here?'

'No, the home place is about five miles away,' he said, as if it belonged to a different archipelago in the great ocean of Carlow. The measures of time and distance were those of a country person, reflecting Mullins' deep-rooted sense of place.

His office was well-organized, as I expected. His assistant Katrina sat at one end, while Willie's desk was at the other, neatly stacked with faxes and mail, a laptop at the ready. The shelves held rows of form and stud books, and there were many trophies, plaques, and photos, including a splendid montage of his four Cheltenham bumper winners – Whither Or Which ('96), Florida Pearl ('97), Alexander Banquet ('98), and Joe Cullen (2000).

Some of the trophies were engraved with his name, awards for his own triumphs.

'You were a good rider,' I said.

A half-smile. 'Good enough.'

He was being modest, a fitting trait for royalty. More than once he'd been Ireland's amateur champion, just as

Jackie had been the women's champ in the 1994-95 season. It was Paddy Mullins who was responsible for putting Willie in the saddle while his son was still in boarding school, despite Paddy's protestations about wanting his boys to choose another career. Arriving home for a weekend visit in 1973, Willie discovered his father had taken out a licence for him, and he was scheduled to ride in a Fairyhouse bumper that very Sunday. Among his greatest moments as a jockey was a win in the National Hunt Chase at the Festival on Paddy's Hazy Dawn, in 1982.

It still amazed me how many Irish trainers had a similar background, their lives joined to horses from childhood and linked to them forever after. Willie doubted he could do anything else, really. 'I'd go bananas in a regular office,' he said, although that doesn't mean training is simple for him. Instead, it was like dodging bullets. I thought his season had been below average to date, for instance, and had only begun to gel with such big horses as Hedgehunter and Florida Pearl hitting their stride at last, but he disagreed, believing a trainer is always going to be a little frustrated and should learn to cope with it or else. Six of his horses had failed to scope clean that morning and would miss their weekend races, he said.

'Why do you do so well in the bumper at Cheltenham?' I asked him. The Bumper has become an Irish specialty, with the English winning it only twice in the past decade.

'We have a better programme,' Mullins told me. 'There's good prize money in Irish bumpers. If you've got a good horse in England, you go off jumping right away.'

He has a dozen or so flat horses in the yard, as do most of his peers, so that he can compete during the summer when the National Hunt has less to offer. If a horse runs well on the flat, it will be relatively easy to sell, plus some flat horses turn into hurdlers or even into chasers on occasion. For his Grade One horses, Willie maps out a campaign in advance, but for the younger ones – the juveniles and novices – he drops them in wherever it seems appropriate, just to see what happens. 'Separates the wheat from the chaff,' he said.

'Lots of chaff,' I said, and he agreed.

I changed the subject to Florida Pearl, and Mullins brightened considerably. I was thinking about Richard Johnson flying over to ride the horse in the Normans Grove Chase, and without mentioning the words 'betting coup', I inquired as gingerly as possible if the booking should have been read as a sign of Willie's seriousness. 'No, it was just that all the A-list Irish jockeys were unavailable,' he said, putting my paranoia to rest, 'and Richard had been on Florida Pearl before.' Given the Pearl's age and his problems last year, Mullins was delighted with his horse, all credit due to Grainne Ni Chaba. On the weekend just past, he'd entered Florida Pearl in both the Ritz Chase at Ascot and the Kinloch Brae at Thurles, even though the horse's probable target was the Irish Hennessy.

'If you have a horse that can go to Ascot,' I said, 'why bother entering it at Thurles?'

Another half-smile. 'In case the grandstand at Ascot had burned down.'

Mullins swears by multiple entries. For the Festival,

he plays a kind of poker. He'll enter a horse such as Davenport Milenium in races at different distances, then wait until the last minute, when everybody's cards are on the table, before declaring himself. The strategy has some obvious merits. Since 1994, Willie has had more Festival winners than any Irish trainer, seven to Edward O'Grady's six. 'I've got about twenty-five entries this year,' he reckoned, 'but I may wind up with only six runners.' His guess was way off – he wound up with seventeen.

Yet the buy-in isn't cheap. Each Festival entry costs £110 and has to be paid far in advance, sometimes before a horse has proven it deserves to be there. The policy, reasonably new, had upset some trainers, who considered it unfair and merely a way for Racecourse Holdings Trust, Cheltenham's parent organization, to raise more prize money. Phillip Hobbs had been the most vocal critic. He had forty entries at that point, but only two confirmed runners in Rooster Booster and Flagship Uberalles. A promising French horse was set to arrive at his yard soon, and though he hadn't even seen it, much less watched it run, he felt compelled to enter it in a Festival race or two to cover himself.

In response, Edward Gillespie, Cheltenham's MD, had suggested the racecourse was trying to stimulate the ante-post market – the more entries, the longer the odds, leading to more interest from punters hoping to cash a big bet – but the idea that RHT would show such concern for the welfare of bookmakers sounded a trifle far-fetched to most. In another move that had a few trainers scratching their heads, RHT was expanding the Festival to four days in 2005, a decision that Mullins, who is invested in the sport's history and traditions, opposed.

'I'm on the anti-side, preferring three days of top-class racing,' he said, when queried by the *Post*. 'If there are new races that ought to go in, I'd get rid of one or two of the handicaps to make room. I am sure it will be financially rewarding for Cheltenham.'

I could hear the rain drumming on the roof, heavier now. Mullins had some calls to make, so he sent me back up to the gallops, where Florida Pearl would soon be working. 'I'll be there in five minutes,' he shouted as I went out the door, but he was on farmer's time. With only a flimsy fold-up umbrella for protection, I waited twenty minutes before he joined me. The riders going around, all well protected against the rain, were amused to see me there, a stranger drenched to the skin. How the stranger must adore horses! As at other yards, many of them were from abroad – Pakistan, India, Finland, the Ukraine – and had been hired in a variety of ways, through agencies, by word-of-mouth, or by contacting Willie via his website. The heavy winter ground was making it tricky for the lighter riders, those destined for the flat. A jockey has to be strong to pull together a horse who acts up or refuses to perform, and horses can be as contrary as we are in nasty weather.

I finally abandoned my umbrella, its spokes decimated by the wind, and resigned myself to a case of bronchitis. I watched Florida Pearl come up from the stables with Alexander Banquet. The horses were pals and lived in adjoining boxes. Every star horse has a sidekick, apparently, a Tonto for every Lone Ranger. Did they always work together? 'Not always,' Willie said, as precise as ever. 'But often. They can both be lazy and like a bit of competition. Alexander Banquet does nothing on his own. Florida Pearl's not so bad.'

The horses trotted through the mud, off to complete two one-mile circuits of the newer B-shaped gallop. On Florida Pearl was Tracey Gilmour, his long-time lass, as tuned in to his psyche as anyone could be. Florida Pearl *is* a beautiful athlete and seemed to know it, aware of his standing above the others, all perfectly sculpted muscle and princely action. Alexander Banquet is more rough-hewn, not so finely composed, with something of the bar-room brawler about him, able to take a few knocks without coming unglued. He has stamina to spare and can plod along for a few extra furlongs without tiring. A little Rottweiler named Sybil nipped at Florida Pearl's heels, and Florida Pearl let out a whinny, but Alexander Banquet wanted nothing to do with Sybil and looked ready to trample her.

As the horses began their first circuit, Willie and I talked about Ruby Walsh, his jockey of choice, who still finds time to ride for Mullins up to three times a week, complicating an already hectic schedule. Again I listened to a litany of praise for Ruby, yet Willie also expressed an almost paternal concern for him, as if being away from Ireland for such long periods must be hard on Ruby's soul. 'It's a rough life,' he commiserated. 'On the motorways all the time, day after day.'

Somewhere on the farm Be My Royal, now retired with a tendon injury, was roaming. I'd saved up until the last to ask Mullins about the morphine scandal, thinking I might touch a raw nerve, and I did.

'Zero tolerance! That's an impossible standard to meet,' he said heatedly. 'Red Mills stated as much to the Jockey Club four years ago! Sure, we lost in court, but we got a jury of the people. It's all out in the open now. What do they call it? Natural justice.' Clearly, this was a matter of principle for him. Like Red Mills, he'd seen his good name suffer by innuendo. I detected an Irish pride, too, along with a distaste for the English way of doing things, strictly by the rules, where the Irish are inclined toward sympathy and forgiveness.

'You're still pretty pissed off,' I said.

He brushed aside the comment. 'Ah, let the solicitors handle it.'

Better to consider Florida Pearl's chances in the Hennessy, as we did when he walked me to my car. Could Florida win it a record fourth time? Mullins thought so. He pointed toward the sculpture on his lawn. 'Do you recognize that horse? That is Florida Pearl.' He'd met Rupert Till, the artist, at an exhibition of Till's work. 'We got to talking over a couple of beers, as people do, and I mentioned that I'd always wanted a horse sculpture, and the next thing I knew he just showed up with this one day. It's supposed to be Ruby, even though Ruby never won on Florida Pearl. Notice anything wrong?'

I checked it over, but it looked pretty accurate to me. The jockey was even wearing goggles. 'Can't say I do.'

'Rupert took Ruby's measurements, but he also used a photo of Paul Carberry. Ruby doesn't have the same body type as Paul, or the same style of riding. So it comes out in-between.' There it was, that meticulousness again. 'Anyway, it's something different,' Willie mused. He made a half-hearted attempt to remove the Christmas lights, but the strings kept catching in the wire mesh, so he did what most men would do under the circumstances and postponed the chore to get back to a job he knew he could handle. 'See you racing!' he yelled as I departed.

In those early days of February, the Irish appeared to be under a black cloud, with nothing going right. The rain continued to fall and flooded the courses at Fairyhouse and Clonmel, cancelling the races. Edward O'Grady, his Cheltenham squad already whittled to the bone, faced another potential loss when Back In Front, after working ineffectively, was found to have an irregular heartbeat and sent to the Veterinary Hospital in Dublin for further examination.

In Limerick, Michael Hourigan came clean about Beef Or Salmon. The horse had a sore muscle in a rear hindquarter, he said, probably the result of his fall in the Gold Cup last year. His jumping hadn't been the same since, so he was receiving some physio, and though he was ninety-five percent right, he would skip the Hennessy and go straight to Cheltenham.

In Kilkenny, Connolly's Red Mills threw in the towel and mailed cheques for any forfeited prize money to the connections of all forty-six horses in England and Ireland who'd tested positive for morphine, an estimated payout of about a half-million pounds when legal and specialist fees were included. The company accused the Jockey

Club of upholding a technical interpretation of its rules 'at the expense of fair play'.

Only Paddy Power Bookmakers rose above the storm. If you brought your girlfriend or your wife into any shop on Valentine's Day, she would receive a free box of Butler's chocolates and a chance to win a trip to Paris for two.

The clouds parted for the Hennessy Gold Cup and presented us with a perfect Sunday afternoon at Leopardstown, sunny and cold, with a few daffodils already blooming in weak little patches by the parade ring. Anticipating a large turnout, the bookies were eagerly preparing their pitches, among them Francis Hyland, the head of the Irish National Bookmakers' Association. If anyone doesn't fit the raffish image of a turf accountant, it's Hyland, who was once a dealer on the London Stock Exchange. He was dressed as if for a bullish round of trading in a topcoat, tie, and pinstripe suit. Only his worn-looking shoes, scuffed and muddy from tramping from course to course, hinted at his profession.

Though I knew a little about the bookmaker's art by now, having met the Old Bookie, chatted with the weather-beaten gents on the Thurles train, and lost money to the likes of Paddy Sharkey, I needed more information to fill out the big picture, and Hyland was the ideal person to supply it since he takes a scholarly approach to his work. An authority on Irish racing, he has written histories of both the Irish Derby and the Grand National. He began his lecture with a short course on the tools of his trade, known collectively as a joint. Bookies have been using them for centuries, with no need to change anything. 'It's all designed to be cheap and portable,' he said. The tools included a long, hollow, telescopic pole that Francis extended to its full length and tied to a fence with some twine. He attached a cash tray for coins to it, and then his slate, and finally an umbrella holder. The one modern touch was a laptop that Francis's only employee used to record bets and issue receipts.

I was intrigued by Hyland's leap from being a broker to a bookie, as dramatic as any of Best Mate's, but he said racing has always fascinated him. In 1974, when the stock market was in a slump, he took a year off to try and write his history of the Derby, and also have a shot at book making. He did well enough (meaning 'I survived') to continue full-time. His career on the London exchange gave him a slight edge because he'd honed his skill with numbers in an arena where, as he put it, 'There isn't any finish, and the betting is all in-running.' Yet he didn't want to create an impression that his job was uncomplicated. He was quick to dispel the common perception that bookies just stand on a box and accept handfuls of cash from stupid gamblers. 'The punters in Ireland aren't mugs,' he said. 'They're very well informed. This is the only business I know where insider trading is legal.'

'But tips . . . ' I said, my voice trailing off as I remembered all the worthless ones I'd heard and sometimes foolishly heeded.

Hyland clarified the matter for me and explored its

ambiguities. Real inside information does exist, he believes, and he protects himself against it by being a shrewd student of faces. 'In this game, faces are very, very important,' he insisted, and I could feel him reading mine, inspecting it for nervous tics of a devious nature. If he finds a punter regularly backing horses of Noel Meade's, say, and winning every time, he assumes that punter must have a line to the yard and will remember his face. (The very notion of internet betting alarms Hyland, because it's so faceless.) But it's equally true that the Irish tend to accept any tip as valid, a grave mistake since most trainers are wary and rarely tell anyone a horse is going to win, because if the horse loses, they'll never be forgiven. 'Do you know what William Hill once said?' Francis asked. '"People with inside information have made me a rich man."'

I was enjoying Hyland's spriteliness, his sense of fun. His pitch is about two hundred yards from the rails, the preferred position between the reserved and ordinary enclosures. 'A rails bookie at Leopardstown might pay about two hundred and fifty thousand euros for a pitch there,' he said, and maybe a little more for a premium spot, but the price drops drastically after that because most punters are lazy and won't do much walking. A pitch only a few yards past Hyland's might cost ten grand less, and so on, to the outer reaches of the ring, a region as isolated as the Skelligs. On an average day, the bookies' take at Leopardstown might be about six hundred thousand euros, Francis guessed, with about eighty percent of it going to those on the rails.

To compensate for his position, Hyland delivers service. 'It's what I sell,' he said, with a theatrical flare.

Two Dubliners 'in the know'. There are few places on earth where hot tips are embraced so readily, like pieces of the Holy Grail.

The morning after. A Dublin pub in Temple Bar, where you can hear the rattle of empty beer kegs everywhere.

TOP Edredon Bleu steals the prize in the Oil Chase at Clonmel, defeating Beef Or Salmon.

BACKGROUND Over they go. Yet horses also bash right through a flight of hurdles sometimes, so the hurdles must be repaired frequently.

LEFT Hardy Eustace springs a 33-1 surprise in the Festival's Champion Chase. The horse's regular rider, Kieran Kelly, had died in a freak fall at Kilbeggan back in August.

NEAR RIGHT
John P McManus,
Ireland's largest
owner of jumpers,
and Noel O'Brien,
the senior Irish jumps
handicapper.

FAR RIGHT A man
with the gift of the gab
– Paddy Power, the
bookmaker.

RIGHT Father Sean Breen,
the racing priest from County
Kildare, has been attending the
Festival since 1963, when Arkle
won his first Gold Cup.

ABOVE Henrietta Knight, famous for her infinite care and patience.

RIGHT Willie Mullins calls Florida Pearl 'a beautiful athlete'. The horse would win his fourth Irish Hennessy at Leopardstown.

ABOVE Many consider Paul Carberry (right) the best natural horseman in the game, while Timmy Murphy's stock has risen dramatically since he gave up the drink.

FAR LEFT Tom Burke, Leopardstown's racing manager.

LEFT Barry Geraghty, Moscow Flyer's superb jockey, had five winners at the Festival in 2003.

ABOVE The packed stands at Cheltenham during the Festival, host to over 50,000 racegoers each day.

RIGHT Jessica Harrington, Eamonn Leigh and Barry Geraghty, with Moscow Flyer after a big win.

BACKGROUND A point-to-point at Comber. These races are the cradle of the sport, and though they can be brutal, they've produced such stars as Best Mate and Florida Pearl.

TOP LEFT Moscow Flyer likes to watch the traffic zipping by on the N9 motorway below his special paddock at Harrington's yard in Moone.

TOP RIGHT Pretty Solerina, the fairytale mare.

LEFT Formerly of the London Stock Exchange, Francis Hyland sometimes mans his pitch in a pinstripe suit.

RIGHT Beef Or Salmon's patchy jumping has been a trouble spot, but he's still young enough to have a real shot at the Gold Cup.

BELOW The unsaddling enclosure at Down Royal, in Northern Ireland.

Doom-and-gloom for Ireland. Azertyuiop wins the Queen Mother after Moscow Flyer's fall. 'Jaysus, what a relief!' shouted jockey Ruby Walsh.

Knight with Terry Biddlecombe, who can't hold back the tears when Best Mate wins a Gold Cup.

Iris's Gift holds off Baracouda in the Stayers' Hurdle, following a plan Barry Geraghty cooked up.

Jim Culloty pilots Best Mate, a true leaper, in the 2004 Cheltenham Gold Cup.

'I'm their bank, I'm their cloakroom attendant. They leave their coats and bags with me. They use my mobile. I cash cheques for them, and if they argue about the odds, I'll adjust them ever so slightly. In essence, I am their servant.' A few customers have credit with him and can bet 'on the nod', but he doesn't like to grant the privilege because people will wager more than they normally do and often get into financial difficulty. Bad debts are bad for business, so Hyland's strategy is to keep his customers afloat rather than let them drown.

I got to thinking about Nosey Flynn and also T.P. Reilly. Was English racing really more honest than Irish racing? When I mentioned Reilly's theory to Hyland, he gave me a withering stare, as though he couldn't believe my innocence. 'All racing is bent!' he cried. 'Everyone knows that! Racing's bent, football's bent, darts is bent, any sport with betting is bent!' He wasn't referring so much to fixed races as to the shifty ways a trainer can manipulate the handicap system to his advantage and still stay within the rules.

'How many times have you seen it?' Hyland asked. 'A trainer has a horse that loses time after time. The horse runs in the wrong races, or at the wrong distance, or at the wrong racecourse, with Jimmy Unknown riding. And when the horse's mark is low enough for a win, surprise! Mr Unknown has been fired, and Ruby Walsh is the new jockey!'

'Do jockeys really matter that much?' I asked, playing devil's advocate.

'Ruby is a stone better than an average professional jockey, I can tell you that,' Francis said. 'Ruby, and also

Carberry and Geraghty. And in a bumper, a top amateur rider is worth three stone more than the average amateur.'

In the past, before bookmaking was tightly regulated, high-street bookies were known to pay jockeys to throw a race when they were on the favourite. A jockey's life could be harsh back then – drinking was the norm, and a rider often died as broke as the average boxer. At times, a poor Irish family would send off a small, skinny boy as an apprentice, just so they'd have one less mouth to feed. Though race fixing isn't so blatant anymore and doesn't exist at the highest levels of the sport, I'd read a recent article about how the stable staff at any yard can supposedly inhibit a horse's performance. They can deny the horse any water the day before a race, for example, then bring it to the track and allow it to drink its fill, or they can let a horse gorge on hay the morning of a run. According to the article, they can also dose a horse with ACP, an animal tranquillizer hard to detect in a urine sample.

When Francis began checking the card for the first race, I was astonished at how little mental energy he spent. He didn't even bother to consult a *Post*, only a list of entries torn from a newspaper. With scarcely any deliberation, he had the field reduced to three possible winners. That wasn't any great mystery, he felt. He simply searches out the good jockeys and trainers, and there aren't very many. It's possible to toss out more horses from the equation than ever before, he said, because the quality of Irish racing in general has declined in recent years, except at the top of the game.

'We used to have about three thousand horses in training,' he estimated, 'and five hundred were OK, five hundred moderate, and the rest couldn't keep themselves warm. Now we have almost six thousand in training, and five hundred are OK, five hundred moderate, and the rest are useless.' Besides, as he pointed out, a bookie isn't looking for the form horse. All that concerns him is the horse that the public likes. If he doesn't get the odds right on the jolly, he'll blow his margins completely.

My session with Hyland had been very productive. I'd gained the clearest picture yet of what an on-course bookie requires to be successful – a decent head for numbers, some psychological insight into his clientele, ample operating capital, the balls to take a risk, and the intelligence to know when to take it. Francis had those attributes and earns a substantial living, although he is, by his own admission, in the minority. As I'd suspected at Thurles, most on-course bookies were struggling to get by. But what makes for a successful gambler? When I put the question to him, he echoed J. P. McManus: impulse control. A punter must be patient enough to recognize good value.

'Show me someone who bets only three or four times a year,' Hyland said excitedly, 'and I'll guarantee that person will be a winner. The more you play, the less chance you have of coming out ahead. In effect, you pay me a commission on every bet.'

Most punters are doomed, though, and lose control under pressure, especially on the last race – pure gravy for a bookie. If they are ahead, they'll look to double or triple their earnings since they're playing with the house's money, and if they're in the hole, they'll dig down deeper in an attempt, often fruitless, to break even. How well I knew the syndrome! I glanced at the crowd milling around the ring and saw it the way Francis might, as a horde of impulses barely held in check, fish about to be fried, and I vowed to avoid my usual mistakes – confusion, thinking too much, probing the entrails of birds, and so on – when it was time for a flutter.

For once, I was admirable, even virtuous. I actually kept my vow and stuck to my plan. I didn't have a feel for the first two races and waited until the third, the Deloitte Novice Hurdle, a Grade One, to make my move, backing Colm Murphy's Brave Inca. Although Murphy, a former accountant, was indeed new to the game, as Father Breen had noted, he showed immense promise as a trainer. Away from the track for about two months, Brave Inca was up against a hard-hitting field that included Newmill, Mariah Rollins, and the heavily favoured Watson Lake, but the horse delivered a dynamite run over the last 100 yards to beat Newmill and secure a Festival berth in either the Royal & SunAlliance or the Supreme Novices, depending on the state of the ground.

Another good field was entered in the following race, the Dr P. J. Moriarty Novice Steeplechase, also a Grade One. From among such standouts as Hi Cloy, Mossy Green, Xenophon, and Pay It Forward, I settled on Pizarro, blocking out the fact that his sire was called Broken Hearted, as dubious a name as You Need Luck. The distance of about two miles and five furlongs was short of Pizarro's best, but he still went off at even money. I had a hunch that Edward O'Grady was due for a score, and so did the other punters. Barry Geraghty rode Pizarro hard from two out, but his horse held on to squeak out a victory over Mossy Green.

Next up, we had a handicap hurdle with nineteen runners, an intimidating number, so rather than squander my profits, I controlled my impulses and retreated to the Jodami Bar, an appropriate choice since Jodami had won the Irish Hennessy three times from 1993-95, a feat Florida Pearl had matched and would soon try to surpass. With Beef Or Salmon on the shelf, I believed in the Pearl. The other horses didn't scare me in the least. Cloudy Bays and Be My Belle were stepping up in class, and Rince Ri probably needed more than three miles. Harbour Pilot hadn't competed over fences since last year, while Le Coudray, favoured at a startling 15-8 on account of his second to Best Mate in the Ericsson, was getting more credit than he deserved. At 5-1, Florida Pearl looked juicy, so I placed my bet in the ring, although not with Francis Hyland, whose intelligence scared me away.

Sometimes when I place a bet, I want to go back a few seconds later and plead with the bookie to cancel it and refund the money, as people do when they drop a letter into a mailbox and go through agonies of regret immediately afterward, wanting to stick an arm down the slot to retrieve it. But at other times I experience a profound sense of well-being, entirely regret-free, as if the result of the race were pre-ordained, and that was the feeling I had with the Hennessy. I never worried when Cloudy Bays grabbed the early lead because I was certain he'd fade, and he did at the fourth-last, yielding to Florida Pearl and Harbour Pilot, who were soon clear of the others with Richard Johnson tackling Paul Carberry, a Leopardstown veteran, who knew the track well and had an advantage.

That might have caused my certainty to disappear, but

it didn't. I remained steadfast, sure the fates would intervene on my behalf, so I hardly blinked when Harbour Pilot, who'd been jumping well, seemed to lose his bearings at the second last, smashed into the fence and deposited Carberry on the turf, leaving Florida Pearl alone in front. The race wasn't over yet, though, because the riderless Harbour Pilot, a free radical, veered wildly toward Florida Pearl at the last fence. For a few seconds, it looked as if the two would go down in a heap, but the Pearl scraped by and kept on to deny the fast-closing Le Coudray by three lengths.

Afterwards, Johnson suggested the loose horse was a help rather than a hindrance, forcing Florida Pearl to focus instead of dawdle as he often does with an easy lead. He and Willie Mullins were over the moon. 'I think I would have cried if he'd been caught on the run-in,' Willie said. Now Florida Pearl was back in business big-time and might even go to Cheltenham for another crack at the Gold Cup. I was quite happy myself as I pushed through the crowd and lined up to collect my money. My fifty euro bet had blossomed five-fold, so I stopped at the Jodami Bar again and rewarded myself with a glass of champagne.

Whatever J. P. McManus felt about another near-miss for Le Coudray, he must have been gratified by Baracouda's win at Sandown that same weekend. Carrying twenty-six pounds more than Yogi, the runner-up in the Tote Scoop 6 Handicap Hurdle, the great French stayer had walloped his opponents and looked invincible. McManus did have a problem on another front, however, one involving the 25.49% share of Manchester United he owned with his friend and business partner John Magnier. The club's most rabid fans had distributed a leaflet, Just Say Neigh, to a capacity crowd at Old Trafford on Saturday, urging everyone to do their best to disrupt the pair's racing interests. The leaflet was a gesture of support for Sir Alex Ferguson, who had taken on McManus and Magnier in a world-class wrestling match.

Rock Of Gibralter, a very special racehorse, was at the heart of the dispute. After a smashing season as a two-year-old in 2001, the colt was even better at three and had reeled off a string of five straight Group One wins on the flat that made his value at stud enormous, a perfect example of the programme for nurturing and developing stallions devised by Coolmore, the powerful group of Irish racehorse owners and breeders. Sir Alex was Rock Of Gibralter's half-owner, at least in theory, since Magnier had apparently given him a share in the horse as a gift, and he felt entitled to his piece of the cake. But Magnier reportedly contended that the gift did not include any stallion rights; those belonged to Coolmore alone. The absence of any paperwork added to the confusion, so Fergie had turned to the courts for resolution and filed a lawsuit.

Magnier and McManus, just as hard-nosed, had put the club and Ferguson under intense scrutiny, asking its directors to answer ninety-nine questions about United's finances, affairs, and transfer dealings. That was all too much for the United loyalists, whose leaflet supplied Coolmore's phone numbers and email addresses. What right did those Irishmen have to be mucking about in English sport? Some boyo had already tagged a wall at

Magnier's home in Fermoy, scrawling an obscenity in red letters four feet high. Worse still, the loyalists had staged a protest at Hereford during the races, marching onto the course with banners that read 'Quit the horseplay, Coolmore!' and 'United Not For Sale!', and delaying the action for a full twelve minutes.

Bad enough, you might say, but now the zanies known as United4Action were threatening to infiltrate the Cheltenham Festival on Gold Cup Day. Heresy! Sacrilege! The outrage of the jumps fraternity can scarcely be exaggerated. The threat beggared belief, but the group had to be taken seriously. They were buying up tickets as fast as they could and claimed to hold eighty-eight for the Tattersalls Enclosure. The group's dispatches to the media were also becoming more volatile and guerilla-like in their ardour. They spoke of 'cells' being activated on a mission to cause 'immense embarrassment' to McManus.

Somewhere in deepest, darkest Manchester, the spirit of Che Guevara must be alive and well, I thought, although desperately perverted. United4Action offered the Cheltenham officials a way out, of course, simply by allowing a peaceful demonstration on Gold Cup Day. If that smacked of blackmail, so be it. I felt for Edward Gillespie, who already had enough contingencies on his plate. In all the planning for the Festival, all the imagining of potential disasters – a pregnant woman going into labour, say, or a disgruntled punter throwing a punch at a bookie – nobody in his right mind would have considered the possibility of an attack by . . . football commandos!

*　　*　　*

When I set out to arrange a visit with Tom Costello, I was surprised how accommodating Tom Jr was on the phone. I hadn't anticipated such a friendly welcome because of all the talk about secrecy. After we worked out a few details regarding the best time to see his father, I packed a bag and drove through the farms of the Midlands, then around Lough Derg with its backdrop of bogs and mountains and along the Shannon River near Limerick, sensing with each passing mile that I was entering a part of Ireland where tourists are infrequent and the local traditions remain intact. It was tranquil, isolated, misty country, ideal for Costello's private way of doing business.

Horse country, too, it has always been. Not far from Newmarket-on-Fergus lies Turret Hill, across from Dromoland Castle. The turret dates from the 1740s, built so that Sir Edward O'Brien could watch his horses gallop. A stable block on his estate was inscribed with the motto 'In Equis Patrium Virrus', or 'Through horses a nation receives its strength'. Sir Edward liked to gamble on his horses, naturally, and fell into such financial jeopardy that his son, a Dublin attorney, hoped to curtail his spending. In a furious letter of reply, Sir Edward berated him and said, 'I neither play cards or dice, keep neither whores or hounds . . . and I should have been in my grave long since, choked with fat and eaten up with infirmities and disorders, had it not been for the exercise and amusement my horses afforded me.'

Tiny Newmarket-on-Fergus was drowsy, still asleep centuries after Sir Edward had departed from this earth. The only people about were some workmen hammering away in a gutted structure adjacent to The Hunters Lodge. I saw nowhere else in town to stay for the night, but the lodge's front door was locked, and the desk in the little lobby was vacant. Luckily, the owner was one of the workers, pitching in to renovate his restaurant, and he was happy to rent me a room, although he warned me I'd be his only guest. How could he be so sure? Strange, I thought. Even a bit creepy. Alone inside, I felt the musty staleness of a place long unoccupied and imagined Sir Edward's ghost afoot.

After bolting my door against the spirit world, I called Tom Jr to let him know I had arrived and to confirm my appointment. He had suggested I meet his father in the late afternoon, around five o'clock, but he gave me directions to his own home rather than to the famous Fenloe House I'd seen photos of in Henrietta Knight's book. That made me slightly uneasy because of Costello's reputation for being cold toward outsiders, particularly writers. 'No, I don't let the press in,' he once told Michael Clower of the *Post*, overlooking the fact that Clower *was* the press. 'I'm only a small farmer and lead a quiet life.'

Still, I'd been able to find out a fair bit about Costello in advance of the trip by consulting the public record. His story was again typical of the rural Irish. As a boy, he rode and raced ponies, a common pastime for a lad 'on the other side of Ennis'. In those days, every farmer had a mare he worked and mated to a local stallion, selling the foal for whatever price and glad for some extra income. Costello's father, a leading show jumper, dealt in half-breeds in large quantities, so horse-trading was in Tom's blood from early childhood.

As a young man during the war years, in the late 1940s when racing was banned in Ireland, he 'flapped' horses in the north, where lots of American soldiers were stationed and waiting for orders. With little else to spend their money on, the GIs gambled on anything – craps, poker, or the races. Often Costello left for Ulster in May and didn't return until August. The prize money was excellent up there, and though the racing did have handicappers, the scene was still very scrappy, with a horse running under one name this week and a new one the next, moving from town to town. Later, Costello held a proper trainer's licence. He had an excellent strike rate and even won the Irish Grand National with Tartan Ace in 1973. His ability to lay out a horse for a race and score a betting coup was almost unrivalled.

Yet he seems always to have been more involved in the speculative aspects of the game, in the buying-and-selling of stock. He has no interest in breeding horses because a breeder gets stuck with nature's lot. Instead, he appears to thrive on the liberty of swapping and the thrill of discovering a special foal or yearling, a most inexact science. It's said that he pays more attention to the look of a horse than to its pedigree, and that he owns about twelve hundred acres in Newmarket-on-Fergus, most of it on good limestone, where his 120 horses have plenty of room to roam.

In the late afternoon, I drove to Tom Jr's place, a big yellow house on a high hill, with a stable and a wonderful expanse of land around. Like his four brothers – John, Tony, Adrian, and Dermot – he has an operation similar to his father's, although on a smaller scale. His brothers were inclined toward the business since they were boys, he said, but he came to it more slowly, considering other things before he dived in. A clean-cut, soft spoken, gracious man in early middle age, he was a good amateur jockey despite being six foot tall and had even ridden a Cheltenham Festival winner, Over The Road, in the National Hunt Chase in 1988.

For a while, we stood outside the house and chatted in a light mist. I kept expecting Tom to direct me to Fenloe House, but it became clear as the minutes ticked by that I wouldn't be meeting the Old Lion as arranged. Tom was apologetic and offered a reasonable excuse. His father, now seventy-two, had been suffering from kidney problems, and after a period on dialysis, he had just undergone a transplant. He still conducted his business as usual, but he hadn't yet recovered fully from surgery, so his energy flagged at times, as it had that afternoon. I was disappointed after the long drive. Though Ted Walsh had mentioned Costello's health problems, I couldn't shake a feeling that the Old Lion was being true to form.

But Tom Jr was quite capable of serving as a stand-in. He works closely with his dad and is well versed in every aspect of the trade. It isn't as ragged as Walsh had portrayed it, not any more. When I brought up the story about paying suspicious farmers with cash from a satchel, Tom smiled. 'They'd ask to have the money wired to their bank now,' he said. But the Old Lion does still feed the rumour mill, so there's always a buzz before he runs a solid prospect in a point-to-point. He's also adept at playing down the merits of a horse someone wants, thereby increasing their determination to buy it and the price. Ancient tricks, I thought, that any trader in a Cairo bazaar or San Francisco flea market would recognize.

Tom Jr outlined the rigorous Costello programme for me. His father buys up to thirty foals and a few yearlings annually in private deals with farmers and at the sales, he said, and they are transformed into racehorses as quickly as possible, before they become set in their ways. The males are gelded when their testicles are still small and their sexuality is undeveloped. As two-year-olds, the colts and fillies are broken and learn to jump over low poles without a rider on their back. They do this in a big indoor arena that resembles a circus tent, completing twenty rounds and forty jumps on an ordinary day. The routine makes jumping fun and also second-nature to them, while it burns off their fat and creates muscle.

In the spring, as three-year-olds, the horses are very quietly ridden, cantering for six to eight weeks. Costello has a set of fences, three all-weather gallops, and grass gallops everywhere, each presenting a different option for the trainers, ordinarily his sons. At four, the graduates of the programme are ready to be shown off and sold unless they're lemons. The point-to-point season around Clare divides in two, Tom told me, with a short autumn season from October to November and a longer one from January until June. The British trainers who are repeat customers (Paul Nicholls, Martin Pipe, Robert Alner, and Henrietta Knight, to name a few) pay closer attention to the second season because the form book says more winners come out of it.

'There's plenty of trust in this business,' Tom continued, 'so we like to work with people who've bought from us before.' The Costellos cherish and protect their valuable name, and are proud that it stands for quality. Turnover matters to them, too, so they never hang onto a horse for long, regardless of how tempting it might be. As Tom put it, 'If there's a good one here, he's for sale.'

Scouting for foals is a part of the business Tom enjoys, a kind of talent search. It's a gambler's game, because he's always at risk. There are no guarantees, so even a shrewd buyer can get stung. 'Gambling runs deep in the Irish,' he laughed. 'I have a feeling we might die without a bet, even when we're losing.'

It's true, he confirmed, that his father has a gift for spotting a racehorse, one that Tom tries to copy. He couldn't describe the process exactly, as if putting it into words would rob it of its mystery, but when he studies a foal he might take in twenty different aspects of its being, although not consciously. He'll check the foal's conformation, say, and how it moves, and whether it has a bold outlook. It's as if the Costellos enter a meditative state, almost like a trance, that encourages the exchange of information between species, an act of surrender any poet courting the muse would understand.

Knowing Tom Jr's history with Best Mate, I asked the obvious question.

'Will he win the Gold Cup again?'

'He should. Cheltenham brings out the best in him. It's a unique course with those big fences. It lends itself to a good gallop, so jumping is very important, and Best Mate has always been a beautiful jumper. You pay for every mistake, though. A horse has to put in a flawless round to win.'

In the gathering dusk, Tom walked me to the stables and introduced me to Bannow Strand, the current talk of Ireland, who was supposed to be as good as, if not better, than Best Mate at the same stage. Adrian Costello had trained the horse, a creature of myth at seventeen-plus hands high, so broad and solid he looked able to carry twelve stone easily, along with three or four jockeys. Everything about him spoke of strength, superiority, and dominion. He is from the first crop of four-year-olds by Luso, and after he trounced a maiden field of point-to-pointers at Tallow, registering the day's fastest time and earning an unprecedented rating of 94, he was the subject of some intense transatlantic bidding before being sold to David Johnson for an undisclosed price, of course.

'He'll go to Martin Pipe in the spring,' Tom said, rubbing Bannow Strand's forehead. If I'd come to Newmarket-on-Fergus for a glimpse of the future, I had a strong sensation I was staring right at it.

Damp from the mist, we warmed ourselves in Tom's kitchen. When I took my tea black, he teased me. 'Jockey's drink,' he said, a reference to the calories I'd avoided by refusing the milk and sugar. He was such an engaging, helpful man, and yet I still felt I'd only seen the very tip of the operation, but that was OK. I had decided the Old Lion's secrets probably weren't that secret, after all. I knew by now how the Irish treat their horses, with love and respect, and I figured those qualities were just exaggerated in Tom Costello. There is a poetic side to buying a foal, an ability to make an imaginative leap that even those who've never read a line of Yeats or Kavanagh would recognize, and Costello obviously has it to an extraordinary degree.

When you couple that with a caring, attentive environment, the chances are good that the foal will develop into
the best possible version of itself.

On Valentine's Day, I stopped at our neighbourhood
Paddy Power shop to enter the draw for that free
trip to Paris. It failed to fall my way, but I didn't dare
object since Imelda and I had been to Paris not long after
we'd met, holed up in a borrowed flat in the Marais and
rarely leaving it, except to dart across the street to a row
of shops for more provisions, stocking up on cheese,
bread, sausage, and wine. On those sweet spring nights,
with our picnic (a dry and successful one, as opposed to
Fairwood) spread out on the sheets, we talked for hours,
listened to music, swapped histories, and had no need for
any world beyond our own.

One evening, we did finally rouse ourselves from bed.
Feeling guilty about not exploring the city, we ventured
out for dinner, only to be caught in a massive downpour,
so we stopped at the first bistro we passed. Through a
steamy window, it looked to be a perfect spot for lovers,
small and intimately lit with candles, but once we were
inside it was as if we'd stumbled into an inn somewhere
in the Black Forest. A wrinkled old woman with the air
of an abused servant directed us to a plank table, order-
ing us to share it with a slovenly man into his second (or
maybe third) bottle of Côte du Rhone, who held the last
of his steak in his hands. He was chewing the meat off the
bone, while he picked at the *pommes de frites* scattered

around his plate. His napkin was stuffed into the neck of his shirt. Once white, it now suggested an improvised work of Abstract Expressionism.

At our approach, he gave us a wave and mumbled a few words, possibly a greeting but more likely a curse. We sat down and took in the décor. It consisted of crayon drawings tacked to the walls, surely the work of someone's grandchildren. Toward the rear of the room was the *pièce de resistance*, a big brick oven where the proprietor (and probably the grandfather), daringly dressed in a lime-green shirt open almost to his navel, cooked meat over a blazing wood fire. Resting on a butcher's block by his side was a haunch of raw beef, and he carved it up as necessary when the orders came in, slicing it off the bone. The scraps of fat and gristle he tossed on the floor, where the dogs – there would be dogs – made a meal of them.

We had a marvellous time, of course, and sensibly drank only one bottle of wine. In the morning, Imelda had to return to Dublin, so she caught her Ryanair bus to the airport at the James Joyce Pub, where copies of Joyce's books, not even first editions, were kept in a locked case to prevent anyone from reading them, an irony that would have had the author in stitches. All at once I was alone and bereft, facing a few more days in Paris on my own before I flew home to California on the ticket I'd bought at the start of my trip, and the city, in an instant, lost its appeal.

I turned to the horses for solace. I rode a taxi to the Bois du Bologne for a card of flat races at Longchamp, and though I won three of my first four bets, relying on such well-known names as André Fabre to guide me, I was still glum and unable to concentrate on anything but Imelda. Now I was just another lonely American guy, pitiful somehow, who had become an item of gossip at the patisserie where the young woman behind the counter used to give me a friendly wink. The clerk at the wine shop, formerly chatty, also regarded me with suspicion, as if I were drinking too much of his product, and that was true. As I lounged around the flat with the lights out, I listened to 'our' music and poured glass after glass of red wine, every inch the broken-hearted romantic.

I flew home as intended, but I only stayed two weeks. Instead, I dropped by my storage locker, where the artifacts of my life are still filed – fifty cartons of books, 500 LPs on vinyl, a nearly complete set of Topps 1952 baseball cards, and some truly awful furniture and kitchenware I couldn't imagine unpacking if I ever did settle in California again – grabbed a few essentials, and bought a one-way ticket to Dublin. I had no idea what to expect and trusted only the depth of my feelings, believing that even if I fell flat on my face, it would be a harmless embarrassment no worse than any other I'd visited on myself and others. It was a gambler's play, and I got lucky. Such were my thoughts on Valentine's Day.

On Sunday evening at O'Herlihy's, T.P. Reilly and I conducted our regular review of the weekend's racing. The action in England had been instructive, we agreed. At Newbury, Azertyuiop sparkled once again in in another big chase, while Geos saved the on-course bookies an estimated two-hundred-and fifty thousand pounds by beating the hapless Rooster Booster in the Tote Gold Trophy Hurdle. Iris's Gift, though only second in the Pertemps Handicap Hurdle at Haydock, had conceded twenty-five pounds to the victor Tardar and looked a real prospect for the Stayers' Hurdle at the Festival, particularly since this was his first outing of the season.

The races at Gowran Park, by contrast, had limited appeal. We found it hard to get excited about the stalwart Rathgar Beau's win in the Red Mills Chase, although Georges Girl went onto the Festival shortlist after taking the Red Mills Trial Hurdle. Solerina failed to run in the Boyne Hurdle at Navan, because she'd contracted the same flu that had afflicted so many horses at Christmas. That was a shame, since the Boyne was to be her first attempt at three miles and a potential guide to how she might fare against Baracouda and Iris's Gift at Cheltenham.

There was so little action during the next week I didn't even go into a betting shop. The owners and trainers in Ireland were treating their best horses like prima donnas, worried about every sniffle and false step, while also trying to stay ahead of the handicapper. With the Festival so close, no one would take an unnecessary chance. As if to demonstrate that fact, Brave Inca was withdrawn from a race at Naas simply because Colm Murphy didn't like the way the horse was working.

On the other hand, Beef Or Salmon was working well, if you listened to Michael Hourigan, having had a race-track canter at Thurles. Beef Or Salmon would be schooled over fences to restore his confidence, Hourigan said, but his horse was still on target for the Gold Cup. The big news, though, was Martin Pipe's Our Vic, another Tom Costello discovery, who had streaked home in the Reynoldstown Novices' Chase at Ascot. 'He is a serious horse and a class above the rest in the Royal & SunAlliance Chase,' the Old Lion predicted, a sage assessment I committed to memory.

For Barry Geraghty, last year's Miracle Man, the approach of the Festival meant even more stress than usual. He had to hustle at double-time to meet the demands of all those who wanted his services, squeezing the sap out of every minute, so when I pulled up at his family's farm near Batterstown, in Meath, to talk about his riding arrangements for Cheltenham, it came as no surprise that he was out doing an errand in his jeep. The farm had belonged to his grandfather, and he lives there now with his parents and siblings, who still work the land with Barry helping out when he can, which isn't very often.

His mother Bea answered my knock and chased away a barking dog. She showed me into a bright living room where Barry's younger sisters, just home from school, sat by the fire watching a teenage sitcom on TV. 'You can talk to those two while you're waiting,' Bea joked. That didn't seem like a bad idea, really. I thought the girls might have an interesting opinion or two about their brother, but I waited for the sitcom to be over and the credits to roll before I said a word, thereby avoiding a colossal adult error.

'Barry's doing well, isn't he?' I asked Holly, breaking the ice. Holly is fourteen and was still in her maroon school uniform.

'He's flying!' she replied, her voice soaring. She'd been at Leopardstown for the Hennessy and approved of the way Barry won on Pizarro. 'I wish he could have got a little more out of Le Coudray,' she said, with good reason.

Somehow the talk drifted to Macs Joy, a horse of Jessie Harrington's, who had lost a sizeable purse in the Matthews Carpets Handicap Hurdle that day after being disqualified for interfering with Timmy Murphy on Kilbeggan Lad. And who should Macs Joy's jockey be? None other than the unfortunate Andrew Leigh, who was suspended for careless riding. Did Andrew deserve it? Holly shook her head. She didn't think so. Neither did Jessie, who'd lodged an appeal.

Then Barry swept in, his car keys in hand. He has a restlessness about him, the sort of person who taps a foot on the floor and can't sit still. When I relayed Holly's praise to him, he grinned and said, 'Well, they're not always so nice. They criticize me, too.' For some privacy, we moved to a dining room down the hall, where a few of Barry's trophies were stacked up. There were trophies all around the house, crystal bowls from Waterford and sterling silver cups, enough to stock a small museum.

The Macs Joy incident was on my mind, so I asked Barry's opinion. 'Well, you know how it is with the stewards,' he said. 'Andrew's never been to court before, has he?' Timmy Murphy, a canny old pro, had done a much better job of pleading his case, he implied.

Bea brought me some coffee and wondered if her son wanted a Coke, but he declined. 'I might eat something later,' he told her, a sentence he must have uttered a thousand times by now. The calories had him at their mercy. He used to be able to shed eight or ten pounds in a day without any fuss, he said, but the best he can currently do is six pounds, and that with some effort. As he talked, I noticed a world-weary quality in his eyes, even a hint of sadness, as if he'd seen too much too soon, but then the weariness would vanish in a second, and he looked engaged and enthusiastic again. There was a curious duality about Geraghty, I thought, recalling Michael Hourigan's formula for what a jockey needs – an old head on a young body. That seemed to sum up Barry's personality. His favourite movie is *Pulp Fiction*, for instance, but his favourite singer is Robbie Williams.

He left school at fifteen and began riding shortly after. Too tall and heavy for the flat, he signed on with Noel Meade as a conditional jockey and had his first winner in January 1997, making such steady progress through the season he had sixteen wins by the end of May. There was nothing magical about that, he felt. He put it down to hard, hard work. He rode out in miserable weather, mastered the game's political intrigues, and learned how to keep his trainers happy, so he was mildly offended whenever someone suggested he's an 'overnight success' because of his five winners at the Festival. Yet he did allow that he'd been very lucky over the past couple of years. He has a strong constitution and hasn't been seriously hurt for a while, although that hasn't always been the case.

'I once broke my back twice in twelve months,' he said with a smirk, as if in the presence of the blackly comic. He had to wear a full body cast for ten weeks the first time and twelve the second, and it would have been much hairier if the surgeon, who'd previously patched up a knee for him, hadn't designed the cast with a zipper so he could shower. He never really believes it when he is injured and once rode out with crushed vertebrae, denying the pain, and if something does feel wrong after a fall, he tells himself it's nothing, that he'll be over it in the morning. He doesn't dwell on his accidents, nor does he like to think about getting older. 'I'll always be the kid,' he said, but he knew better.

When the Hennessy came up in our conversation, I carried on about how much fun it was to see old Florida Pearl shine again, forgetting that Barry was on Le Coudray. His affable manner changed in a flash as he reacted to the slight, his eyes cold now, and I saw the steely resolve that separates a great jockey from an average one.

'You want to win them all, don't you?' I asked.

'Yeah, I do,' he admitted, but he was aware that skill and hard work alone weren't enough to do the trick. 'You know that book Richard Pitman wrote? *Good Horses Make Good Jockeys*. That's the truth. If you don't have the horse beneath you, it doesn't matter how good you are. You have to be lucky.'

Barry seemed obsessed with luck. He'd used the word a number of times, and when I pointed it out to him, he insisted, 'But so much of it is luck,' and cited Kicking

King's loss to Central House at Leopardstown at Christmas as an example. 'A sixty-five grand race, right?' he asked, still sounding a bit wounded. 'Tom Taaffe had Kicking King at the top of his game, better on the day than when he won last time out, and he just clipped a fence and fell – not even a bad mistake, just a novicey one! Ah, well, there'd be no *craic* if things were going right the whole time,' he reminded himself.

'Do you enjoy riding in England?'

'I love it,' he said eagerly. 'There's such a buzz! I grew up watching Ascot and Cheltenham on TV. Here in Ireland it's more of a family affair, more traditional.'

Speaking of luck, Geraghty hoped it would come his way again at the Festival. Last year, he had picked up some key mounts unexpectedly. He was only booked on Inching Closer in the Pertemps Final Hurdle at the start of the week, and his ride on Spectroscope in the JCB Triumph Hurdle fell into his lap at about the same time, although he'd won on the horse for Jonjo O'Neill before. At present, his agent had four solid rides lined up in Kicking King, Pizarro, Back In Front, and Moscow Flyer.

'Moscow's the ace in my pack,' he revealed, and that was music to my ears. Maybe I should forget about The Pattern, I thought, and quit being such a superstitious throwback. 'He's the best I've ever ridden.' But Geraghty was also high on Pizarro's chances after the horse's run in the Moriarty. The pace and distance of the race didn't suit Pizarro, he said, nor did his stamina come into play as it would at Cheltenham over three miles. 'It's very tight there,' he explained, 'and so competitive it's hard to get a pure run. The uphill finish is very tough. If you stand there and look at it, you wouldn't want to walk up it. It's an honest test.'

'What about Back In Front?'

'The vibes are good. He's had the heart problem before.'

A jockey has to be sensitive, talented, and ingratiating to be the primary rider for three top-flight trainers such as Harrington, O'Grady, and Taaffe, performing a balancing act as he chooses among their horses without causing offence, and Geraghty brings it off admirably. Though he's mature beyond his years, he showed his boyish side again when he alluded to a pub in Kells where he is a part-owner. We were considering a trip to it for a drink, but it was getting late.

'Maybe you could put a photo of the pub in your book?' he asked. I doubted I could do that, I told him, but I did promise to mention The Arches Bar, soon to have a nightclub, where Barry can sometimes be found pulling pints on a Saturday night.

In spite of Geraghty's positive read-out, the vibes on Back In Front were not so good, alas. The horse wouldn't be going to Cheltenham. After the episode with his heart, he turned up lame in his near foreleg. Vets, physios, chiropractitioners, and even a farrier had examined him, all to no avail. Edward O'Grady described himself as 'hugely disappointed', as he had every right to be. He might have seventeen Festival winners, but he'd never won the Gold Cup or the Champion Hurdle, Back In Front's intended race. With all the ups-and-downs O'Grady had endured lately, you'd need somebody other than Pierce Brosnan to play him in a movie, I thought. You'd have to cast an actor with a dazed, shell-shocked look, someone like Christopher Walken.

Snow was on the Wicklow Mountains when I drove to Moone for a last visit to Jessie Harrington's yard before the Festival. I could feel the tension in the air and almost hear a whispered prayer that trouble would stay outside the door. Jessie had already lost Imazulutoo and would probably lose Spirit Leader, as well, who didn't have her ordinary sparkle and was only ninety percent right. That reduced her Cheltenham squad to Moscow Flyer, Colca Canyon for the Arkle, and Macs Joy and Green Belt Flyer for the County Hurdle.

Horses were on the move as usual, a second lot headed for the gallops. Down below in an open field, where four sturdy birch fences were set up, Jessie and Eamonn, both on horseback, were supervising a schooling session. As I watched, a pair of horses approached the first fence at a fair clip. I suppose I was unprepared for an accident because this was just for practice, but one horse clobbered the fence and unseated his jockey, poor Andrew Leigh, who left the saddle upside-down, a foot caught in a stirrup. The horse shook him off after dragging him along for a few yards, and he hit the ground with a thump, smashing his left wrist against it.

I had seen dozens of falls by now, but they still terrified me. Andrew appeared to be OK, grinning as he brushed the grass and dirt from his clothes. It was a sheepish grin, to be sure, but he carried it off with grace and pretended his wrist, purple and swollen, belonged to another person. After Eamonn conducted an inspection, he sent the lad to Jessie's house to pack the wrist in ice prior to a trip to Naas for a hospital X-ray. Meanwhile, riders were chasing the loose horse around the yard, joined by a bunch of grooms on foot. It looked like a round-up in Texas.

Eamonn isn't the sort of man to sigh in public, but I guessed he must be sighing inwardly, as parents do. When the schooling session was over, I walked up to the house with him to see how Andrew was doing. Two men I'd never met before were hanging around the kitchen. They were shy and tentative, as if they'd arrived by chance and were waiting for instructions on what to do next. Pat Abbey and Brian Willis turned out to be part-owners of a horse, and they were new to the role and still wet behind the ears, members of a twenty-person syndicate. The members were all employed at a pharmaceuticals company in Kildare. Their horse, La Dearg (meaning Red Dawn), was a four-year-old gelding, as yet unraced.

'We inteviewed other trainers, but Mrs Harrington is one of the best,' Abbey said, in his sober way. He was the more talkative owner, and the one most infected with racing fever. He'd even had a fling at being a jockey, but he quit to accept a job at a 'meat factory', as he called it, and later switched to pharmaceuticals. Willis kept quiet and looked a bit puzzled, as people do when they decide to try something unique and different, and can't tell whether they like it yet. But he was definitely a fan and had been at Leopardstown when the stewards screwed

Andrew Leigh over his ride on Macs Joy – or such was the spin he and Abbey put on the incident.

'Andrew wasn't cheeky enough in the stewards' room,' Eamonn told them, reiterating what Geraghty had said. 'He needs to fight his corner.'

'It's your man Timmy Murphy,' Abbey said. 'He's been around for years. How could you trust him? He'd tell the stewards what they want to hear.'

Just then, Andrew walked in, still looking sheepish. He had a wet towel wrapped around his bum wrist, the ice having melted, and a slash of blood across the bridge of his nose. I figured he must be upset and maybe a little embarrassed, so I tried to cheer him up by saying he was having a pretty good season for a seven-pound claimer.

'A pretty good season?' he asked, laughing. 'At times!' The memory of all the tumbles and suspensions was still vivid, but he had no intention of giving up and said he'd be riding at Limerick later that week for Gerald Cully. It's a cliché to say that racing is about dreams, but I did feel surrounded by dreamers in the kitchen, each with his own vision of transcendence.

We all snapped to attention when Jessie entered, like schoolboys caught fooling around by the teacher. The new owners were desperate for a word about their horse, any word, but Jessie didn't know enough about La Dearg yet to advise them. Instead, she suggested we go up to the gallops for a look at him. He was in the morning's third lot. While the horses circled in a sand ring as a warm-up, Abbey grabbed a spot by the fence and Willis fetched his infant son, Gary, snuggled in cute winter clothing, from a car seat. Babysitting was probably the price he had to pay for investing in a horse, I guessed, such forfeits being common in most marriages.

Abbey and Willis were chomping at the bit, frustrated as they tried to pick out La Dearg from the crowd. 'Is that him?' Abbey asked, pointing. 'I think that's him.'

'They all look the same,' Willis protested. He had his hands full with Gary, who was wriggling like a bug. 'At least four or five of them do.'

The rider on La Dearg caught onto their plight and signalled to them. 'He's a nice one!' she shouted, patting a robust chestnut with a white blaze. The owners waved at her appreciatively. They were beaming. There he was, their horse!

The horses left the sand ring for the gallops, where Jessie waited. She was on horseback again and had the look of a general posing for an equestrian statue. She was riding Moscow Court that morning, a hurdler with two wins and four places to his name. 'He'll make a grand chaser next year,' she told us. She noticed Gary for the first time and smiled. 'How old is the little fella?'

'Nine months,' his dad said, chucking him under the chin.

'I became a grandmother for the second time nine days ago,' Jessie said, turning her horse to join the rest.

I didn't stay for La Dearg's debut. I went over to Moscow Flyer's paddock instead, where he stood very still, watching the traffic. He would have one last racetrack gallop to sharpen him, then it was off to Cheltenham. What was going on in that rarified head of his? Maybe Tom Costello would know, but I didn't. I tried to communicate with him, anyway, asking if I should forget about The Pattern and back him in the Queen Mother Chase, and I think his reply was, 'It's up to you.' After that, I was left to ponder all the dreams afloat in the world, my own included, wondering if some day in the distant future Gary Willis would sit down with some friends over a pint at Punchestown, or even Thurles, and remember the time Jessie Harrington had smiled down on him from a very great height on a cold winter day.

Andrew Leigh didn't fare well at Limerick. His horse, Batang, an import from Germany, was a 10-1 outsider in a two-mile maiden hurdle. Early in the race, at the crest of a hill, Batang began to gurgle, so Andrew eased up on him. That was the right thing to do, but when the horse seemed to recover a few seconds later, Andrew went back to work on him and drove him to a decent sixth-place finish behind Rabble Run, who was ridden by his old nemesis, Timmy Murphy. Would Murphy always pop into the picture whenever a problem arose? The notion might well have crossed young Andrew's mind.

Batang's stop-and-go performance led to an inquiry. Gerald Cully told the stewards his horse did gurgle on soft ground and that Leigh could have been closer to the pace halfway through, but otherwise he was satisfied with the ride. Yet when the Turf Club vet examined Batang, he couldn't find anything wrong, so the stewards judged the trainer and jockey to be in violation of Rule 212 which states that 'every horse shall run on its merits, and the rider shall take all reasonable measures to ensure his mount is given every opportunity.' Cully was fined 800 euros, Batang was banned from racing for forty-two days, and Andrew received a ten-day suspension, one more bump on the rocky road to Experience.

On the last day of the month, a Sunday, there was a grand show after the races at Leopardstown. Standing by the rail at twilight, I watched nearly fifty horses bound for Cheltenham being put through their paces. As befuddled as Pat Abbey and Brian Willis, I couldn't identify any of them except for Mouse Morris's ghostly Rostropovich, all white from head-to-toe. The track didn't provide a commentary, but I gathered that Florida Pearl was out there somewhere, as were Solerina, Hardy Eustace, Golden Cross, Hasanpour, and Sadlers Wings.

Willie Mullins had about fifteen horses on the course, many of them prospects for the Champion Bumper. Rule Supreme, still an iffy jumper, was being schooled over fences for the Royal & SunAlliance Chase, and again he crashed into one and banished Ruby Walsh from the saddle. Timmy Murphy, David Casey, Jim Culloty, and all the other jockeys on the course were focused single-mindedly on the Festival now, and some were sampling horses and trying out rides before they reached a final decision. Cheltenham was gradually taking over the available space in everybody's brain.

My own Festival plans were fixed at last. From a travel agent in Kildare, I had ordered a brochure about Cheltenham package tours. The hotels in town were already full, and frighteningly expensive, so I was left to choose between two inns in Stratford-upon-Avon, about twenty-eight miles from the course, and the Twigworth Hotel, advertised as 'popular with our clients' and also under new management, not necessarily a recommendation in my view. But beggars can't be choosers, so despite my affection for the Bard and Stratford's literary cachet, I settled on the Twigworth at a cost of about eight hundred euros for three nights, including dinners and airfare. My tickets to the Festival were extra, so I was down more than a grand before I ever set foot on the Promised Land.

March: Festival

So my long winter's education was coming to an end. The many miles I'd clocked around Ireland amounted to a diploma of sorts and qualified me as a graduate of the jumps academy, hardly an expert but still entitled to attend the Festival and offer an opinion. I had paid my dues, as they say, cold and wet for days at a time, had won and lost money – I was ahead by the paltry sum of 209 euros – and had drunk pints in pubs both quaint and unruly, and that, I believed, stood as my own peculiar badge of honour, on a par with Andrew Leigh's bruised wrist and blood-stained nose.

With a week to go, the Irish were preparing for their annual migration, more than five thousand strong. Their march to Cheltenham had started in earnest after World War II, the catalyst being Vincent O'Brien, arguably the finest trainer of racehorses ever, whose assault on the English and their big prizes enlisted an army of followers. In those lean times of post-war shortages in England, O'Brien's countrymen did not depart for the Festival empty-handed. They packed a full Irish breakfast, bringing

235

bacon rashers, eggs, and puddings both black and white, as well as bottles of Jameson and Powers and even jugs of bootleg poteen to fortify themselves and any relatives stuck with jobs in London.

Even before I opened a biography of O'Brien, I could have guessed at the story of his childhood, so familiar were its elements. Born in Churchtown in 1917, Vincent learned to ride as a boy, and later schooled point-to-pointers and hunted with the Dashing Duhallows, Ireland's oldest hunt club. He had no interest in formal education and dropped out at fifteen to join Fred Clarke's training centre at Leopardstown. His father, Dan, held a permit to train his own horses, loved a game of cards, and mistrusted ginger-haired women as a source of bad luck. Vincent was his amateur jockey and served as his assistant, taking over the yard when Dan died in 1943.

O'Brien operated on a shoestring back then. The prize money in Ireland was still ridiculously low, so most trainers supplemented their income, or tried to, by gambling. In contrast, the Cheltenham Festival featured purses worth a relative fortune, and the stakes in the betting ring were quite high since England was awash in black market currency after the war, and a bookmaker's cheque was one way to launder it. Those incentives weren't lost on O'Brien, who had the advantage of being anonymous and secluded in the Irish countryside, where his privacy could be guaranteed. Beyond the scope of rumours, and far from prying eyes, he set in motion a plan to sting the bookies with ante-post wagers on his little-known horses, the only way to survive.

He conducted his first Cheltenham foray in 1948 with

Cottage Rake, who was delivered to him three years earlier as a six-year-old. O'Brien was always patient with his stock, never hurrying the horses along. Cottage Rake jumped well, and had some class in his pedigree and enough speed to have won good races on the flat, and that helped him beat Happy Home in the Gold Cup – an astonishing triumph for a young Irish trainer on his initial trip to the Festival, and a huge gamble landed to the bargain. Barrels of stout lined the streets of Churchtown on O'Brien's return, fuel for an all-night party where the bonfires blazed. He was also celebrated in Dublin with a special banquet at Jammet's, whose chef created such inspired dishes as Le Potage Vincent and Les Poussins à la Rake as a mark of respect.

The next year, as an experiment, O'Brien sent his horses to the Festival by plane. Trainers usually relied on the ferry, as they do today, although the route went from Rosslare to Fishguard in those days. For the three-hour flight from Shannon to Bristol, O'Brien requisitioned a converted bomber for Castledermot, Hatton's Grace, and Cottage Rake, who was a feisty traveller even overland and kept his handlers occupied for the whole trip by almost collapsing. However ill-at-ease while in transit, the Rake won the Gold Cup again, and once more in 1950, while Castledermot triumphed in the National Hunt Chase, but it was Hatton's Grace, a horse with a big heart, who provided the major surprise.

Small and furry, with a pronounced dislike for cold weather, Hatton's Grace had bounced from yard to yard until O'Brien accepted him as an eight-year-old in '48 – too old, really, for a Festival bid over hurdles, according to received wisdom. In fact, the horse had run at Cheltenham that spring and hadn't even been placed, another strike against him. As patient as ever, O'Brien coaxed Hatton's Grace out of the doldrums and entered him in the Champion Hurdle, which Hatton's Grace won at a starting price of 100-7. Yet his trainer had the foresight to back him heavily at ante-post odds of 33-1, 25-1, and 20-1, so he made another killing.

Twice more Hatton's Grace would win the Champion Hurdle, while Knock Hard added another Gold Cup to O'Brien's collection in 1953. Through the decade that ended in 1959, O'Brien had twenty-three Festival winners, a record without parallel, and he tossed in three Grand Nationals for good measure. Perhaps it was inevitable that he would transfer his talent to the more lucrative field of flat racing, where he again set benchmarks rarely equalled, winning six Epsom Derbys, five Sussex Stakes and July Cups, four 2000 Guineas, three St Legers, and so on, with such great horses as Nijinsky, Roberto, and The Minstrel. Ultimately, he moved from Cork to Tipperary, where he still lives on the Ballydoyle compound, well into his eighty-seventh year.

Others helped to forge a link between the Irish and Cheltenham, of course, with Tom Dreaper and Arkle being vitally important, although Dreaper's run of successes actually began with Prince Regent, who won the Gold Cup in 1946. Dreaper tallied twenty-six Festival winners in all, a total yet to be matched, but it was the flair and bravado of Vincent O'Brien that captured Ireland's attention, invoked its sense of pride, and demonstrated a home truth that might have been written into the constitution – the Irish will travel many a mile to watch one of their own defeat the English.

The casualty list for the Festival continued to grow, with Florida Pearl forced to join the ranks of the fallen. He was observed walking oddly around Willie Mullins' yard, and after a veterinary exam he was found to have an injured ligament. It wasn't serious, but the only cure was rest. I spoke with Grainne Ni Chaba, who had checked on her former patient with Tracey Gilmour, and she told me Florida Pearl was in good form despite the problem. 'He doesn't know he's hurt,' Grainne said, meaning that he wasn't in any pain, but she hoped his owners would retire him before he came to a terrible end as Dorans Pride had done.

As for Best Mate, he'd yet to hit a snag. He kept sailing along in Wantage, but the anxiety was taking a toll on Henrietta Knight. An intruder had stumbled into her yard around Christmas, probably just a drunk sleeping it off in a vacant box, yet the incident was scary enough for her to hire some security. Her superstitions were also reeling out-of-control. To placate any malign forces, she'd ordered a load of hay, not straw, for delivery on Gold Cup day, and she had already put bets on all Matey's rivals. Long into the night, she sat up writing replies to her star's fan mail and irritating her husband, who wished she'd give it a rest and get to bed.

Meanwhile, organizations all over Ireland were holding Cheltenham preview evenings where, for the price of a ticket, punters could hear trainers, jockeys, and tipsters of varying stripes and worth expound on the Festival. I boycotted those in Dublin because I had no use for inside information any more, particularly when it was bandied about in public and hence devalued at source. Instead, I met Noel O'Brien, the country's senior National Hunt handicapper, for lunch at the Stand House Hotel to see if I could learn anything of value. He is no relation to Vincent O'Brien and was such an indifferent rider as a boy in rural Kildare, in fact, that he never shared the common dream of becoming a pro.

'Talking is not a problem with me,' O'Brien said when he breezed in. He has the elfin, red-haired look naive tourists expect to encounter when they visit the Emerald Isle, and he does leap into a conversation with both feet. Spirited and witty, he told me he'd always loved racing and could remember when Kildare kids were let out of school every April to attend the Punchestown Festival. He was so enthralled by the races he invented a game to simulate the National Hunt, cutting out paper horses and having them 'jump' over obstacles, like his shoes. Some horses were better than others, naturally, so Noel handicapped them by using a staggered start, an early indicator of his future career.

Even before he finished his leaving exams, O'Brien had a job lined up in the accounts department at the Turf Club. Only seventeen, he was star struck at first, in awe of the famous people he met. Four years later, he applied for a job as an assistant National Hunt handicapper, although not with any confidence because he was so young. 'I was still riding my bike to the office, and the other applicants showed up in cars,' he said. 'One was driving a Mercedes!' During his interview, he developed a case of stage fright and could only speak in monosyllables. He thought he was sunk but got lucky – luck again! – when a board member asked what he knew about Adirondack, a horse of Dermot Weld's. Strictly by chance, he knew everything about Adirondack from his private studies and recited it chapter-and-verse, and that led the board to take him seriously.

As much as he coveted the job, it had a single drawback. He wouldn't be allowed to gamble any more because it was against Turf Club rules – not that he was a major plunger, but he still felt deprived. Inside he was going, 'Oh, God, this is going to be awful!', and he gripped his head between his hands and made an agonized face to show me the extent of his suffering. He was relieved when he discovered his work could generate the same buzz as betting, since it involved the same element of comparison. Tutored by Captain Louis Magee, his boss, an army man who was strict but fair, he was taught to handicap a horse on its best form – on who it beats, not who beats it – but soon realized the job was wholly subjective.

'Logic goes out the window,' he said in a chipper way, as if the absence of logic were fun. 'Too many anomalies. It's always a judgement call, regardless of the data.'

For Noel, the bottom line is to try and make each handicap as evenly balanced as possible. He does his analysis at home, where he has a massive bank of statistics on computer, and he also relies on the Turf Club's file of videos. In theory, a 20-1 long shot should have the same chance of winning as a 2-1 favourite, but when a 2-1 favourite comes home by ten lengths, Noel has to scratch his head and wonder what went wrong. In any case, the result often displeases more people than it pleases, and O'Brien swears he's always unpopular in one quarter or another for piling on too much or too little weight. Regardless of that, he feels the top-level Irish races are more competitive than ever for reasons I'd heard before – increased prize money, good horses staying in Ireland rather than being sold abroad, and fine jockeys riding them.

'Ruby Walsh, Barry Geraghty, and Paul Carberry, it's almost a Golden Age,' Noel said, impressed with the array of talent.

Gradually, I nudged the conversation toward Cheltenham. Did O'Brien have any special favourites among the Irish runners? Yes, he did. His two top choices were Sadlers Wings and Kicking King. I wrote the names down, but the pen trembled in my hand when he said next, 'I doubt Moscow Flyer is a sure thing.' Could he be referring to The Pattern? No, he just believed Azertyuiop was honestly to be feared, a noble adversary with every chance to steal Moscow's crown. That wasn't what I hoped for, so I was glad when his comments became more general. He praised the Queen Mother Chase as the most exciting race on the card, the best test of speed and stamina, and reminded me, too, that anything could happen at the Festival.

'It's often an unfancied horse who wins,' Noel said. Some horses stumble under the pressure, while others, touched by the heroic, rise to previously unimagined heights.

My lunch with O'Brien failed to have the desired effect. Among the coterie of so-called authorities plying their trade, he was a real one, someone who earned a living by being informed, and though I was still ahead for the season, I worried that I might not be up to the task at Cheltenham. Insofar as I had a method, it was to drink my mystical pint, cross out inferior horses as Francis Hyland did, focus on the best trainers and jockeys, and make a selection. That was all right for the majority of Irish races, but at the Festival I'd be hard-pressed to find a single horse to discard and felt the way a student does when he hasn't cracked the books before an exam.

So off to O'Herlihy's I went for a nightly grind. Reilly joined me in a corner booth, envious that I was going to the Festival, while at the same time teasing me about it. 'Must be nice to have that kind of money,' he said, as if he hadn't gone himself two years ago. He brought a file of study materials with him – his special form book, the results of key races culled from the *Post*, and some feature articles about racing personalities clipped from tabloids and magazines. Knowing that Tony McCoy ate Jaffa cakes with his tea didn't seem significant to me, but for Reilly every factoid, no matter how trivial, was a tile in the grand mosaic.

We weren't alone in our behaviour. Ordinarily, my stop at the newsagent took no more than a minute or two, but now I lost track of the time as I listened to Brian analyse the races, then contributed my own two cents. Other punters in Dublin were wracking their brains to invent a credible excuse for missing work on Gold Cup Day. Food poisoning, a sick child, a car crash, all the old stand-bys would be in play. Anything could, and probably would, happen. Priests might desert their confessionals and beggars might leave their posts, while every bus, train, and tram in Ireland was guaranteed to be a little late when Best Mate launched his run.

What Imelda made of this frenzy I can't say for certain. Wisely, she let it swirl around her, no more than a minor distraction. She knew better than to judge me by my current hyperactivity, aware that it wouldn't last. Not a critical word did she say about the papers and notes spread over the dining room table, nor did she tune out when I discussed my betting strategy with her, even faking some interest. I would borrow a page from Father Breen, I told her, and confine myself to just a few bets every day rather than spreading my limited skills over the whole card, although I didn't follow through.

The worst of it was the trilby episode. I'd seen the hats in a window at Coyles on Aungier Street, a display marked with a sign that said 'Cheltenham', but they'd been sold by the time I decided I had to have one. Inside the shop, amid the bare and dusty shelves, the aged proprietor was huddled by a gas fire. He complained that his next shipment of trilbys was stranded on the Naas Road. 'I could have sold six this week alone!', he groaned, as if that might equal a record. 'When I did business with England, the shipment would be here by horse-and-cart the same day it arrived at the North Wall.' So I settled for a waterproof hat from Marks & Spencer that resembled a trilby. What this would mean in terms of luck, I had no idea.

As for luck, Guillame Macaire had none. Just before the Festival, Jair du Cochet fractured a cannon bone while doing a final piece of serious work in France. The fracture couldn't be repaired, so the horse was put down, and the Gold Cup lost more of its allure. Macaire sounded inconsolable. 'He was like a member of my family,' he said, perhaps regretting the harsh words he'd spoken previously about Jair du Cochet. 'For some seconds before the end of the gallop, I was dreaming of Cheltenham. A few seconds later, I was looking at a horse on three legs.' If destiny really had a darling, Best Mate appeared to be it.

On the Monday of Festival week, I joined a host of Irish punters on a charter flight to Birmingham, the nucleus of a group who'd signed up for the same package deal. There were coaches waiting for us at the airport, and on our ride through the Cotswolds, dreary-looking at the tattered end of winter, my heart sank as we progressed toward Twigworth. In my fantasies, I'd pictured a jolly English village with some shops and pubs, where gents with faces like Toby jugs played darts and shared flagons, but our hotel was an island unto itself in the midst of open farm land, with only a gas station to keep it company.

It was a decent hotel, at least, rather like an American motel, clean and neat, with friendly staff. The management understood the needs of its guests. In my room, I found a complimentary packet from William Hill containing a pen, some blank betting slips, and a booklet instructing an innocent person, should any exist in the vicinity, on how to place a bet. (Hill's flagship shop in Cheltenham opened at eight in the morning during the Festival, so the poor unfortunates with steady jobs could bet on the way to work.) The inescapable *Post* was outside my door before breakfast, and the early prices for the day's races were chalked on a board by the breakfast room. We were as isolated as shepherds on the Isle of Man, and as distant from the world's concerns.

That evening, I hung out with the others at the bar after dinner, the choices for entertainment in Twigworth being limited. Our group was composed mostly of men, although a few women, wives and girlfriends, were included. The men might not have had much in common under ordinary circumstances, differing in their age, professions, and relative means, but all that mattered here were the horses. Some fellows were so knowledgeable about the Festival's history they matched Reilly, a feat I had considered impossible. I heard more about Istabraq and Dawn Run, Desert Orchid and, yes, Arkle, listening to a veteran of many trips to the Cotswolds tell the tale of Arkle's rivalry with Mill House, an English giant of seventeen hands.

The two met first in November 1963 at the English Hennessy, I learned, the same year that Mill House had won his only Gold Cup at Cheltenham. It wasn't Arkle's day at Newbury. Despite a five-pound advantage, he slipped after jumping the last open ditch and finished third, beaten by eight lengths. Little wonder, then, that Mill House was favoured to win a second Gold Cup the following spring, 8-13 against Arkle's 7-4, but the Irish horse was foot perfect this time out, showed effortless acceleration, and reversed the decision by five lengths while shaving four seconds off the track record – sobering news for Mill House, who had turned in a career-best performance and still lost.

In their next engagement, at the '64 Hennessy at Newbury, Arkle conceded three pounds to his opponent. Under Willie Robinson, Mill House went into the lead as he'd done before, and Pat Taaffe on Arkle was soon with him, the pair locked together stride-for-stride until the fourth last, when Arkle picked up and flew home ten lengths to the good, a margin he extended to twenty lengths in the '65 Gold Cup. With Mill House injured in 1966, Arkle won his third Gold Cup easily, by thirty lengths with a shamrock threaded through his bridle, although he was inattentive at times because he lacked competition and almost fell, striking a fence with his chest and scattering the birch.

Arkle won just one more race, the SGB Chase at Ascot in December, before his legs began to bother him. Tom Dreaper reported that his horse was occasionally lame, but some other vets who examined Arkle disagreed, saying he was only 'pottery'. As with Back In Front, nobody could pinpoint why he was hurting. He appeared to improve after a summer at his owner's farm in Bryanstown, near Maynooth, and received 160 cards on his birthday, but he also had some stiffness in his hindquarters now and was diagnosed with arthritis, officially retiring in October 1968.

Yet he responded fairly well to treatment and was judged healthy enough to go to England for Wembley's Horse of the Year Show the next autumn. He paraded twice daily, behaved like a movie star, and ate whatever he pleased – a bunch of hydrangeas, for instance, and all the fruit off a vendor's cart. His theme song, chosen by his owner, Anne, Duchess of Westminster, was 'There'll Never Be Another You', but his reprieve did not last long. Once he was home in Ireland again, his arthritis grew more severe. Often he lay idly in his box and had trouble standing up. He finally became so crippled he had to be put down, in May 1970. Buried in a field at Bryanstown, his gravestone bears a single word – ARKLE – as if to consecrate his uniqueness.

Until past midnight I stayed in the bar and listened to Arkle's story, more dramatic with each new pint, waking to a grey dawn and realizing I'd gone to bed without a glance at Tuesday's card, so I sat at my Twigworth mini-desk to make amends. I had allowed myself a betting bank of £500 for the Festival, a pittance by Cheltenham standards, though not by mine, and I intended not to lose it – no, more, I wanted to go home a winner, bragging all the way to Dublin and bearing elaborate gifts for the family. In fact, I was so fired up I couldn't wait for the tour bus to leave for the racecourse and instead ordered a mini cab, whose driver gouged me for twice the normal fare.

Well, it's the way of the world, I told myself, resisting the temptation to view it as a bad omen. Everybody gets screwed at the Kentucky Derby and the World Series, too. Besides, I was delighted to get to Cheltenham as quickly as possible. The traffic was already snarled up on the main road, and racegoers were crossing it at random, sometimes risking life and limb. Amid the ceaseless stream of cars, I saw some impressive horse boxes, the expensive air-conditioned kind, and also some humble one- and two-horse vans from smaller yards, pulled along behind a trainer's 4x4. Familiar names were boldly inscribed on the sleekest, showiest boxes – Martin Pipe, Jonjo O'Neill, Paul Nicholls, and Phillip Hobbs, a convoy of British-based jump racing's elite.

At 10.30 am, with a mild flourish, the attendants threw open the gates. The press of flesh was immediate and substantial. I squeezed through a door and was carried along in a sort of scrum into The Centaur, a new addition since my last visit. It was a noisy, brilliantly lit, Vegas-style auditorium with six bars, several food stands, a Coral betting shop, a handful of bookies, and fruit machines for the terminally bored. On a stage beneath a monster screen for showing the races, a lounge-act band was churning out some brassy pseudo-jazz I didn't really want to hear in the morning, if ever. The Centaur was a universe apart, and some fans occupied it as cosily as a couch in front of the TV, avoiding both the fresh air and the sight of a horse all day long.

Though The Centaur's bars were already busy, I chose not to compound last night's folly and instead attended an HRI press conference, held in a suite in the Tented Village. On the panel were Jessie Harrington, who looked a little tired, Noel Meade (relaxed), Edward O'Grady (amused), Barry Geraghty (intense), and Noel O'Brien (eager). The atmosphere was much more formal than in

Ireland, and that had a distancing effect. The intimacy I so enjoyed on the Irish circuit, that sense of being inside rather than outside the racing, was gone, replaced by the demands and anxieties of the Big Time, with all the attendant hoopla.

The session started with a question for O'Grady. Did he have many commitments? 'Lots of commitments, but not many runners,' he replied, his wit still sharp. How would his horse John Oliver do in the Supreme Novices' Hurdle? 'He's like the little girl with a curl in the middle of her forehead,' O'Grady said. 'When he's good, he's very, very good, but when he's bad . . .' A reporter apparently interested in gender issues addressed himself to Jessie. 'We're always hearing about Henrietta Knight's feelings. You must have feelings, too?' he blurted out, as if only women had emotions.

Jessie wisely ducked the question. Rather than discuss her feelings, she spoke about the Queen Mother Chase and how much easier it was to bring Moscow Flyer back this year, an optimistic note I liked. She claimed there was less pressure, too, although I didn't buy it, not after seeing how difficult it is to get an Irish horse to the Festival in one piece, much less win a race in England after all that hard travel and before a home crowd. Since the 1998-99 season, Noel Meade had just one winner from forty-two runners, Willie Mullins two in forty-two, and O'Grady two in twenty. Only Jessie was an exception, with four winners from nine entries, the best of the bunch by far.

At noon, with the races still two hours away, I sat on the steps of the parade ring and watched a master-of-ceremonies conduct interviews with such luminaries as

Martin Pipe and John P. McManus, who looked as cool as ever in spite of the stakes. He had five horses entered that afternoon, three in the Champion Hurdle, yet he radiated serenity. When a groom led Istabraq into the ring, shipped to Cheltenham from McManus's farm in Limerick, the fans applauded heartily and Istabraq responded with a powerful buck, as a man might tip his hat to an admiring crowd. It was a lovely moment and all about the horse, as Ted Walsh might say.

In another hour or so, the moment had fled, and I was in a frazzled state. As impatient as I was for the Festival to start, I dreaded the challenge ahead. If I hoped to achieve my goal of going home a winner, I had to kill off my partiality toward the Irish, block any sentimental bets, try not to be confused, and stick to my plan with the icy calm of a hit man. In my belated study period at the Twigworth, I'd only had time to look at the first two races and had chosen Brave Inca in the Supreme Novices' and Well Chief in the Arkle Chase. My third pick was Chicuelo in the William Hill, but that was no more than a stab in the dark.

Ireland was well represented in the Supreme Novices' with seven runners, two from Willie Mullins' yard, Arch Stanton and Euro Leader. Ruby Walsh had won on both horses, but he would be riding Paul Nicholls' Albuhera. As for Barry Geraghty, he'd made a late switch from Garde Champetre to John Oliver, a suspicious move. Had O'Grady whispered a secret in Barry's ear? I thought about it, but a hired killer can't afford to be swayed by such trifles, so I put twenty to win on Brave Inca at 7-2. At first, I thought I'd kissed the money goodbye because Arch

Stanton looked unbeatable, but he fizzled out as rapidly as he'd caught fire, and Conor O'Dwyer on War Of Attrition stormed into the lead at the second last. Yet Barry Cash on Brave Inca was right there with him, casting a long shadow, and the two battled up the hill until War Of Attrition surrendered over the last fifty yards.

All at once, the famous Irish victory cry rose around me, a bellow of sheer unadulterated joy that had in it the roar of the ancient kings, of Finn McCool and Brian Boru, and also a touch of Molly Malone's melodious pitch for cockles and mussels, and most definitely the echo of well-oiled voices bouncing off the cobbled streets of old Dublin through an eternity of late-night exits from a thousand different pubs. Men were holding up fistfuls of pounds, raising pints of beer and singing, off-key at times and yet unashamedly, with force and vigour, the whole of it dwarfing the little preview I'd got at the Open. When Brave Inca passed by on his return trip, the crowd ran along the rail to accompany him, waving and reaching out, a couple in tears, and Barry Cash smiled and thanked them with a salute of his whip, a god on horseback for a while. Young Colm Murphy was waiting for Brave Inca in the winner's enclosure. 'That's the nearest I've ever been to a heart attack,' he said.

So the Irish were off to a soaring start. It was as if they'd all been dosed with helium and were hovering a few feet above earth. Their momentum was building, too, since they held some fine cards in the Arkle, up next, with Central House, Colca Canyon, and Kicking King. As often as Kicking King had been touted to me, by everyone from Geraghty to Noel O'Brien, I took a twenty-quid flyer on Well Chief because Tony McCoy preferred him to Puntal, another from Pipe's yard. Jockeys don't always make the right choice, but I had a hunch about McCoy. I believed *he* believed the horse was special, even though Well Chief had just one chase (and one win) behind him, in a lowly Grade E affair at Taunton.

Had any jockey ever looked as grim and determined in the paddock as McCoy? I doubted it. Nearly thirty, with a face so starved of fat it was almost skeletal, his cheek and jaw bones in sharp definition, he had an air of utter misery. 'Yes, and I'll stay miserable,' he once said grumpily, 'and I'll keep winning.' As Britain's leading jockey every season since 1995-96, McCoy had almost one hundred and ninety winners going so far this season into the Festival, and a strike rate of twenty-six percent. He was stronger and fitter this year from a strict routine of workouts and riding better than ever, down low in the saddle for a better grip on his horse.

Cocky, aggressive, and strong, those were McCoy's trademarks. In the Arkle, he kept Well Chief out of trouble at the back, while Geraghty pushed Kicking King up with the pace. Thisthatandtother, the favourite, came to grief at the second fence, and five other horses fell or unseated their riders in a very sloppy race. With so many gone, McCoy saw a clear path on the inside and went for it. Well Chief was just too much for Kicking King, who had to settle for the second spot, as he'd done in the Supreme Novices' last year. A momentary silence descended on the Irish and their sympathizers, but my own feet were still a few inches above the ground.

There was a story behind Well Chief's success, I later heard. Pipe, the master manipulator, had pulled off another stroke, laying out his horse for the Arkle over the past two weeks. Every day, Well Chief had been schooled over thirty fences to counteract his lack of experience in chases, a fact that didn't appear in the *Post* or travel very far beyond the confines of Pipe's Pond House. Serious punters steered clear of Well Chief because he was so lightly raced, and that allowed David Johnson, his owner, to back him at 33-1 ante-post, while small fry like me, who were out of the loop, were thrilled to get him at 9-1.

My ledger was a thing of beauty. I had two wins in two races for a profit of £250. Now my job was to sit tight and enjoy the scenery until the William Hill, but I fell into the usual trap. Over stimulated and absolutely certain I was in tune with the universal flow, I abandoned my three-bet plan and wagered fifty pounds on Rigmarole to upset Rooster Booster in the Smurfit Champion Hurdle.

Phillip Hobbs' horse looked eminently beatable on paper. Only three ten-year-olds had won the Champion in its seventy-four year history (although Sea Pigeon and Hatton's Grace did win it as eleven-year-olds), and the Rooster had disappointed in most of his races this season, the excuse being that he failed to get the fast pace he requires. His one magnificent run, in the Tote Gold Trophy at Newbury, where he gave away seventeen pounds to Geos and only lost by a stride, might have been costly since he'd used up a lot of energy. Furthermore, three horses in the field (Geos, Intersky Falcon, and Rigmarole) had defeated him at level weights. Still, race goers liked him and sent him off at 11-8, with Rigmarole behind him at 4-1.

The race set up ideally for the champ. Hardy Eustace, one of four Irish entries and dismissed at 33-1, took the lead at a good gallop, so Richard Johnson had no worries about the pace. Like Rooster Booster, Hardy Eustace had been quirky this season, losing all four of his starts and suffering from sore shins, but you wouldn't have guessed it by his current run. Wearing blinkers for the first time, he ran loose and free and rebuffed every challenge until Rooster Booster came at him. The grey horse was electrifying as he slashed through the field, but Hardy Eustace had no fear, and the Rooster's surge fell short by five lengths. Again that monumental roar engulfed us, though many couldn't help remembering the late Kieran Kelly and knew Dessie Hughes and Conor O'Dwyer would speak of him, causing a few more tears to be shed.

What a brilliant afternoon for Ireland! Exactly as described in the anecdotal literature, I got carried away. So I'd just lost fifty quid, so what? The mad energy had me in a whirl. Hired killer, my eye. I couldn't control a single impulse and started on a string of sorry wagers.

In the William Hill, I forgot all about Chicuelo, who was a loser, and instead backed Marlborough, another loser. Next, I bet on the loser Jasmin D'Oudairies in the Kim Muir and after that, hoping to win some money back on the Pertemps Final Hurdle, the last race ('pure gravy for the bookies'), I picked the loser Keepatem, a 4-1 favourite beaten by Creon, a 50-1 long shot. It did little to soothe my flayed nerves when I saw that

J. P. McManus owned Keepatem and Creon, and no doubt had the good sense to have a flutter on both.

Later that night, as I lay in my lonely Twigworth bed, I closed down my accounts. I was ninety pounds ahead, a better result than I deserved, really, given the error of my ways. Down the hall at intervals, I heard my fellow guests retreating from the bar, their voices hoarse from all the talk, drink, smoke, and cheering. They were busy constructing a narrative that would become the myth of this particular Festival, each player's tale of glory or woe a strand in it. Still to come were the myth's core events, the Queen Mother and Gold Cup, after which the story would be over and ripe for countless re-tellings. Such were the lofty thoughts of a bone-weary punter on the edge of sleep.

On St Patrick's Day, Moscow Flyer had a walk over the course in the early morning mist. 'He's himself,' Eamonn Leigh said on TV, a gnomic remark I chose to interpret as positive. Moscow figured mightily in my plans for that afternoon. I had talked myself out of all that silly, superstitious business about The Pattern, replaying Barry Geraghty's words in my mind time and again. 'He's the ace in my pack,' Barry had said, and I believed him. The horse had already trounced Azertyuiop once this season, so why shouldn't he do it again? I couldn't see any rational reason, so Moscow would be my banker, the key element in a new plan to beat the bookies.

I had been a virtuous punter the night before. Rather

than swap lies with the lads until the wee hours, I did my homework, retired early, and slept well. I had a feeling of clarity and focus, but it began to fade almost as soon as I arrived at the racecourse and met with distractions – people in costume, for instance, among them two short chubby guys dressed as leprechauns, who'd painted their faces green and were boozily hamming it up for the crowd. Green was everywhere, in fact, as in a Lorca rhapsody, with green shirts and ties, green scarves and socks and maybe even green underwear, green dresses and green beer, along with garlands of green shamrocks being sold at the gates by vendors who had the nerve to back them with a guarantee of luck.

Arkle, Mill House, Cottage Rake, and Istabraq, they all had bars named in their honour at Cheltenham, and the green hordes had already commandeered them with the authority of an invading army. No glass or bottle would go untipped today, not when there was a patron saint to be celebrated. The shepherd boy who brought Christianity to Ireland and banished every snake would be toasted repeatedly with a fierce, partisan energy, so I sought refuge from the bedlam in the Head On Stand where, for an extra fifteen pounds, I could buy a seat to call my own, no small thing when some fifty thousand fans are searching for a place to rest.

Fundamentalist, Pizarro, and Moscow Flyer. Someday they too might be honoured with a bar at the racecourse, but for now they were my selections in the first three races. Of the trio, I was least secure about Fundamentalist in the Royal & SunAlliance Novices' Hurdle, concerned that Sadlers Wings might be as remarkable as Willie

Mullins suspected. The gelding, a former flat horse, had won his first maiden hurdle by thirteen lengths, but Inglis Drever, the season's outstanding British novice, looked an even bigger danger. Unbeaten in his three starts over fences and proven at the distance, Inglis Drever had the fourth-highest *Racing Post* Rating of the past decade and drew solid support at 7-4.

I liked Fundamentalist because he had impressed me in a race at Haydock in February, where he finished second to Royal Rosa, a filly with a bright future, plus Nigel Twiston-Davies, his trainer, had a yard near Cheltenham and often did well at the track. Carl Llewellyn, his much-battered stable jockey, let Fundamentalist relax at the rear of the field, then cranked him up from three out, followed closely by Inglis Drever, who seemed in an ideal spot until he blundered at the second last. There would be no catching Fundamentalist now, I figured, already tallying the return on my bet, but the horse refused to make it easy and grazed the last hurdle, so the race was on again, with Inglis Drever thumping up the hill in a fury, only to fall short by half-a-length.

I let go of the breath I'd been holding. I'd put twenty pounds on Fundamentalist at 9-1 and showed an overall profit of £270 so far. As ever when I'm winning, I regarded this as a mere prelude to the riches yet to come and imagined how I'd spend my windfall, maybe on a trip to California to fish for trout. More important, though, was a special gift for Imelda, so I ducked into the Tented Village and did some window shopping. An exclusive pair of boots from Dubarry of Ireland? Or a pashmina woven by hand from the fleece of a Tibetan Capra Hircus goat? That sounded exotic, but I was leaning toward a simple gold bracelet when I had to leave for the Royal & SunAlliance Chase.

I put fifty pounds to win on Pizarro, hesitating only a bit. Our Vic, the horse that Tom Costello had praised, was intimidating. He'd won three straight hurdles for Martin Pipe, then switched to fences and demolished a Grade 2 field at Ascot, so the odds on him were 11-8 – too short, I thought, when you had such other contenders as Mossy Green, who'd narrowly lost to Pizarro in the Grade One P. J. Moriarty at Leopardstown. As if to prove my point, Our Vic banged into the very first fence and jumped sketchily throughout, while Royal Emperor committed blunder after blunder and shook up Dominic Elsworth so thoroughly that the jockey dropped his whip.

Yet both horses survived their mistakes and stayed close to Mossy Green, the pacesetter. On the second circuit, Pizarro made an awkward jump over the water. He might have been spooked because Irish courses don't have water jumps. At the fourth last, the race got very messy. Calling Brave, who'd been error-free, clobbered the fence and lost his rider. A revitalized Pizarro was travelling sweetly through the scramble, but Mossy Green misjudged the tricky second last, fell, and brought down my horse. David Casey on Rule Supreme, probably the worst jumper of the lot but still upright, swung wide of the fallers and gained some ground. Our Vic was tiring, and Elsworth lacked a whip to drive Royal Emperor home, so Rule Supreme held on to become the third Irish winner at the Festival, and the only one from Willie Mullins' seventeen entries.

The Irish were still waving their flags when the horses entered the paddock for the Queen Mother Champion Chase. I'd placed my bet early, £200 to win on Moscow Flyer at 10-11, and stood in the front ranks to watch the Harrington team get him ready. The yard at Moone, the beech and lime trees, the Wicklow Mountains, and even Ireland itself seemed a galaxy away, and I saw Moscow as a stout-hearted country horse up against the city slickers. Not that he looked like a bumpkin – no, he looked splendid because of all the work and care Jessie, Eamonn, and the others had lavished on him. I only hoped he would concentrate, really concentrate, and do the job for which they'd so thoroughly prepared him.

Azertyuiop did not look as good. He was sweaty – excellent, I thought, may buckets of the stuff pour out of him. I counted Ruby Walsh's bad-luck streak as another advantage for our side. Ruby had ridden five losers yesterday and two today, and he'd just taken a tumble on Mossy Green, but in truth Barry Geraghty wasn't doing much better. He hadn't been on a winner yet, either, and had hit the deck when Pizarro was brought down, so egos were bruised all round. That made both jockeys hungrier than ever to come out on top. The tension between them was reflected in the opposing colours of their silks. No costume designer could have done a better job. Walsh was as bold as a crocus in bright yellow, with a red star from the Mao era on his chest, while Geraghty wore black-and-white chevrons such as an escaped convict might sport, a thief out to rob the race. They were the only two in it, and they knew it.

The horses who contested the early lead, Cenkos, Ei Ei,

and Eskleybrook, swiftly burnt out, like the fuses that ignite an explosion. Ruby played a waiting game on Azertyuiop, coasting along in mid-division behind Moscow Flyer. To keep my fears at bay, I remembered my talk with Jessie back in October, and how she had explained why the Queen Mother Chase suited Moscow so well. 'The pace is so fast, and the competition so intense, he has to pay attention,' she'd said, whereas his mind wandered during Irish races because they unfold more slowly, only turning into a sprint over the final few furlongs. And Moscow did appear to be attentive and travelling beautifully, at least until he came to the water jump – the same one that had bothered Pizarro – and fouled up.

Some horses find trouble at the water and can even become phobic about it. I had no idea if that was the case with Moscow, but I could see that the slight hitch had upset his rhythm, and rhythm is everything in a fast-paced chase. Even Geraghty, an expert at balancing a horse, couldn't get him right. Before my eyes, I saw The Pattern emerge in gigantic numbers and letters, 111 and then FUB (fallen, unseated, and brought down). Navan, Sandown, and Leopardstown, that added up to three wins in a row, and I knew in a terrible instant of foreboding that something awful was about to happen. Sure enough, Moscow was slow at the next fence, and at the one after that – an open ditch, the fourth last – he lost his timing completely and paddled through it. Geraghty couldn't hang on and landed on the ground.

The collective groan that followed Geraghty's flop was a melancholy counterpoint to that Irish roar of triumph. Countless pounds and euros had dropped into the bookies' pockets, my own 200 among them. I could almost hear the howls of pain in faraway Dublin. Incredibly, Moscow Flyer had done it again, the Number Four his eternal *bête noire*. What a strange animal he was! Had he been watching too much traffic in Moone, scrambling his brainwaves as kids do with computer games? No answer was forthcoming. Moscow would forever be a mystery to us, even to Barry Geraghty, his long-time intimate, who was at a loss to account for the mistake since he wasn't unsighted approaching the fence. 'Stunned about sums it up,' he said later.

For Jessie and Eamonn, it was a bitter defeat, their months of hard, dedicated work smashed in a few seconds. With his adversary gone, Azertyuiop mowed down the other horses, streaking clear by nine lengths. It was a win, all right, but not a definitive one. Instead, it recalled Moscow's contests with Istabraq, those races decided by phantom blows. Even the leprechauns were dejected about the result, an arm around each other's shoulders, locked into a support group. But for Ruby Walsh, who'd swore all along that Azertyuiop was too fresh in the Tingle Creek, not yet himself, the Queen Mother Chase provided a welcome corrective, and he could forget his recent spill and those seven straight losses, stand tall in the saddle, and shout, 'Jaysus, what a relief!'

The rest of the afternoon dragged by for me. I felt depressed, as if I'd fallen myself. I still had some money, but it seemed like chump change after my elaborate fantasies. I could forget about fishing in California, that much was certain. I was too low and blue to sort through the twenty-eight horses in The Coral Cup and passed up the National Hunt Chase, as well, hoisting a Guinness at the bar where the leprechauns, ever less merry, were drinking. In the Mildmay of Flete, I threw away twenty pounds on Fondmort (again), and that left the Weatherbys Champion Bumper, where almost half of the twenty-four entries were from Ireland.

I chose Martinstown, yet another McManus horse, who had won his only two starts in Ireland and been saved for this race since November. Martinstown couldn't keep himself warm. He quit two furlongs out and finished fourteenth, costing me another thirty quid. Instead, Total Enjoyment, a five-year-old mare, stole the show. Her trainer Tom Cooper, a part-timer from Tralee who also works in his family's dental supply business, had a winner on his first trip to the Festival. Everyone in Kerry seemed to know in advance that it would happen, so the bookies were subjected to a huge, million euro plus betting loss. Jim Culloty, a Kerryman, was in the saddle, and the members of the It Will Never Last Syndicate, composed almost entirely of Kerrymen, had backed their mare with such enthusiasm they couldn't resist lifting Cooper onto their shoulders and serenading him with 'The Rose of Tralee'.

Ahead loomed another studious, boring, lonely evening at the Twigworth, a prospect I couldn't abide, so I boarded a shuttle bus to the centre of Cheltenham, determined to do St Patrick's Day in style. I sat next to a postman from Coventry, who looked the way I felt, half-elated and half-wrecked, a function of violent mood swings. When I mentioned the Gold Cup, he frowned. He wouldn't be coming back tomorrow. 'Too exhausting,' he said, and I knew what he meant. As I strolled through town, I was shocked at the sight of normal people doing normal things, like buying shoes. I almost envied them. They had a life apart from racing.

On both sides of the main street, I saw racegoers in little groups, some dazed and some cheery, all drawn as if by pan pipes to the Queens Hotel, a grand old structure with columns out front and a pair of bouncers who could have belonged to the World Wrestling Federation guarding the door. An overtaxed gent was dozing in the lobby with a wilted shamrock curled in his lapel. Possibly he had intended to go to the track, but the undertow of alcohol was too strong. He was the only casualty so far. The night was still young, after all, and a band was just setting up nearby, although I could hear some Irish tunes playing on a tape in a small bar at the back of the hotel, where I found a vacant table, my first bit of luck since Fundamentalist.

Here I held court for a time. I had two empty chairs and could have rented them by the hour to enhance my bank account. First to join me were Harold and Ginger, locals to judge by their tweeds. They'd never been to the Festival before and were exhilarated to have survived it, but they wouldn't do it again, they hinted, though Ginger did have three paying guests at her house, gentlemen from Ireland, and thought they were 'interesting'. Harold knocked back his beer so fast I offered another round, but he declined, his mission accomplished.

Next came a captain-of-industry, an Irishman in exile forced to earn his fortune outside London, which he'd clearly done. He entered to 'McNamara's Band' and whistled along with it, asking for my *Racing Post* so he could check why all his bets today were losers. That should have endeared him to me, but it didn't. He was too pushy. The Queens had been his base for decades, and he felt privy to its secrets and entitled to do as he pleased. He knew the St Patrick's drill well and was in no hurry to finish his drink. Instead, he'd pace himself – instinct control! – and switch to good wine at dinner before moving on to brandy and a cigar.

The captain's wife was more friendly. She loved racing and had travelled the world in pursuit of it. She'd been to Australia, New York, Kentucky, and even Hong Kong, she said, while I glared at the captain as he flipped the pages and sang 'The Wild Colonial Boy'. Why did I have an urge to strangle him? It was a low thing to feel, but his air of entitlement so annoyed me I gave up my seat and my table for the crush at the bar, where a giant from Kerry was holding forth. He was in on the Total Enjoyment caper and drank to the mare, Jim Culloty, Tom Cooper, and Kerry itself. I had a pint in my hand, but he bought me another one. 'God's Country', he mumbled, listing toward me like a derelict building about to collapse. I promised to visit Kerry some day and bought him a pint, and he bought me a pint, and I bought him a pint, and he tried to buy me a pint, but I finally escaped.

The bar was jammed now. Among the punters I noticed pair of working girls, one in a skirt that barely existed. I'd read an account not long ago of how poorly low-grade hookers fared among the Irish at Cheltenham in the old days. 'They're only interested in cards and horses,' ran the apocryphal quote. It's 2-1 the redhead will go home empty-handed, I said to myself, my brain in Paddy Power mode. The drink was getting to me, and I was still angry at the captain, who was lording it over the room. He'd invite a chum to sit for a minute or two in a precious chair (my chair!), then dismiss the poor guy and summon the next in line. His losing bets were my only solace. May they haunt you forever, captain, I muttered.

In search of fresh air, I elbowed my way to the lobby, where the band had started playing. They were so loud you practically had to stand on another person's toes and shout into an ear to be heard. The hotel resembled a deafening echo chamber, but nobody seemed to mind – quite the opposite, in fact. All the noise and palaver and marginal behaviour were linked to a more general release the Festival encouraged, a chance to drown the cares of everyday life. Here were managing directors and judges clinking glasses with shopkeepers and farmers, and maybe burglars and dope fiends. There were no class distinctions, no banal discussions of mortgage payments or children in need of orthodontia, and especially no moral imperative to better yourself. Instead, they let it all hang out. For many of them, the Festival was as good as it got.

Hunger spared me from total ruin. On the brink of being seriously tipsy, I excused myself, located an Italian place down the street and ordered some pasta. I felt desperate, though, because I had nothing to read. The menu was no help, either, being short on digestible prose. The captain had my *Post*, damn it, and I imagined it had gone that way for him since birth, his every desire fulfilled. A kindly waitress, sensing my distress, loaned me a wrinkled, sauce-stained tabloid. It was missing a few pages, including the sports section – the sports section is always missing – but on the news pages I saw a feature about Best Mate, who was only hours away from his 'appointment with destiny', as the tabloid's overwrought reporter put it.

A light rain fell in beads against my window on the morning of the Gold Cup. The guests were sleeping in at the Twigworth, victims of St. Pat's. On most doorknobs I saw a sign that said 'Hangover Recovery In Progress', the hotel's semi-clever version of 'Do Not Disturb'. The breakfast room was quiet, the staff subdued. On the coach ride to the course, the passengers rarely spoke. Our mood was sombre, even respectful. We had a sense of occasion, I suppose, a feeling we were part of something special. If the day went well and Best Mate won his third Gold Cup, we'd be telling our grandchildren about it in years to come, and if we didn't have any grandchildren, we'd corner strangers and bend their ears.

The coach dropped us in a car park around noon. I stepped over some puddles as deep as little ponds. Though it was dry and cool now under a grey sky, the rain had done its work and softened the ground considerably. The official going was 'Good (Good to Soft in Places)', an edge for the Irish horses, although also for

267

Best Mate. Despite the dreary weather, the fans weren't deterred in any way and set a Cheltenham attendance record of 57,463. I looked around for the Man Utd guerillas, but a mild scolding from Sir Alex had nipped their rebellion in the bud, and they were no longer threatening to march down Cleeve Hill in camouflage and interrupt the races with a flurry of smoke bombs.

We arrived early enough that I found room to stand at the Arkle Bar and order a much-needed coffee, wistfully recalling when I was still ahead of the game, but yesterday I'd returned most of my profit to the bookies. I was almost even now, an unacceptably wishy-washy state, the province of people who store pennies in jars and never cross a street against a red light. Better to win or lose big than go home untouched or unscarred by the experience, I thought, but once again I'd neglected to do a thorough job of studying the form, having lingered too long at the Queens. Always an excuse, as my teachers used to say.

The Triumph Hurdle, the afternoon's opener, was a devilish affair featuring twenty-three lightly raced, four-year-old novices. So much depended on luck I'd intended to give the race a wide berth until I noticed Hasanpour's name on the card – Hasanpour, my newsagent's selection, an enticing echo from Dublin! Charlie Swan told the *Post* he liked his horse's chances, too, and explained that a virus had affected his last outing, a bad one. I had to grip my left wrist with my right hand to prevent access to my wallet, but it worked, and I was glad that it did, because Hasanpour was pulled up. The first five finishers were all long shots at odds of 16-1 or worse, with Phillip Hobbs' Made In Japan the winner at 20-1.

The Stayers' Hurdle appeared to be another race to avoid, although for a different reason. The marvellous Baracouda, twice a champion, looked unstoppable. French-bred, out of Pêche Aubar by Alesso, a stallion from the States, Baracouda was among John McManus's most valued possessions. He had reportedly purchased the gelding, and also First Gold, from the Marquesa de Moratalla after meeting her at a London dinner party in 2001. The Marquesa sensed a kindred soul, it was said, who'd treat her horses humanely, but the estimated six-figure price tag must have had some influence over her decision to sell.

Finding a flaw in Baracouda's armour was a thankless task. His overall record was formidable, with sixteen wins and four seconds from twenty-one starts. Only two things counted against him, a tendency to idle in front and the fact that older horses fared poorly in the Stayers'. Over the past eleven years, sixty-four eight-year-olds had tried the race, but just three had won, and Baracouda was a nine-year-old. His primary competition would come from Iris's Gift, a close second to him in 2003, losing by only three-quarters of a length. But Iris's Gift was bothered by niggling problems all winter, and Jonjo O'Neill felt his horse's training had been less than ideal with just that single impressive run at Haydock behind him.

Trends aside, I still believed in Baracouda, but I couldn't stomach the odds of 8-11. Though Solerina tempted me, I realized it would be a sentimental play – betting with the heart, not the head – and so for the sake of a little action I put twenty pounds on Sh Boom, a stable mate of Iris's Gift, who had a solid win over the course and seemed to be improving. But current form would prove to be deceptive again, and an X factor – the wiliness of the Irish, with Barry Geraghty as its instigator – would have a more profound effect on the result.

Geraghty had learned some things about Baracouda last year and warned Gary Hutchinson, the jockey on Solerina, who loved to be in front, not to go too fast or he'd be handing over the race to the French horse. That sounded sensible to Hutchinson. He was already concerned about Solerina's ability to stay three miles, so he agreed to co-operate and conserve the mare's energy for a late sprint. By keeping a tight hold, he effectively served as a pacemaker for Geraghty on Iris's Gift. Thierry Doumen was content to have Baracouda in mid-pack, within easy striking distance of the leaders. When Geraghty moved past the tiring Solerina two out, Doumen let his horse loose, and Baracouda closed briskly at the last hurdle, but Geraghty's little intrigue reaped its dividend, and Iris's Gift drew clear over the last fifty yards.

Every Festival develops its own thread of meaning, a strand of occurrences that ultimately define it, and the one we were witnessing might well be called the Graveyard of Champions, with Rooster Booster, Moscow Flyer, and Baracouda all upstaged. Only Best Mate still held his title, and we'd know soon if Matey would be the exception to the rule or another fallen idol. Certainly, no horse could have been nurtured toward his goal with more care or patience, each in infinite supply thanks to Henrietta Knight and her devoted crew, who had tuned Best Mate so minutely he might have been a sensitive instrument for detecting tiny disturbances in the atmosphere.

The Gold Cup in 2002 came seventy-eight days after Best Mate's last race, for example. In 2003, the spread was seventy-seven days, and this year it was eighty-one days, an extraordinary degree of precision. Again the horse had just three preparatory races, the same as last year, with the Ericsson substituted for the King George. A skilled squad of specialists saw to Matey's every need, as well. He had a physio to insure his back muscles were in good order, and an equine dentist to deal with any painful teeth. Jackie Jenner was almost saintly in her attentions. As if that weren't enough, Best Mate was receiving more fan mail than Arkle now, with over eight hundred cards, often with sprigs of clover or heather enclosed, mailed to Knight's yard to wish him luck.

For Knight, the planning and precision didn't stop with the horse. Every human movement had to be plotted, too, and made as identical as possible to Gold Cup days in the past. She wore the same blue suit as before, the same blouse and hat, and her lucky pearls, of course, while Terry Biddlecombe retrieved his own lucky hat, a bashed-in old trilby, from the cupboard where it gathered dust between its annual one-off appearance. Their house guest, Andrew Coonan, head of the Irish Jockeys' Association, had gone home to Kildare on Wednesday, just as he'd done in the past two years, and Knight would dine at a Tote luncheon and watch the race on TV (if she could bear to) in a press tent behind the weighing room, the same as she did last year.

Whether or not you subscribed to the worth of Knight's precautions (and who could be critical of her, after what the infuriated fates had done to Moscow Flyer?), Best Mate appeared to be unbeatable. He looked tremendous in the parade ring, possessed of a curious nobility only the finest horses have. Where was the danger, I wondered? Beef Or Salmon was still too green, while Harbour Pilot was too risky despite his decent finish in 2003. A highly strung type, he'd lost some weight on his journey to the Cotswolds, plus Beef Or Salmon had defeated him both times they had met. What about First Gold? Francois Doumen insisted his horse was in excellent form, yet First Gold had only won a single race in England, the King George in 2000, prompting McManus to buy him, and had run just once this season, again in the King George, where he finished third.

Keen Leader, Barry Geraghty's mount, was getting some play. Undeniably, the horse had class, but his record was too in-and-out for my taste. As for Truckers Tavern, second in 2003, he'd blown every race since then. No, the only two outsiders who appealed to me were Therealbandit and Sir Rembrandt. With Therealbandit, I knew Martin Pipe and David Johnson were taking a chance. Their horse liked Cheltenham, with two wins in novice chases there before a fall in the Pillar Property Chase, and he'd have less trouble among experienced older horses in the Gold Cup than he would have among the sloppy novices in the Royal & SunAlliance, but only one novice had ever won the Gold Cup, and that was Captain Christy in 1974.

Still, there was some good money for Therealbandit, second favourite at 15-2 to Best Mate at 8-11 – wishful thinking, maybe. For my own part, the more I watched Sir Rembrandt in the paddock, the more convinced I became that he had an outside chance. True, you'd doubt it on his recent form. His last good run was in the Welsh National in December, after which he'd been pulled up in the Pillar and had weakened in the Aon Chase. Robert Alner couldn't account for his decline, but Sir Rembrandt had forgotten all about it, at least by the look of him. He had real presence and a magnificent aura of health, so I took a blind stab and put twenty pounds on him to win at 33-1, a wager I would come to regret.

For the Gold Cup, I had an invitation to the Horse Racing Ireland suite, high up among the corporate and members' boxes in the privileged precincts of the grandstand, a wonderful treat. From such an elevated position, I could see the full panorama of the racecourse without having to fight through a crowd, and I felt like a potentate among such dignitaries as Paddy Mullins and Father Breen. As I helped myself to some food from a buffet, a young waiter tapped me on the shoulder. He was still a teenager and bore all the normal burdens of adolescence, with braces on his teeth, blotches on his face, and a crop of unruly hair. On a crumpled napkin, he'd written, 'First Gold, £2'. Would I place the bet for him with the tote? Servers weren't allowed to gamble while on duty, he said.

I agreed to help him out. Why wouldn't I facilitate the dreams of a fellow dreamer? But I was curious why he'd chosen me from so many other eligible candidates, attributing it to my gentle nature at first, then realizing it could be interpreted just as easily that I was the only fall guy in the room. Whatever the reason, I did his bidding and put a fiver on First Gold myself, because the napkin *had* to be an omen, even though I was aware First Gold was an eleven-year-old, and that no horse older than ten had won the Gold Cup since What A Myth in 1969. Ah, well, not to worry. I shrugged, topped up my glass of wine, and gave the lad his ticket. He could keep it as a souvenir.

We moved out onto a balcony for the race. The weather had conspired to increase the drama, providing an operatic backdrop. Above the deep green expanse of the racecourse, the sky was a thundery purple, and the air had a stinging bite, as sharp as a wake-up call. The horses followed a team of red-coated huntsmen onto the track and acquired a shimmering grace in the fine mist. They must have been aware of a heightened moment. They would recognize it from the intense focus of the crowd, I thought, and maybe from a sound most of them had never heard before, the slightly altered breathing of nearly sixty thousand human beings knotted together in a rapturous state of suspense.

All the hype, all the boozing and carousing, even the fruit-machine frenzy of The Centaur, they were swept aside as if by a cosmic broom, and we were delivered to the heart of the matter and understood our purpose again. It went that way at every major sporting event, be it the Super Bowl or the World Cup final, because in the modern age the event itself was often buried under so many layers of commerce its essence was obscured. But there always came a revelatory instant such as this, when everyone remembered the why of it and snapped to attention, ready to witness the impossible forward pass, the amazing penalty kick, or the making – or unmaking – of a champion.

For the jockeys, it was all business. They said as much themselves. Any anxiety they might feel about the importance of the Gold Cup or the immense stakes involved vanished the minute the tape flew up. They could have been at Thurles, so little did the externals concern them, and their only injunction was to ride the best race they could, according to their plan. For Jim Culloty, who'd walked the course with Terry Biddlecombe, that meant clinging to the inside rail where the ground was marginally better, even though the tactic was risky because a horse can get pinned on the rail. For Paul Carberry, the job was to 'sit and suffer', as Noel Meade phrased it. Harbour Pilot could become finicky and frustrated when asked for a jump or a run, so Paul's instructions were to let the horse dictate.

From the start, First Gold took the lead. He set a good pace, too, tracked by Harbour Pilot. Beef Or Salmon and Therealbandit were held up, while Sir Rembrandt was slowly away, to my distress. Best Mate kept to the inside as intended, a few lengths behind the pace-setter. What a joy it was to see him jump! His indifferent performance in the Peterborough was a distant memory, eclipsed by his return to superior form. Now he was so exact he jumped each fence in the same measured way, hitting it dead right, with the middle of his body poised over it. It was a picture-perfect display and full of prowess. Sleek and streamlined, he never wasted an ounce of energy, nor did

Culloty have to whisper a single word to him. Matey was a natural – a true lepper, as the Irish say.

Truckers Tavern, Alexander Banquet, and Irish Hussar were the first to drop from contention, no surprises there. Therealbandit jumped like the novice he was and never really had an impact on the race, another gamble lost. The speedy pace burned up Keen Leader's energy, and when he blundered four out, he was gone. First Gold also botched that fence, but he hung onto the lead, although he was clearly fatigued. Best Mate, on his heels, began to quicken. As the horses approached the third last, it looked as if Matey would break free again in his patented, headlong rush, but instead the unimaginable happened. Paul Carberry loomed up on Harbour Pilot and boxed in Culloty and Best Mate behind the leg-weary First Gold, trapping them on the rail.

This was a brilliant, aggressive bit of riding. In essence, Carberry had called Culloty's bluff. If you think you deserve special treatment, he was saying, you've got another thing coming, you cheeky bugger. Any jockey worth his salt would have done the same – and Culloty knew it – but his supporters disapproved. They were at Cheltenham to see history made, not a mean trick only an Irishman would pull, so they cheered loudly for Best Mate, except in our suite, where the chant was 'C'mon, Paul!' Culloty had to move fast and take decisive action. He checked his horse for a second and swung wide to get outside both First Gold and Harbour Pilot for an unobstructed run. That was brilliant, too. It cost Best Mate a step or two, but I hardly noticed because Sir Rembrandt was storming up the hill.

Could Sir Rembrandt really win? It was too far-fetched, and I didn't dare believe it for fear I'd jinx the horse. As First Gold receded into the mist, Best Mate and Harbour Pilot jumped the second last together, but Sir Rembrandt committed a minor error and that, I figured, would be the end of him. But no, he was all heart and picked up again, a force still to be reckoned with – the wild card in the deck. At this point, the script called for Best Mate to accelerate as usual and assert his right to join the pantheon of Gold Cup immortals, only that didn't happen. For once, he was in a serious battle – a real bare-knuckle fight. Harbour Pilot wouldn't roll over for him, and Sir Rembrandt kept gaining ground, but Best Mate dug deep, struggled on, and proved his mettle, beating my horse by a half-length.

The crowd went crazy. This was the result they'd craved, a fulfilment of every expectation and desire. Henrietta Knight burst from the press tent to hug her teary-eyed husband, while the Irish gathered around Carberry to congratulate him on the superb ride. The debate over whether Best Mate was better than Arkle, or vice-versa, raged in all the bars and would continue long into the night. I glanced at the teenage waiter, who stared disconsolately at his Tote ticket. His dream of riches was in tatters, as was mine, by a measly half-length. Since Sir Rembrandt was a 33-1 long shot, why hadn't I backed him each-way? It was another riddle, as unanswerable as those about Moscow Flyer. Evidently, I still had a few gaps in my education that needed to be closed.

For the Irish, there were no more winners at the Festival. Ted Walsh came close with Never Compromise in the Christie's Foxhunter Steeplechase, second to the ancient Earthmover, as did Charlie Swan in the Grand Annual with Ground Ball, who made St Pirran work for the victory. No horses from Ireland ran in The Cathcart Challenge Cup, won by Our Armaggedon, and the five entered in the Vincent O'Brien County Hurdle failed to get a place. Ruby Walsh, substituting for an injured Robert Thornton, took the County Hurdle on Sporazene and earned the top jockey award despite his abysmal start, with three wins from fifteen rides.

I cashed one of my four bets – the one on St Pirran – and looked over my ledger. Sad to say, I never recouped my losses and finished in the red, down by £120. It could have been much worse if I hadn't controlled my impulses and resisted the temptation to go for broke on the County Hurdle. That lesson, at least, had sunk in. I felt strange after the last race, though, and I suspect others did, too, because our little bubble of fantasy, a universe unto itself, had abruptly burst. It shouldn't have come as a shock that the Festival was over, and yet it did. Sheep still grazed on Cleeve Hill, but the horses had gone away. Our real lives were out there waiting for us, dimly glimpsed but beckoning, and as the shock began to wear off, I became eager to reclaim my own.

Then I was hurtling through the night on a coach bound for Birmingham Airport, a Festival veteran who'd been at Cheltenham on the day Best Mate won his third straight Gold Cup. Already I was working on my version of the race, polishing up one aspect of it at the expense of another to brighten the narrative. The story would stand me in good stead at O'Herlihy's, when I was even more aged and grey and surrounded by callow youths hungry for such tales. They would regard me as an authentic and reliable source of historical information, and I would try not to disappoint them, although I had a fairly strong feeling I'd lie about my bet on Sir Rembrandt and say I backed the horse each-way. Would I admit to coming home a loser? That's an interesting question, I thought, touching a box in my jacket pocket, the one with a gold bracelet inside. It depends on how you look at it.

Away

Winter again. On a cold morning just after Christmas, I walked from the house to the garden shed where I work, casting an eye toward the wilted runner bean and pea plants that used to grow like ivy at the height of summer. No birds were at the feeder nearby. The sparrows who outnumber and ordinarily out-manoeuvre the bluetits were gone for the moment, flying over Dublin on an errand known only to themselves. I remembered Gautier's white pigeons at Ascot, those poor hirelings of the bookies, as I switched on an electric heater. I was in a dreamy mood, subject to idle fancies in the way of Moscow Flyer.

Whenever I thought about Moscow lately, I recalled 'Pick Yourself Up', the Jerome Kern tune. It could serve as the horse's theme song. He was terrific at starting over. Only two weeks after his disaster in the Queen Mother, Moscow dusted himself off and tackled Aintree's stiff fences in the Martell Cognac Melling Chase, acting as if nothing untoward had happened at the Festival. He destroyed his opponents over two miles four furlongs, longer than his ideal distance, then moved on to Punchestown in April and won another good race before being turned out for his holiday on the grass.

I hoped Moscow Flyer would meditate while he ate his fill and further straighten out his head, and when he returned to the track it looked as if he'd done so. He was a model of clarity in the Fortria Chase at Navan in October, again the start of his campaign, but Jessie would send him to Sandown next for a rematch with Azertyuiop in the Tingle Creek Chase, his fourth race after three wins. If he fell or unseated his rider, it would be too much for anyone to bear, forcing the punters to admit that the universe operates on random principles only Henrietta Knight truly comprehends.

As ever, Knight was babying Best Mate, who'd become an industry since the Festival. He had his own line of clothing (for human beings) that would be sold at Cheltenham, where the Courage Enclosure had been renamed in his honour – better than a bar, even. At henandterry.com, Matey's admirers could follow his progress toward his seasonal debut in the William Hill Chase at Exeter in November, a race created especially for him over a course he favoured. Jim Culloty had a broken thumb, so who'd be his jockey? Knight preferred Timmy Murphy, but Jim Lewis wanted Tony McCoy. They held a summit meeting, and Murphy got the nod. Old feuds, they say, die hard.

If Best Mate honestly was a wonder horse, his third Gold Cup didn't prove it. According to the form book, he'd beaten a weak field, at least by historical standards, and the comparisons to Arkle seemed ever more far-fetched.

His run at Exeter, deemed so important to the nation that the BBC broadcast it live on a weekday, further lowered his standing. Though just three horses took him on, including Sir Rembrandt, he had to struggle to squeak by Seebald, who only had a four-pound advantage. Our champion didn't appear to be so special anymore.

For Michael Hourigan, the William Hill was heartening. He still believed in Beef Or Salmon's Gold Cup chances and ran him steadily through the autumn, beginning with a warm-up chase in Limerick. His horse shone in the James Nicholson Chase at Down Royal, defeating Kicking King at level weights, only to have the decision reversed in the Durkan Chase at Leopardstown over too short a trip. But all the racing kept Beef Or Salmon in fine fettle, so when Knight decided to skip the King George VI again in favour of Ireland's Lexus (formerly Ericsson) Chase, Hourigan's leading light was ready.

First, though, we had the Tingle Creek in early December. I watched the race at O'Herlihy's, where I was finally accepted as a fully-fledged regular and could be as cranky as anybody if I arrived for a pint and found someone sitting in my chosen spot – a table close to a gas fire that I swore I deserved, being a Californian and not yet entirely accustomed to Irish winters. On the other hand, so many foreign things were old familiars to me now, and I liked that sensation of belonging, of being a link in the chain of community, liked coming home through the early dark to see Imelda's sons turning into young men, even as I got older and ever-so-slightly wiser.

On a living room wall, we'd hung a new painting of Imelda's. Working from photographs, she had pictured us both in youth, herself as a college girl in Amsterdam and me as a proto-hippie circa 1969 – long hair, cool shades, I was headed for San Francisco to join the revolution. She had managed to bring the images fluidly together, as if that were destiny's desire as well as our own. O mystical lady! Often I stood before the painting and pondered the thousands of miles I'd travelled in my life, blindly at times, and I'd feel a deep respect for the great unknown that haunts us all, even the horses. All the falls I'd taken, all the missteps and false starts – no wonder I identified with the jumpers.

In the Tingle Creek, I backed Moscow Flyer once more, and not for peanuts, so I was panicky before the race and ordered a medicinal whisky to calm my nerves. Superstitions are mere phantoms and meant to be ignored, I reminded myself, yet when Moscow jumped tentatively at the ninth fence, I feared that he was as doomed as any figure from Greek tragedy. For a few seconds, I glanced away from the TV screen, expecting to hear the bad news, but Moscow was soon back in stride and briskly disposed of Azertyuiop to reclaim his title as the sport's premier two-mile chaser.

So The Pattern was laid to rest, along with sundry demons. The world, it seemed, was an enlightened place, where reason ruled. It followed, then, that Best Mate would improve on his showing at Exeter, as he'd done after the Peterborough last year, and demonstrate his superiority in the Lexus, but Beef Or Salmon wasn't a gawky adolescent anymore. With Timmy Murphy suspended, Paul Carberry grabbed the ride and never had it so easy. While Matey laboured throughout, Beef Or

Salmon glided along with such energy that Carberry couldn't hold up the horse and was forced to relax when his mount put in a superb jump at the third last and took command.

Beef Or Salmon by seven lengths! Passing the finish, Carberry's high spirits got the better of him. He rose up in the saddle, looked back at Jim Culloty, and gestured with his hand, as if to say, 'Hey, c'mon, Jimmy, catch me if you can!' There were echoes of Cheltenham in the gesture, traces of the last time the two Irishmen had locked horns, when Culloty escaped from the trap Carberry had set for him, so this was sweet revenge. For his antics, Carberry received a slap on the hand from the stewards, but it had no effect on the celebrations. Off to Lanzarote went Michael Hourigan and his Queen.

The ground at Leopardstown was against Best Mate, said Henrietta Knight. But she also said something far more telling: great horses win on any ground, so Matey might only be a very good horse. Still, her champion would be at Cheltenham to face Beef Or Salmon again, and possibly Strong Flow and Kingscliff, and probably Kicking King, who had won the King George in sensational style, except for a blunder at the last fence. The contenders were lining up, and the Festival was looming.

I wondered dreamily if I'd return to the Cotswolds in the spring, balancing the potential fun against the certain expense, another toss-up. As I edged closer to the heater, I saw a solitary bluetit land on the bird feeder, hasty and uneasy, its little eyes flicking about, on the lookout for that bossy gang of sparrows as it pecked at the seeds and gulped them down in a hurry. Then with a noisy flurry of wings the sparrows descended, back from their mysterious errand, and the bluetit disappeared. Where did it go? Into the slipstream of eternal questions, maybe, where people ask: Has anybody seen my hat? What's for dinner? Who'll win the Gold Cup?

Acknowledgements

I am most grateful to Tamso Doyle of Horse Racing Ireland, who provided the introductions, the racing know-how, and the general good cheer that made the writing of this book so much more pleasant than it might have been. The *Racing Post* was an indispensable tool, particularly the dispatches of Michael Clower and Tony O'Hehir, its chief Irish correspondents, as were the richly informative pages of *The Irish Field*. Of the writers listed in the biography, I am most indebted to Raymond Smith, a fine racing journalist, whose books were a helpful source on both John P. McManus and Vincent O'Brien. 'T.P. Reilly' is a pseudonym, as is 'O'Herlihy's', a necessary precaution to protect my table by the gas fire.

My heartfelt thanks to the trainers, jockeys, and bookies who gave so generously of their time, poured tea into me when I was cold, and answered my sometimes boneheaded questions with grace. Without their assistance, there'd be no book at all. In the text I say, 'I reckoned I'd never lived in such a hospitable country as Ireland,' and that still holds true. As Willie Mullins says, 'See you at the races!'

Bibliography

Broderick, Jacqui, *The Shane Broderick Story* (Merlin Publishing, 1999)

Fitzgeorge-Parker, Tim, *Vincent O'Brien: A Long Way From Tipperary* (Pelham Books, 1975)

Herbert, Ivor, *Arkle: The Classic Story of a Champion* (Aurum Press, 2003)

Holmes, Richard, *Sidetracks* (HarperCollins, 2000)

Kavanagh, Patrick, *The Green Fool* (Penguin Books, 1990)

Knight, Henrietta, *Best Mate: Chasing Gold* (Highdown Books, 2004)

Lyons, Larry, *The Gay Future Affair* (Mercier Publishers, 1983)

McCoy, A P (with Steve Taylor), *McCoy: The Autobiography* (Michael Joseph, 2002)

O'Flaherty, Liam, *A Tourist's Guide to Ireland* (Wolfhound Press, 1998)

Oh Ogain, Daithi, *Myth, Legend, and Romance* (Ryan Publishing, 1991)

O'Neill, Peter and Boyce, Sean, *Paddy Mullins: The Master of Doninga* (Mainstream Publishing, 1995)

Pipe, Martin (with Richard Pitman), *Martin Pipe: The Champion Trainer's Story* (Headline Books, 1992)

Reynolds, James, *A World of Horses* (Creative Age Press, 1979)

Sheedy, Kieran, *The Horse in County Clare* (Colour Books, 2001)

Smith, Brian, *The Horse in Ireland* (Wolfhound Press, 1991)

Smith, Raymond, *High Rollers of the Turf* (Sporting Books, 1992)

Smith, Raymond, *Vincent O'Brien: The Master of Ballydoyle* (Virgin Books, 1990)

Wilde, Lady, *Ancient Legends, Mystic Charms, and Superstitions of Ireland* (Chatto & Windus, 1975)

Index